The Frontier World
of Edgar Dewdney

Brian Titley

The Frontier World
of Edgar Dewdney

UBCPress / Vancouver

Printed in Canada on acid-free paper ∞

ISBN 0-7748-0730-X

Canadian Cataloguing in Publication Data
Titley, E. Brian.
  The frontier world of Edgar Dewdney

  Includes bibliographical references and index.
  ISBN 0-7748-0730-X

1. Dewdney, E. (Edgar), 1835-1916. 2. Northwest, Canadian – Biography.
3. Politicians – Canada, Western – Biography. 4. Northwest, Canadian – History.
5. Indians of North America – Canada – Government relations – 1860-1951.* I. Title.

FC3217.1.D48T57 1999   971.2´02´092   C99-910695-3
F1060.9.D48T57 1999

This book has been published with a grant from the Humanities and Social Sciences Federation of Canada, using funds provided by the Social Sciences and Humanities Research Council of Canada.

UBC Press acknowledges the financial support of the Government of Canada through the Book Publishing Industry Development Program (BPIDP) for our publishing activities.
Canadä

We also gratefully acknowledge the ongoing support to our publishing program from the Canada Council for the Arts and the British Columbia Arts Council.

UBC Press
University of British Columbia
6344 Memorial Road
Vancouver, BC V6T 1Z2
(604) 822-5959
Fax: 1-800-668-0821
E-mail: info@ubcpress.ubc.ca
www.ubcpress.ubc.ca

Contents

Introduction

This story takes place in the latter half of the nineteenth century in what are now the Canadian provinces of British Columbia, Alberta, Saskatchewan, and Manitoba. The West, as we shall call it, was experiencing breathtaking change in this period, and the upheavals and convulsions that transformed society are central to our narrative.

The frontier is an expression often used in association with this time and place. The concept is useful, although lacking in precision. Sometimes defined as the outer edge of a zone of influence, jurisdiction, and civility, the frontier might also be seen as an idea or attitude. Frontier conditions imply wilderness – tracts of terra incognita awaiting occupancy, a social and economic blank slate on which an invading culture could make its mark. Frontiersmen and women in this context are intrepid adventurers who brave physical hardships to tame the new land and whose labours pave the way for a material nirvana to be enjoyed by themselves and their descendants.

This rough-hewn image of pioneer folk persists, and with good reason, but Western Canada as a destination was more complex than a mere haven for land-hungry peasants. While the region drew its share of the ordinary and unremarkable, it also attracted those who considered themselves a cut above the rest. Unable, for whatever reason, to maintain social status at home, well-bred Britons looked to the West, and to British Columbia in particular, as a realm where they might either live to respectable standards or return home to do so after having profited from their adventures. It was to this class of immigrant-adventurer that Edgar Dewdney belonged.

Whatever the personal motivations of Dewdney and his fellow migrants, and those motivations varied greatly in individual cases, the newcomers were part of a colonial project that envisaged the re-creation of a British society far from home. The project also anticipated unrivalled economic returns through the efficient harnessing of human and physical resources. In some ways, a rationally ordered society geared to profitability was easier to create in the colonies than in tradition-bound Europe. Hence, the political and economic development of Western Canada was always a mix of the rugged individualism so readily associated with the American frontier, and the sentimental attachment to feudal symbolism and class privilege so characteristic of British imperial outposts.

These tensions and contradictions were at the heart of the dialectic that marked the political, social, and economic evolution of the West. And Edgar Dewdney was never far from the centre of the most vital decisions and actions. He experienced the gold rushes of the 1860s, building key pathways to the British Columbia interior and trying his hand at prospecting and mining. The entry of the Pacific colony to Canadian Confederation was by no means a foregone conclusion, and Dewdney was a participant in the vigorous debates that preceded the union in 1871. In the decade that followed, the completion of the Pacific railway was the major preoccupation of British Columbia politicians, and Dewdney, as MP for Yale, was at the forefront in reminding Ottawa of its obligations. More importantly, perhaps, he championed the route with a western terminus at Burrard Inlet that ultimately prevailed, in spite of keen opposition from Vancouver Islanders.

As lieutenant governor of the North-West Territories in the 1880s, Dewdney wielded virtually autocratic power. There, he presided over the gradual democratization of political institutions in the region, ensuring that the will of the people was constrained by his wisdom and experience. There, too, he played his most significant role as Indian commissioner. Colonialism is about land and race. What ought to be done with the displaced or conquered peoples who had lived unchallenged in the newly acquired territories? In the Prairie West, marginalization with a touch of forced labour (that is, work for rations) dressed up in the language of a *mission civilisatrice* became the Dewdney solution.

He continued to keep his finger on the pulse of the West after leaving his Regina posts, first as minister of the interior and later as lieutenant governor of British Columbia. And he was a player in the enduring tribute to greed that engulfed the West as the century drew to a close, the Klondike gold rush. He was not just an eyewitness to history; he helped to make it. In many ways, his career is a metaphor for the maturing western frontier. His exploits tell the story of a region experiencing staggering change.

Biography is akin to necromancy. We exhume the bodies of the dead – skulldiggery, if you like – and breathe life into them. But we cannot question them, and our reconstruction hinges largely on the fragments they leave behind, whether deliberately or accidentally. In Dewdney's case, a formidable dossier of private papers and public documents testifies to his deeds and motivations. The records, however, relate mainly to the various offices he held, and this focus inevitably becomes our concern, too. The paper trail does not permit much insight into his youth or personal life. The reader expecting a *chronique scandaleuse* – a tiresome idiom all too familiar in popular writing today – will be disappointed. The man had his shady side, to be sure, but because it was motivated by avarice rather than lust, Dewdney's life hardly qualifies as the stuff of breathless revelations.

People are interested in others of their kind, especially in the fortunes of individuals who have some claim to pre-eminence. This remains so in spite of the puzzling attempts of some social historians to write of a past peopled with nameless collectivities. There is, nonetheless, no impulse towards creating an idealized biography here. I do not consider Dewdney a great man or a nation builder. Rather, I see him as a type – a representative of that class of adventurer who saw in the western frontier an unprecedented opportunity for self-aggrandizement.

The Frontier World
of Edgar Dewdney

CHAPTER I

The Trailblazer

Throughout much of the 1850s, Britain's Pacific Northwest attracted little interest in the homeland. To those who had heard of the place, it was a remote, untamed wilderness of rock and timber where fur trader and Indian held sway. There was some truth to this image. New Caledonia, the mainland territory between the Rocky Mountains and the ocean, was part of the Hudson's Bay Company's commercial monopoly. Vancouver Island, although a Crown colony since 1849, was under a ten-year lease to the company on the unlikely condition that it promote settlement. The company's chief factor, James Douglas, doubled as colonial governor from his headquarters at Fort Victoria. The inhospitable if romantic image persisted, and there was little incentive for Britons to make the long voyage to this distant outpost of the empire. The land-hungry could find what they wanted with much less trouble in the United States.[1]

The obscurity of the Pacific Northwest did not survive the decade. In fall 1857, prospectors from Washington and Oregon Territories found gold in the Fraser River. Within a few months, news of their discovery reached California, sparking off an influx of fortune seekers. Throughout 1858 they came, 30,000 in all, some striking it rich in sandbars near Fort Hope and Fort Yale.[2]

The gold rush captured the popular imagination not just in the United States but also in Britain. London *Times* correspondent Donald Fraser came north from San Francisco to witness the excitement first-hand, and his vivid accounts captivated readers in the homeland.[3] Among the captivated was a young Englishman named Dewdney who was about to explore the career opportunities a worldwide empire offered the ambitious and adventuresome.

Edgar Dewdney was born on 5 November 1835 in Bideford, Devonshire. Although little is known of his parents, Charles Dewdney and Fanny Hollingshead, they were clearly people of means because they afforded their son an education available only to the wealthier classes. The young Dewdney went to school in Bideford, Tiverton, and Exeter before going on to Cardiff to study for the profession of civil engineer.[4] Tall and athletic, he loved sports and had that inexplicable fondness for cricket peculiar to the English and those colonized by them. Indeed, he was an accomplished player and once served on the South Wales team in a match against All England. The game would remain one of his abiding passions throughout his long life.[5]

Dewdney moved to London after completing his studies and worked for a year as private secretary to John Lorry Rickards, who had been in India during the mutiny of 1857. Rickards was a principal informant to Solicitor General Sir Fitzroy Kelly on that event, and Dewdney wrote out the information. India intrigued the young engineer, and for a while, he contemplated pursuing his career in that jewel in the imperial Crown. The empire offered exciting prospects to a man of his training; there were roads, railways, and bridges to be built, and fortunes and reputations to be made.[6]

At this time, the newspapers were filled with stories of the Fraser Valley gold rush, and Dewdney realized that he could do better for himself in this new land. He reasoned that it would take but ten years in a country paved with gold "to put together a competency" with a view to returning to England and a life of gentlemanly leisure. Already acquainted with the political scene in London, he secured, through Charles Kemeys-Tynte, MP for Bridgewater, an introduction to Colonial Secretary Edward Bulwer Lytton.[7]

Lytton was the first occupant of the Colonial Office to take an active interest in the Pacific Northwest. Using the gold frenzy of 1858 as an excuse, he cancelled the Hudson's Bay Company's control of the mainland, turning it into the Crown colony of British Columbia. To discourage American annexationist designs, he sent out a detachment of 165 Royal Engineers under Colonel Richard Clement Moody; they were to build roads and fortifications and maintain a military presence. And he handpicked key officials for the new colony, the most notable of whom was Matthew Baillie Begbie, a Cambridge graduate, who became chief justice.[8] Begbie was to personify British law and order in the gold fields.[9]

It is not surprising that Lytton encouraged Dewdney in his plans to seek his fortune on the banks of the Fraser. He offered the engineer no official appointment, however, but rather a letter of introduction to James Douglas, governor of the two colonies of Vancouver Island and British Columbia.[10]

And so, armed with this letter and with £150 in his pocket, Dewdney set sail on 5 March 1859 to embark on a new life. Travelling on a steamer of the

Hamburg mail line, he arrived in New York on 20 March after a stormy passage. There, he lingered for two weeks, squandering most of his money on high living. The spendthrift inclinations that were to plague him throughout his career were already causing him trouble. But, as he put it, "with a strong constitution, lots of confidence in myself ... I proceeded on to my destination with a light heart." The remainder of his journey was by sea to Panama, across the isthmus by train, and from there again by sea to Victoria, where he arrived on 13 May.[11]

Victoria had few attractions or amenities in 1859. The old company fort still stood guard over the harbour. A few stone structures on the waterfront hinted at prosperity, but most buildings were of crude timbers and hastily constructed, a legacy of the excitement of the previous summer. Streets were quagmires of mud, and sanitation was rudimentary.[12] The rough-and-ready shape of the island capital was typical of settler outposts in both colonies at the time. Few newcomers had put down sufficiently deep roots to improve their properties, and many had little intention of staying. Most of the gold miners had given up on the Fraser by now and had returned home. But about 5,000 of them remained, determined to try their luck elsewhere in the interior.[13] They comprised by far the largest element in the non-Native population and were the most transient. The British-born – officials, soldiers, missionaries, Hudson's Bay Company personnel, and the like – numbered around 1,000 but constituted a political and social elite. The Natives, declining in numbers because of disease, were estimated at around 30,000 and were increasingly resentful at the intrusions on their domains.

These intrusions were not about to end, for the new arrivals sought ways and means of exploiting the land to best advantage. In spite of challenging topography and poor communications, the possibilities were enormous, and Dewdney had no reason to be disappointed with his chosen destination. Gold mining was the most lucrative enterprise and would remain so for at least a decade, but a man needed luck to succeed. Servicing the miners was probably a more certain way of doing well. There was money to be made also in the fur trade and in lumbering. Sawmills were springing up to provide building materials for new and expanding communities. Agriculture had never been one of the great attractions of the colonies, but some tried their hands at it after arrival. By 1859, farms had spread north from Victoria to the Cowichan Valley.[14] There were opportunities, too, in government service – in fact, there was no shortage of activities a young energetic immigrant with the right connections could turn his hand to.

Anxious to make a good impression, Dewdney donned his best clothes – frock coat and tall hat – before calling on Governor Douglas. The old fur trader examined the letter from Lytton, and on learning that his visitor was a civil engineer, suggested he approach Colonel Moody, commander of the Royal Engineers and commissioner of lands and works for British Columbia. Dewdney explained to the colonel that he was virtually broke and needed immediate employment. Moody, who was about to leave next day for the mainland to lay out the site of its capital city, invited him along as head of the civilian surveying team working on the project.[15]

Elated, Dewdney returned to his quarters. He was staying at the Cushing Hotel, a flimsy structure thrown up to accommodate the gold miners and a lively spot after sundown. He hardly slept that night, his bedroom being directly above the saloon where he could see the revellers through cracks in the floor.

The next morning he was up early, packed away his good clothes, and put on an old velveteen shooting coat, corduroy pants, and a fur cap. Thus attired, he went on board *The Beaver*, the Hudson's Bay Company steamer that was to take them to the mainland. Before long, Colonel Moody and his family arrived, followed by Governor Douglas who came to say farewell. Douglas, with an oblique reference to the change of clothing, remarked: "Good morning, Mr. Dewdney. Glad to see you prepared for work. Hope to hear great things of you."[16] Dewdney was already somewhat in awe of the governor whom he later described as "a man of splendid presence," although "rather pompous."[17]

The Beaver slipped away from the wharf at eight in the morning amid cheers from the assembled well-wishers and a salvo from the Fort Victoria cannon. The crossing was slow, and they reached their destination at ten at night, deep in the Fraser delta where the north arm branches off the river. There, on the right bank for strategic reasons, Moody had chosen the site of the new capital city which he named Queensborough. A few months later, at the suggestion of Queen Victoria, the city was renamed New Westminster.

The site was covered with magnificent trees – fir, cedar, hemlock, spruce – and the surveyors, civilian and military, worked hard to clear them.[18] Dewdney's contract lasted from 18 May to 20 June when Moody cancelled it in order to hire a former Royal Engineer who had recently arrived in the colony.[19] Although now out of work, Dewdney was pleased with the pay – $250 in American gold coins – American and British money being used interchangeably in the colony.[20]

While carving New Westminster out of the forest, Dewdney met an old friend named Lee whom he had not seen since 1858 when they had lived in the same boarding house on Northumberland Avenue in London for a few months. Lee now proposed that they go into business together cutting hay on Sea Island near the mouth of the Fraser which he had already explored. Dewdney mentioned the idea to Moody who offered them $100 per ton for up to 100 tons. (Moody had many mules and horses to winter.) Neither Englishman knew much about farming, and so they teamed up with a Canadian, Silas Brouse, who was experienced in the matter and whom Dewdney had met on the voyage from New York.

Using Dewdney's money, they purchased food and farming equipment and set up camp on the island. Weeks of hard work followed while Dewdney learned with some difficulty the art of swinging a scythe. The mosquitoes were relentless, and he began to think that haymaking at $100 per ton was not the bargain it appeared to be when he had made his initial investment. In the end, the venture came to naught, because the nine or ten tons that they harvested had to be used to pay off debts. Dewdney was back where he started: broke.[21]

While busy with his haymaking venture, Dewdney first came into contact with the Native Indians of the region. The Musqueam and Squamish peoples were active in the Fraser delta and made occasional visits to his camp on Sea Island. He described them as "very saucy and independent," and he was clearly annoyed when once they helped themselves to a pot of beans from his campfire. Reports that they were implicated in "various murders and piratical excursions" against prospectors en route to the diggings gave him further cause for concern.

The Indians, of course, were only defending their territory from the invaders, but few newcomers could see it this way. Dewdney was not easily intimidated and fear of attack never stood in his way. Indeed, he loved to tell the story of how he participated in the hunt for a Squamish "desperado," John Chinaman, so named because of his oriental appearance. Another story with which he regaled listeners for years to come concerned his role in the capture of Silpaynim, a Musqueam who was wanted for "a number of desperate acts." In this case, Dewdney physically overpowered the Indian after luring him from the forest with a bottle of whiskey while talking the Chinook jargon.[22] These early encounters gave him a poor impression of Natives and his unsympathetic views hardened with time. Although he came to depend on them as packers and guides during his years of prospecting and road building in British Columbia, he resented the Natives' lack of subservience and their insistence on being paid decent wages for their labour. His attitude reflected all too well the colonizing mentality that regarded Aboriginal inhabitants as a regrettable nuisance.

During 1959, the gold excitement was moving north along the Fraser, beyond Lytton and into the Cariboo. A year later, the fortune hunters were exploring the country east of Quesnel where fabulous strikes were to be made. Meanwhile, others were trying their luck with encouraging results in the Similkameen Valley, on the eastern side of the Cascade Mountains.

The roving Judge Begbie was the key to law and order in the shifting eldorados that were opening up the colony at a fast pace. He was assisted by local gold commissioners who were stipendiary magistrates with the power to settle claim disputes. Most commissioners were new arrivals who had been recommended by Colonial Secretary Lytton, and many of them were Irishmen of the Dublin Castle persuasion.[23] Peter O'Reilly, the gold commissioner at Hope, was typical, and he became a lifelong friend of Dewdney.

Roads were virtually non-existent in the colony, and the expanding mining frontier demanded that they be built, if only to keep the auxiliary trade (outfitting and so forth) in the hands of local merchants. Government-sponsored road and trail construction provided Dewdney with some lucrative contracts in the 1860s and cultivated his reputation as pioneer pathfinder. In January 1860, he hiked in difficult weather from Hope to Similkameen and back over an old foot trail, reporting to Peter O'Reilly on conditions in the gold fields and on the importance of keeping the trail open to supply the influx of miners expected in the spring.[24] He was hoping for a contract to improve the trail to accommodate pack mules; he got it, but later in the summer.

Meanwhile, he set himself up in business as a land agent and auctioneer in New Westminster. He secured a few contracts from his old acquaintance, Colonel Moody, to sell town lots and to lay out the plans for government buildings that were in the course of construction. In May, Moody made him official surveyor of the fledgling capital, but the job proved inadequate to his financial ambitions. In July, Dewdney was auctioning off town lots in Hope and was about to embark on his first road-building project. In partnership with Walter Moberly, a Canadian, he had the contract to improve the Hope-Similkameen trail to accommodate mules.[25]

Dewdney and Moberly laboured throughout the fall until November when a dispute arose over the route they were taking and Moody's reluctance to advance them cash to pay their workers.[26] The partners abandoned the project, and Dewdney was soon back in New Westminster trying his hand once more as an auctioneer. This time, he was selling seven-year leases to waterfront property on Columbia Street, and with his friend Moberly, he retained two of the leases as a personal investment.[27] This venture was his debut in real estate speculation, a route to elusive riches he would explore repeatedly in the years to come.

At this time, Adam Beaur, a Canadian, hit pay dirt at Rock Creek, about 100 miles east of the Similkameen diggings. This find gave a renewed significance to the Hope Mountain trail. Governor Douglas, with the interests of Victoria and New Westminster merchants in mind, resolved to extend the mule trail to Rock Creek and to improve a section of it to carry wagons.[28]

Dewdney and Moberly won the contract to build the wagon road in January 1861, and the work kept them busy until the summer. The contract called for a road twelve feet wide with bypasses of sixteen feet every 200 yards. All creeks and rivers were to be bridged, and the grade was not to exceed one foot in twelve.[29] With payment at £300 per mile, the road was an expensive undertaking, and the government called a halt when only twenty-five miles had been built out of Hope. In any event, the Similkameen and Rock Creek gold fields were not as lucrative as expected, and the miners were already hurrying off to the Cariboo, inspired by tales of fabulous strikes.[30]

Over the 1860-1 winter, prospectors found gold in the gravel of Williams Creek, causing a stampede into the area. It became the centre of the Cariboo gold rush and the site of the fabled Barkerville. So rich were the strikes on Williams Creek and adjacent streams that Governor Douglas embarked on an ambitious road-building scheme into the area, borrowing huge sums of money to do so. For much of 1862, Royal Engineers and civilian contractors were busy building the Cariboo Road, blasting rock faces, and constructing elaborate cribbing supports in difficult sections through the Fraser Canyon. By 1863, travellers could take a four-horse stagecoach from Yale to Soda Creek, catch a steamer to Quesnel, and carry on to Barkerville by trail.[31] Dewdney was one of the civilians who worked on this project. In partnership with Moberly, he got the contract to build the section from Lytton to Cook and Kimball's Ferry on the Thompson in February 1862.[32] With this done, he went off to see the excitement at Williams Creek for himself, spending the summers of 1862 and 1863 in the area and the winter in between in Victoria and Hope.

Dewdney's reputation as a surveyor preceded him to the Cariboo, and he readily found work there marking out the boundaries between claims. Because many of these claims were immensely valuable, the boundaries had to be clearly identified, and he was able to charge handsome fees for his services. One of the disputed claims he surveyed was a celebrated one. Henry Fuller Davis discovered that the adjoining claims of Isaiah Diller and Joel Abbott covered 212 feet rather than the specified 200, that is, 100 feet per claim. He staked the twelve-foot strip for himself and took $15,000 in gold from this sliver of land before selling it to another. This exploit earned him the name "Twelve-Foot Davis," although he was short in stature. Davis went on to establish himself as a fur trader in the Peace River country.[33]

By 1864, Dewdney had been six years in British Columbia, and the fortune he had sought was still nowhere in sight. He had made lots of money but had spent lots too. Work in fact had been spasmodic, even seasonal, and the cost of living high. Even so, he retained his faith in the country and in himself. Optimistic by nature, he was not easily discouraged, and he could see all around him that men were doing well in speculation and in business. He had a further reason not to give up, a personal motivation that ultimately convinced him to make his life in this new land; a romantic attachment was more and more at the centre of his thoughts.

In August 1860, while on the river steamer *Reliance* between New Westminster and Hope, the captain introduced him to the other passengers. Very soon, Dewdney was on good terms with one of them, Thomas Glennie, a Scot who was planning to homestead near Hope. Glennie had just arrived in the colony from Britain and was accompanied by his wife, Susan Louisa Moir, and her two daughters from a previous marriage, Jane, aged 17, and Susan, who was about to turn 15. The girls had been born in Ceylon where their father had been joint owner of a tea plantation before his sudden death in 1849. Dewdney took an immediate fancy to Jane who was described as "lovely and dainty in every way."[34] It was a most fortunate encounter for him because eligible non-Native women were in extremely short supply in both colonies. Glennie built a substantial house for his family on the 160 acres he pre-empted along the Coquihalla River, two miles from Hope. The Glennies were settled in by Christmas 1860, and a month later, some household effects they had sent around Cape Horn, including Jane's rosewood piano, were delivered to the door. By then, the family was actively involved in Hope's lively social scene – parties and dances at the company fort, horse races, and the like. Dewdney would always be found at such events, unless he was away road building, never losing a chance to spend time with Jane.[35]

As early as 1862, some of their mutual friends in the community were even laying bets that the two would be married before long.[36] But it was not until 25 March 1864 when Ned and Jeannie, as they called one another, tied the knot at the Anglican Christ Church in Hope. The wedding party included Jane's sister, Susan, her mother, her stepfather, and Peter O'Reilly, who had left Hope in 1862 but returned for the occasion. The ceremony was followed by lunch at the Hudson's Bay Company fort, hosted by William Charles, the chief trader, and his wife, Mary Ann. After lunch, the bride and groom boarded the *Reliance* en route to New Westminster, retracing the journey on which they had first met less than four years previously.[37]

For several more years, Dewdney's career pattern was as before: contractual work of varying complexity and remuneration that often kept him away from home for long stretches at a time. Some of the jobs seem unchallenging at first glance, but they invariably involved travel over difficult terrain, sometimes in appalling weather. His assignment to inspect a bridge built by Thomas Spence at the confluence of the Thompson and Nicola Rivers is a case in point.

In March 1865, Dewdney set out from New Westminster, where he and Jane had a house, planning to go by canoe as far as Yale. Five other men, who were also en route up the Fraser, accompanied him. The group included David Oppenheimer, a fellow contractor and land speculator who would do well for himself in the Vancouver real estate boom in later years and become mayor of the city. The river was choked with ice, however, and they only made it to Matsqui Island when they were forced to return to New Westminster. Ten days later, when the ice had cleared, they were able to proceed once more. The winter had been a severe one, and progress on foot along the road north of Yale was hampered by heavy snowfalls and slides. At Jackass Mountain, the road was blocked completely, and they had to cross the fallen snow by cutting footholds in it while perching over the precipice of the canyon.

One night, when they were staying at Chapman's Bar wayside house, they were awakened by two Indians knocking excitedly at the door. The Indians reported that they had been escorting Ned Wadham, his wife, and a bag of gold dust worth over $25,000 belonging to a merchant named Beede down the canyon when they had been carried away by a snow slide. They had managed to save themselves, the wife, and the gold, but Wadham had been lost, presumably ending up in the river. The next morning, Dewdney and his party visited the nearby cabin of Pat Ryan, the road foreman, where Mrs. Wadham had spent the night after her harrowing escape. To their surprise, they found her husband there, too, alive and well. Ryan and his men had searched the snow slide for much of the night, digging here and there until they had found Wadham just beneath the surface. Many years later, when he was living in Ottawa, Dewdney loved to tell of this miraculous escape. His listeners were often incredulous, but one day Wadham himself turned up in the national capital as part of a British Columbian delegation, and he was able to confirm this story.[38] Dewdney did eventually get to Spence's Bridge, checked it out, and pronounced it fit for public traffic.[39] The bridge was a substantial structure and lasted until 1894, when it was swept away by flood waters.

Meanwhile, the political landscape of the colony was changing, and new gold discoveries continued to force the pace of exploration, road building, and settlement. James Douglas retired early in 1864 and was succeeded by two governors: Arthur Kennedy on Vancouver Island and Frederick

Seymour in British Columbia. Seymour was a thin, bald, card-playing bachelor who took an active interest in the development of the mainland colony. Shortly after establishing himself in New Westminster, he visited Barkerville and the surrounding gold fields, travelling along the Cariboo Road.[40]

During the governor's absence, reports arrived in the capital of a rich gold strike at Wild Horse Creek, a tributary of the Kootenay River in the far southeast of the colony. The discovery was the work of American miners who had crossed over from Montana. Supplies were coming in from the United States – the easiest route, given the contours of the land – and once again, British Columbia merchants feared they might be excluded from a potentially lucrative trade. Those who tried to transport goods through American territory ran into trouble with customs officials. Seymour came to their rescue by actively seeking out an all-British route to the new eldorado.

In fall 1864, the governor sent out an expedition under George Turner which went by way of Lytton, Kamloops, Shuswap Lake, and the Columbia River but failed to reach the Kootenay country as a result of lack of provisions. Around the same time, another party led by J.J. Jenkins set out from Hope and made it to the Kootenay River travelling via Princeton, Osoyoos Lake, Kettle River, Columbia River, and St. Mary's River, reporting that a trail was possible just north of the boundary. Seymour decided on this route, and money was put in the estimates for that purpose.[41]

When Dewdney arrived back from Spence's Bridge at the beginning of April 1865, Seymour told him that he had been recommended by Peter O'Reilly as the man to build the pack trail to Wild Horse Creek. He wanted it done by September. Dewdney knew nothing of the country beyond Similkameen, but he agreed to take on the job if he could choose his own men and could be assured of enough money to pay them as the work progressed. That was fine with the governor.[42]

In 1863, Britain had withdrawn the Royal Engineers from the colony, but most of the sappers and NCOs had decided to take their discharge and the offer of free land in British Columbia. Dewdney greatly admired these men, and it was former engineers that he chose as his team, including his assistant, George Turner.[43]

When the survey team reached Hope, Dewdney hired eighteen Indians, men and women, to pack their supplies over the mountains to Similkameen. The trip over the old road that he had built in 1860 was slow but pleasant. As they approached the upper altitudes, they encountered snow and the Indians helped them make snowshoes, which they called bears' feet, out of vine maple and rawhide. This trip brought back happy memories for the trailblazer, and he was almost poetic in recounting the experience many years later: "I shall never forget what pleasure and enjoyment I had when walking over the frozen summits on a bright, sunshiny, early morning, the sun dazzling in the snow, which seemed studded with millions of diamonds, and the air bracing and seeming to give fresh life with every breath you drew."[44] They arrived at the Similkameen Valley after about ten days of travel. There, they paid off their packers who returned to Hope. Dewdney observed that the older Indians had been just as good at the arduous work as the younger ones. One couple, Polalee and his wife, both of whom were around sixty years old, were among the best. Polalee's wife, for instance, had carried a barrel of sugar weighing 125 lbs. over the mountains.

The Similkameen had fine potential as cattle country, with thick bunch grass all over the ranges. Yet few settlers had made their homes there at the time. One of the pioneers was John F. Allison, who had established a ranch at Princeton. Allison provided the party with a dozen horses which they used to pack their supplies down the valley. En route, they met Angus McDonald on his way to Hope. McDonald was in charge of Fort Colville, a Hudson's Bay Company post located south of the forty-ninth parallel, and he knew the country well. He advised the party that the road ahead was rough and that they should keep their eyes fixed on a couple of snow-capped peaks barely discernible in the distance – part of the Selkirk Mountains, as it turned out.

The surveyors pushed on, crossing a small range and Osoyoos Lake, over more mountains and into the Kettle River Valley. By this time, the horses had outlived their usefulness, and they were abandoned in the valley. With the beasts sent out to pasture, Dewdney hired Indians to pack their equipment for the remainder of the journey. He now split his party in two, sending one group down the valley with instructions to rendezvous with him at Fort Sheppard, a Hudson's Bay post on the Columbia. Along with three Indians and two whites, he headed off across the next mountain range and emerged at Lower Arrow Lake. Hiring a canoe from local Indians, they made their way down the Columbia to Fort Sheppard, arriving on 27 May. Dewdney realized that the route he had taken was impractical. Fortunately, however, the men who had taken a more southerly route from Kettle River, and who were already at the fort before him, reported that a trail was possible the way they had come.

Indians were playing key roles in these explorations, but Dewdney was annoyed that some of them refused to travel beyond their own locality, forcing him to re-hire at different points. He remained irritated by their sense of independence and by their insistence on charging what he considered exorbitant rates for their services.[45] Even so, he knew that he could not do without them, and they clearly were aware of this fact.

At this point, he decided to leave his men at Fort Sheppard while he explored the Kootenay River from its junction with the Columbia to Kootenay Lake, with some thought of finding a way from the lake through to St. Mary's River. Engaging the services of "a couple of good Indians," he set out in a birchbark canoe, a mode of transport he greatly admired. The trip up the Kootenay was rough going, requiring fourteen portages around rapids and falls. They crossed the lake to what is now known as Crawford Bay and went partly up the valley towards St. Mary's River. But Dewdney came to the conclusion that the ferry across the lake would be too long and, as such, objectionable to packers. The route just would not work, and he returned to Fort Sheppard with his companions, running most of the Kootenay rapids in the canoe.

Because some definite decisions had already been made concerning the Kettle Valley – Fort Sheppard section, he instructed most of his men to retrace their steps westwards from the fort, blazing the line as they did so. He continued eastwards, following the Pend Oreille River, accompanied by an Indian named Peter and a former Royal Engineer called Howell. They crossed the mountains and came out at Kootenay Flats near where Creston now stands. The Indians there were friendly, and one was engaged as packer, another as guide. With this help, the party carried on along the Goat River Valley, skirting the southern edge of the Purcell Mountains. Upon reaching the Moyie River, the going was easy all the way to Wild Horse Creek. A well-tramped trail up the valley was the principal supply route in from Idaho.

In early June, Dewdney arrived at the gold diggings. Several hundred claims had been staked, rockers and sluices were in full swing, and some of the miners were making well over $100 per day from the creek bed. American merchants had cornered the market in food and other necessities and were selling beef, flour, eggs, tobacco, and so forth at astronomical prices.[46] This was the trade coveted by the Victoria and New Westminster merchants, and the planned trail was supposed to divert it into their pockets.

Peter O'Reilly was already on the spot, keeping an eye on things in his role as gold commissioner. On his recommendation, Dewdney hired William Fernie, "an active young man," as his foreman.[47] He also engaged sixty-five men, mainly from the ranks of disappointed miners, as his work crew. Fernie and Howell were put in charge of trail construction from Wild Horse to Kootenay Flats, and an American merchant was contracted to create a supply depot at the latter place to serve their needs.

With these arrangements in place, Dewdney set out for Fort Sheppard accompanied by Louis, a Metis packer, who was carrying enough food to get them to Kootenay Flats. Upon their arrival, they were shocked to discover that the local Indians, who were minding a food cache sent in from Fort Sheppard, were nowhere to be seen. They spent a couple of anxious days and nights assailed by hunger and relentless thunderstorms. At last, they found the Indians, who had moved camp to avoid being pestered by mosquitoes. Their food cache was untouched, and Dewdney was delighted when he reached inside a flour sack to find a bottle of brandy sent surreptitiously by his friends at the fort. He returned to the fort by canoe via the Kootenay River, shooting the rapids once more along the way.

Fort Sheppard became his centre of operations. It was about halfway along the chosen route and had easy access to Fort Colville, a major Hudson's Bay Company post from which supplies could be had. He began to hire work crews to build the trail in various sections east and west of the Columbia, and he arranged for the creation of supply depots along the way. Chinese workers built the section just west of Fort Sheppard. A substantial Chinese population lived in the colony, many of them working in the gold fields, especially in sites abandoned by whites.

As the work progressed, Dewdney travelled back and forth along the line ensuring that all was going well and that supplies were in place. By the end of the summer, the trail was almost complete, and he paid a final visit to Wild Horse Creek. There, O'Reilly advanced him $25,000, mainly in gold dust, and he set off along the trail on horseback, paying the work crews as he went. At Kootenay Flats, he met Judge Begbie en route to Wild Horse to hold the assizes.

By mid-September, trains of pack mules and horses were able to go from Hope to the Kootenay gold fields along a trail entirely in British Columbia territory. Dewdney returned to New Westminster where he settled his accounts with the colony's treasury department. The entire bill came to $74,000, and not one item of expenditure was questioned. Indeed, Governor Seymour complimented Dewdney for the efficiency with which he had done the work.

The Dewdney Trail, as the route to the gold fields became known, was a four-foot-wide, meandering serpentine highway that hugged the American border while passing through some of British Columbia's most rugged and spectacular scenic terrain.[48] It was Dewdney's greatest achievement to date and secured his reputation as one of the colony's pioneer pathfinders. And the prominence thus acquired paved the way for his later entry into politics.

The 1865-6 winter was harsh in the interior, and when the snows melted in spring, the gold at Wild Horse seemed to vanish along with it. The diggings proved to be shallower than first imagined, and the miners moved on, mostly to Big Bend, northwards along the Columbia River.[49]

The trail never had a chance to profit the colony as intended. The eastern section fell into disuse, but the western half became an important route into the interior valleys for settlers and cattle drovers in the years ahead.[50]

The gold excitement continued to spring up in unexpected places, and Governor Seymour persisted with his policy of blazing trails into the diggings. There was no shortage of contracts for Dewdney. In March 1866, he worked at Lillooet, reporting on the shape of roads. He was also about to build a trail up the Bridge River to Tyaughton Creek where men had found the yellow metal.[51] A little later, he was busy on another trail, this time from Cache Creek to Savona on Kamloops Lake.[52] This trail was part of the governor's plan to create a route via the Thompson River to the Big Bend gold fields.[53] While in the area, Dewdney surveyed reserves around Kamloops, giving the Indians not what they wanted, but grazing land that he considered more suitable for their purposes.[54] In this matter, his thinking mirrored that of the authorities in the colony's capital. There were no Indian treaties in British Columbia and, consequently, no land entitlements. In assigning reserves, government officials usually acted in an arbitrary manner, keeping settler interests at the forefront.

Throughout Dewdney's travels, Jane was living alone in New Westminster. Her husband considered the interior far too rough for her sensibilities. Shortly after they had wed, her stepfather, Thomas Glennie, disappeared, leaving his family homeless and broke. He had never made a go of the homestead, and he turned out to be a spendthrift and ne'er-do-well. In 1865, Jane invited her mother, Louisa, and younger sister, Susan, to live with her in New Westminster. They agreed and quickly entered into the lively social activities of a very "agreeable community." Dewdney's brother Walter and two of their sisters, Charlotte and Fanny, came to British Columbia around this time and also settled in New Westminster.[55]

Dewdney's work had kept him constantly on the move over the years, which was less than satisfactory to his wife. In 1867, with a more sedentary life in mind, he purchased land at Soda Creek. He built a house, made some improvements, and tried his hand at cattle ranching.[56] He was not alone. All along the road to the Cariboo, ranches were being marked out in the semi-arid grasslands, often by Americans investing their profits from the gold fields.

Meanwhile, Louisa and Susan returned to Hope where they opened a school. A couple of times each year, John Allison passed through town, driving cattle from his Similkameen Valley ranch en route to markets in New Westminster. On one trip, Allison was introduced to Susan. He was twenty years older than she, but their friendship blossomed into romance, a development noticed by Ned and Jane when they came down from Soda

Creek for a visit in June 1868. The Dewdneys were present when Allison married Susan at the Hope parsonage on 3 September that same year. Two hours after the ceremony, the newlyweds set out on horseback over the Dewdney Trail for Similkameen, she perched on a sidesaddle.[57]

The cattle business was too slow for Dewdney's restless energy and ambitions. The government occasionally sent surveying contracts his way, which he accepted.[58] And he kept an eye on gold-mining developments for that elusive opportunity to strike it rich.[59]

There was no shortage of prospectors to expand the frontiers of exploration. Those who had been disappointed at Barkerville, Wild Horse Creek, or Big Bend were always willing to try their luck elsewhere. Some pushed north beyond Fort George into the Peace River area, and before long, reports that the area was good gold-bearing country began to filter out.

In spring 1869, Dewdney got together a syndicate of Soda Creek ranchers and businessmen to send a prospecting party into Peace River. The partners subscribed a total of $1,200, and the colony's governor, now Anthony Musgrave, contributed $1,000 from public funds. They outfitted fourteen men and sent them north early in the season. Nothing was heard all summer long. In October, the prospectors turned up in Quesnel and admitted to finding promising diggings at Vital Creek near Tatla Lake. News got out, and there was a stampede into the area. Nothing came of it, however; the creek held little enough of the precious metal.[60]

Dewdney had spent a decade in the Pacific colony and had little to show for it in the form that mattered most to him: material wealth. His pattern of migratory contract work was not unusual at the time. Frontier conditions dictated that more people were engaged in seasonal or occasional labour associated with resource exploitation and the construction of towns and transportation infrastructures rather than in agriculture, which was only slowly establishing itself. It was a familiar career path in a community of strangers where few had put down roots and where tradition and concepts of social cohesion were almost entirely absent, save for bonds of common class or ethnic origin.

He had experienced British Columbia in its most romantic transitional phase as it went from a trading colony in the hands of an archetypal concessionary company to a settlement colony invaded by gold diggers and adventurers. Presiding over these dramatic changes was a nervous imperial bureaucracy. In asserting its authority over the rapidly expanding frontier, the administration sought to direct social evolution along an orderly path, ensuring that economic exploitation was conducted according to rules that minimized investor risk.[61] Familiar structures of law and authority – Judge Begbie, the gold commissioners, the Royal Engineers, and the like –

inspired confidence while constraining the freebooting adventurism associated with the frontier in the republic to the south. In an important sense, Dewdney's trail, his most notable achievement to date, represented more than a conduit of trade to the advantage of New Westminster merchants; it was also a line of contact to a remote corner of the colony so that the state could assert its control. The trail, and others like it, were essential arteries of communication, confronting the challenges of geography and ensuring that localities did not develop their own peculiar institutions. In this manner, the trailblazer made his own contribution to stabilizing the colonial state. He was soon to play a more direct role in its evolution.

CHAPTER 2

The Politician

By 1866, the gold colony was in decline. Wild Horse Creek and Big Bend had been disappointing, and the Cariboo had seen its best days. The precious metal was losing its glitter, and the government had accumulated staggering debts in building roads to the gold fields.

In November of that year, the imperial government as a measure of economy amalgamated the island and mainland colonies into the united colony of British Columbia, keeping Seymour as governor. After some clever manoeuvring by island politicians, Victoria was chosen as the capital. It was there that the united colony's legislative council sat. It comprised twenty-three members, only nine of whom were elected. The remainder were either senior civil servants or appointees of the governor.[1] The system ensured political domination by the English and Anglo-Irish elite. The council met in one of the "birdcages," a series of quaint oriental-style pavilions built by a Scottish handyman in 1859. The pavilions were located on the site of the present legislature and were demolished to make way for that building.

The united colony began life with a debt of $1.5 million and a stagnant economy. The future was far from promising and circumstances dictated that some important decisions had to be made.

One possibility was to continue as a British colony. This path was most favoured by the British-born, at least initially. The only problem was that London seemed increasingly unwilling to subsidize remote possessions, especially those as spendthrift as British Columbia.

Another possibility was annexation to the United States, an idea favoured by some Victoria businessmen with ties to San Francisco. The Americans, of course, would have been happy to oblige. Their purchase of Alaska in 1867 showed that their territorial ambitions were as strong as ever.

But the creation of the Dominion of Canada in the same year raised a third possibility – joining Confederation. Understandably enough, this option was supported by the Canadians in the colony. They believed that it would end the social and political privileges of the English and Anglo-Irish elite, which they resented, by bringing in democratic institutions. They also believed that union with Canada, accompanied by a railway through the mountains, would ensure economic prosperity.[2]

Although Canadians tended to be concentrated on the mainland, their most prominent spokesman was an islander, Amor de Cosmos. A Nova Scotian by birth, de Cosmos had been a thorn in the side of the elite ever since he established himself as a newspaperman and political agitator in Victoria in 1858. He had campaigned incessantly for responsible government over the years, and now added Confederation to the reforms he demanded in his articulate, if theatrical, way.[3]

The debates and deliberations surrounding the colony's future did not escape Dewdney's attention. Since his brief sojourn in London, politics had been among his interests, but it had always been a matter of minor concern next to his abiding passion for making money. Now, however, financial and political concerns were inextricably interwoven in the sense that the colony's economy was in crisis, and the return of prosperity would depend on the political road ahead.

Dewdney was close to members of the colonial elite – men such as Judge Begbie, Peter O'Reilly, and Joseph Trutch, the commissioner of lands and works. He shared with them a belief in the superior claim of the well-born to public office appointments and a concomitant antipathy to responsible government. But unlike Begbie and the others, he held no high office and did not fear losing his place should Canada take over. Therefore, he was inclined to be more open-minded and less partisan than many of the elite on the question of Confederation. And while he loved to hobnob with the rich and powerful, he didn't share in their social condescension towards Canadians. Indeed, he had often worked closely with Canadians over the years – Walter Moberly, for example – and had come to respect them.

Initially, Dewdney knew little or nothing about Canadian politics and politicians, but he was willing to learn. One day, shortly before Confederation became a reality, he stopped at Quesnel on his way south from the Cariboo. There he met an old brewer named Kerr who hailed from Upper Canada, and they spent the evening together chatting on Kerr's veranda. Kerr informed his visitor of the momentous political developments taking shape in British North America and in the course of their conversation produced from his pocket his most prized possession – a personal letter from John A. Macdonald. The old brewer was a great admirer of the Canadian leader, and the praise he lavished on the man made a profound and lasting impression on Dewdney. From that moment onwards, Dewdney's interest in Canadian politics blossomed, and he was increasingly receptive to the idea that British Columbia's future lay in a transcontinental British territory as envisaged by Macdonald.[4]

His own entry into the world of politics was apparently unintentional, and his eagerness to participate was far from evident, at least in the beginning. In the elections for the legislative council held in fall 1868, he was returned for the District of Kootenay.[5] This sprawling constituency with a few dozen voters took in the southeastern part of the colony. Dewdney was well known to the settlers on account of building the trail to Wild Horse Creek through the district some years previously. He claimed that the voters nominated and returned him without his knowledge while he was busy at his Soda Creek property. It was a plausible claim because communication was poor and the rules governing the electoral process were far from precise.

The council session lasted from 17 December 1868 to 15 March 1869, and the desirability of joining Confederation was the major issue at hand. Elected members from the mainland supported union with Canada while the Vancouver Islanders were opposed. Most of the appointed members, fearful for their jobs, were opposed. So, too, was Governor Seymour who felt that union was impractical while Canada and British Columbia were separated by the Hudson's Bay Company territory of Rupert's Land. To John A. Macdonald's great disappointment, no resolution in favour of Confederation was adopted.[6]

Where Dewdney stood on the Canadian question at this stage is not clear because he neither campaigned in the election nor turned up for the council session. The press criticized him for his non-attendance and implied that he had not made the journey from Soda Creek to Victoria because travel expenses had not been provided. This he vigorously repudiated, stating that by the time he had received news of his election, the session was so far advanced that he would have missed most of it even had he set out immediately for Victoria.[7]

The truth of this claim is difficult to assess because it is not known when he learned of his election. News travelled slowly, and the journey from Soda Creek to Victoria by stage and steamer took the best part of a week. The leading newspapers in the colony, the *British Colonist* (Victoria) and the *British Columbian* (New Westminster), were run respectively by Amor de Cosmos and John Robson, Canadians who championed union as well as democratic reform.[8] They probably suspected that Dewdney, as a well-bred Englishman, would not be on their side.

Dewdney resolved to attend the next council session, but before it opened, the cause of Confederation was immeasurably strengthened by

changing circumstances. In 1869, Gladstone's Liberals formed a government in London that was strongly supportive of extending Canada to the
Pacific. In that year, too, the Hudson's Bay Company agreed to surrender
its territory to Ottawa, removing an obstacle to union. And on 10 June,
Governor Seymour died while settling Indian disputes at Bella Coola. His
replacement was Anthony Musgrave, a former governor of Newfound-
land, who, upon his arrival in Victoria, received instructions from London
to promote the entry of British Columbia into Confederation.[9]

On 17 February 1870, Dewdney arrived in Victoria after a difficult six-
day journey from Soda Creek. He had travelled by sleigh for part of the way
where the roads were under heavy drifts of snow.[10] This time he would not
miss the session of the legislative council that was opening in the birdcages
as he pulled into town.

The major issue, as before, was Confederation. But now the idea had the
full support of the governor, who drew up a list of proposed terms with
which British Columbia might negotiate union with Canada. Among the
more important demands were that Canada pay off the colony's debt and
build a railway to the Pacific seaboard.

The debate on Confederation opened in the birdcages on 9 March.
Champions of the cause, such as newspaperman John Robson, Lands and
Works Commissioner Joseph Trutch, Attorney General Henry Crease,
and the irrepressible Amor de Cosmos, emphasized the economic advan-
tages of union and its potential to ward off annexation to the United States.
Opponents, such as Dr. J.S. Helmcken, elected member for Victoria,
warned that Canada was too far away and was unlikely to do justice to
British Columbian concerns once the knot was tied.

For the first two days of the debate, Dewdney said nothing beyond a
remark during Helmcken's anti-Confederation speech that hinted at his
support for union. When he rose to address the assembly on 11 March, the
trend was clearly in favour of Canada. He admitted to being unfamiliar
with the intricacies of the question because of his long absence in the
"Upper Country," and he had therefore listened carefully to the speeches
of his colleagues before declaring one way or the other. In the past, he
noted, his constituents had opposed Confederation, but he believed that
they would now support it under the terms proposed by the governor. The
terms were what the country was "fairly entitled to demand" and would
have his support.

As a political debut, it was unimpressive. The speech lacked the passion
and conviction shown by Trutch, de Cosmos, and others; it suggested inde-
cisiveness and an anxiety to please his constituents and the governor.

On 14 March, the council began to discuss the terms of union in detail.

In the days that followed, the terms were sometimes modified by amendments proposed by various members – in effect, British Columbia would be demanding more from Ottawa in subsidies, grants, and services. Members of the council were unanimously agreed on being generous to the colony with Canadian money.

Clause 15 of the terms, however, raised contention. It proposed that the constitutional structure of British Columbia's government not be changed after union with Canada. This proposal roused the ire of several elected members of council, including Robson and de Cosmos, who felt that responsible government was long overdue and should accompany entry into Confederation. But the British-born appointed members were not so keen on democratic structures and argued that the electorate was too small and too thinly scattered throughout the land for such a system.[11]

Dewdney, who had sat silently for several days, joined in the debate on 22 March in opposition to responsible government. Claiming to speak for mainlanders on the question, his principal argument was that nobody wanted it: "I have travelled through this country as much as any Hon. Member of this Council, and I have been brought in contact with all classes, and have mixed with all classes, and I have yet to meet the first individual who has expressed his desire for Responsible Government."

His own constituents in particular, he argued, had no interest in it: "All they want is money to keep their trails in order and a resident magistrate to administer and carry out the laws." People were complaining not about the form of government but about its cost. And the responsible system would only make it more expensive because "speculation and dishonesty would be the order of the day." British Columbia, he observed, was a model of good government and there was no need to change anything.

Opposition to responsible government was his most vigorous contribution to the debate. Although his political views were still at the formative stage, a tendency towards cautious conservatism was clearly emerging. He favoured the gradual evolution of political institutions as a safeguard against mob rule. And he had no time for the uncompromising democratic program of Amor de Cosmos. Indeed, he was already developing a dislike for de Cosmos, and the two men would cross swords frequently during the 1870s. With appointed members in a comfortable majority, Clause 15 remained unaltered.

The debate continued until 6 April with Dewdney contributing hardly a word. In the end, the council endorsed British Columbia's entry into Confederation and agreed to send delegates to Ottawa to negotiate the terms of union.[12]

Some months later, an editorial in the *British Colonist*, probably from the pen of de Cosmos, attacked Dewdney's position on responsible government and described his claim that he had never met anyone in favour of it as "an astounding statement." The writer noted, with relief, that Dewdney had not sought re-election and was back in the interior prospecting for gold.[13] The *British Colonist*, ever since de Cosmos began running it in 1858, had been a mouthpiece for political reform and an unflinching enemy of privilege. Dewdney was now added to the list of those the newspaper regularly accused of "toadyism."

Members of the legislative council received no salaries, and Dewdney's sojourn in Victoria had interfered with his making a living. Before leaving the capital, he reached an understanding with Joseph Trutch that kept him busy throughout the summer surveying pre-emption properties in the Cariboo and Lillooet Districts.[14]

Meanwhile, the mixed reports of gold strikes filtering in from the Peace River country maintained Dewdney's interest in this road to riches. News that a man named Germansen, with his partner, "Nigger Dan," had struck pay dirt on a creek flowing into the Omenica River arrived in November. There was reason for scepticism at first because Germansen, who had worked on Dewdney's ranch, was an inexperienced miner, and Dan was known to be "the biggest liar in the country."[15] But independent confirmation convinced Dewdney that this find might be the big one, and he resolved to stake his claim before the inevitable rush began.

Although the season was late, he set out immediately, going on horseback as far as Fort St. James. The water was still open, and he travelled by boat across Stuart and Tatla Lakes as far as Tatla Landing. From there, he journeyed overland to the Omenica River and then downstream to Germansen Creek. Along the way, he met two Irishmen, Denis and Jim Cane, unrelated to one another as it turned out and not even on speaking terms, and he accompanied them to the diggings. They were moving with all possible haste because it was rumoured that 500 men would be seeking claims on the creek that winter, and they could already see some of the parties on the trail.

Dewdney succeeded in staking the claim of his choice at Germansen. He worked it until the onset of winter forced him to rest. On Christmas Day he left for home, travelling on foot with a 48-lb. pack containing food and his camping gear. A hazardous and eventful journey lay ahead through deep snow and in bitterly cold temperatures. He fell through the ice once but did not go under because of a long pole he was carrying. At Indian encampments and Hudson's Bay Company stores along the way, he found shelter and supplies, and if not for such help, he surely would have perished. The next summer, he hired twenty-four men to work his claim. But the area was so remote and difficult to reach that food and other necessities were in short supply and enormously expensive. At the end of the season, he found that his costs matched his return in gold and no profits resulted from the venture.[16]

He continued to participate but in his habitual manner: trail-blazing and surveying. In May, he was on the Skeena River, where Hazelton now stands, marking a trail eastwards to Babine Lake and on to Tatla Landing and the Omenica gold fields. Because settlers were already moving into the Skeena Valley, he set land aside for a townsite and an Indian reserve. He held an appointment of justice of the peace and in this capacity inquired into cases of theft and other disputes.[17] Ad hoc appointments to these positions had been the practice since the 1850s.[18] Mining continued to interest him, but for the immediate future, he abandoned it as the road to riches. Cattle raising was also losing its appeal, and around this time, he sold his ranch at Soda Creek.

In August, he was back in the Yale-Lytton District surveying preemption claims and pastoral leases. His contract from the Lands and Works Department provided $200 per month and $4 per day in personal expenses while he was on the road.[19] These terms were good, but he still worried about the future. He had reached what he described as a "critical period" in his life, and he sought something with better prospects. Later in the month, when Trutch offered to place him in charge of a surveying party for the Canadian Pacific Railway, Dewdney gladly accepted.[20]

The railway, of course, was the major item in the terms of union under which British Columbia entered Confederation in 1871. The Canadian government of John A. Macdonald, overjoyed at the prospect of extending its domain to the Pacific, agreed to complete the lines of steel within ten years. This project was absurdly ambitious for a country of 3.5 million inhabitants, but for many British Columbians, the promise became akin to a sacred trust. Railway politics were to dominate the relations between Ottawa and its Pacific province for over a decade, and Dewdney became stuck in the middle of the wrangle after his re-entry into public life.

Upon union with Canada, British Columbia was represented in Ottawa by three senators and six members of parliament. The men returned to the House of Commons all pledged to support the government of John A. Macdonald. They were all keen to see the Pacific railway built, and the prime minister was committed to building it.[21] Besides, the federal Liberal leader, Alexander Mackenzie, had described the promise to complete the line within a decade as "an act of insane recklessness," and the Liberal Party's intellectual, Edward Blake, had termed it "a preposterous proposition."[22]

The British Columbia members had barely settled in Ottawa when

Parliament was dissolved in summer 1872. Crimean War veteran and Okanagan rancher Charles F. Houghton did not run in the long and difficult election campaign that dragged on into the fall.[23] His withdrawal enticed Dewdney to re-enter politics, and Dewdney was returned as the member of parliament for Yale.[24] Like the other members from British Columbia, he would support John A. Macdonald, who was as committed as ever to the transcontinental railway. Macdonald and the Conservatives were re-elected, as it turned out, having accepted enormous campaign contributions from Sir Hugh Allan, the Montreal shipping tycoon who was hoping to be president of the railway company.[25]

Dewdney made his decision to return to public life when matters looked less than promising for his career. Neither ranching nor mining had made him rich, and he faced an uncertain future of successive surveying contracts. What he really wanted was a sinecure – a well-placed government appointment with a steady income that would still allow him to speculate in business ventures as he saw fit. He believed that politics might lead to such an arrangement, because it certainly had for several of his friends and acquaintances.

By a happy coincidence, within a month of his election to the House of Commons, such a job came his way. On 20 November, George Walkem, British Columbia's commissioner of lands and works, offered him the post of provincial surveyor general, made vacant by the retirement of B.W. Pearse. Dewdney accepted without hesitation. Everyone assumed that he would then give up his seat in the Commons. But if we are to believe Dewdney's account, his constituents raised a fuss at the prospect of not being represented at the next sitting of Parliament because there wouldn't be time to elect a replacement. He therefore proposed that he keep his seat and the surveyor general position and be granted leave from his duties in Victoria when the House of Commons was in session.[26] The idea was not so strange as it might seem because various forms of "dual representation" were permitted in those days. De Cosmos, for instance, represented Victoria in the House of Commons and in the British Columbia legislature at the same time, and indeed, he was about to become premier of the province while retaining his Commons seat.[27]

Nonetheless, Walkem wouldn't hear of such an arrangement in the case of the surveyor general, whose department was understaffed and overworked. Nor would he accept Dewdney's suggestion that British Columbia would be advantageously represented in Ottawa by its surveyor general because the railway and railway-belt lands were of such critical importance to the province. When presented with an ultimatum, one job or the other,

Dewdney chose to retain his Commons seat.[28] He did so, it seems, under considerable public pressure. An editorial in the *British Colonist*, for example, urged him not to disfranchise his constituents by his selfishness. If he didn't go to Ottawa, the British Columbia delegation would be one man short the newspaper warned, John A. Macdonald would lose a supporter, and the Yale District placed "in a queer dilemma."[29]

With some misgivings, Dewdney gave up secure employment in familiar surroundings for the uncertain world of federal politics. Being a member of parliament did have its appeal, however. It was a prestigious post and his fellow members from the Pacific province, with the exception of de Cosmos, were drawn from the British and Anglo-Irish elite. Besides, the position offered the prospect of further opportunities and connections, not to mention more time with his wife, who had usually been left behind during his surveying assignments. He set off for Ottawa early in 1873 with Jane by his side. They travelled via San Francisco, which had been connected by railway to the east since May 1869. With such modern transportation at their disposal, the journey took a little more than three weeks and can only have impressed on Dewdney the importance of a rail link to the Pacific in Canadian territory.

Ottawa, on the other hand, was far from impressive, apart from the newly built Gothic Revival parliament buildings. Still bearing the scars of its previous life as a lumber town, Ottawa was described in 1872 by Governor General Lord Dufferin as "a jumble of brand new houses and shops, and a wilderness of wooden shanties spread along either side of long broad strips of mud."[30]

Jane Dewdney, who considered herself at home among British Columbia's British and Anglo-Irish elite, found her new abode dreary and its inhabitants even more so. "I never in my life saw such a collection of downright *ugly* and awkward looking men," she wrote to her friend, Caroline O'Reilly (Peter's wife). "Their dancing can only be imagined. My impression of a Canadian ball is that it is better to look on ... than join in." Some Canadian ladies had called on her. "I don't think I'd care much for them," she remarked. Happily, one member of parliament's wife was "quite an English Lady," which meant she was someone with whom to share a dignified cup of tea. Jane also liked Lady Macdonald, and the two women struck up a lifelong friendship.[31]

While the political wives were developing bonds of intimacy, their husbands were similarly engaged. Dewdney met the prime minister shortly before the House met and fell under the old chieftain's spell. Here's how he described their encounter:

He received me in a very kindly manner in his office, and at once questioned me about British Columbian affairs. Knowing that I was a perfect stranger he offered to do anything he could towards giving me information. He made upon me – as he made upon all newcomers – a great impression at our first meeting, and from that day until the time of his death we were fast personal and political friends. He would be about 58 years of age at that time, and I think he would have been picked out in any community as a strong and singularly gifted man. Every man and woman in the country was always anxious to hear him, and, if possible, to come into personal touch with him. He seemed to fill the popular imagination.[32]

All was going well, even the economy, when Parliament opened on a crisp spring day in March 1873. The government had been weakened in the election, but with the support of a number of independents, including the six British Columbia MPs, it could count on a majority of around twenty.

A bill incorporating the Canadian Pacific Railway had been passed the year before. It allowed for a private company to receive 50 million acres of land and $30 million in government grants to build the railway. With the election won, Macdonald awarded the lucrative contract to Sir Hugh Allan, the chief financier of the Conservative victory. And new surveys were going ahead under Sandford Fleming, engineer in chief. Dewdney and his fellow British Columbians in Parliament had reason to be pleased.

But on 2 April, a Liberal MP rose in the House, accused the government of accepting election funds from Allan in return for the railway charter, and demanded an investigation. After much procrastination, an inquiry was agreed to, and as the inquiry proceeded during the summer, the government clearly had a major scandal on its hands. When Parliament reopened in October, Macdonald knew that he had lost the confidence of the country. His support among independents in the House began to slip away, and on 5 November, facing imminent defeat, he and his government resigned.[33]

Dewdney and the other MPs from the Pacific province stood by Macdonald until the end. Their interests were regional rather than national in scope, and their principal concern was that Canada fulfil the terms promised at the time of union. The railway was the major item in the terms, and its future was far from certain with Macdonald, the railway's great champion, out of power.

The new prime minister was Alexander Mackenzie, a dull, Scottish-born stonemason who led a Liberal Party still in the process of formation. Mackenzie was committed to honest, efficient, and economical government – a poor omen for the Pacific railway. He was not against the railway, but he considered the promise to build it in ten years irresponsible. There were good reasons for caution. The Union-Central Pacific Railway, which had reached San Francisco in 1869, was a financial disaster, even though California already had a population of 2 million. And the Intercolonial Railway, which was to link Central Canada and the Maritimes, was costing a fortune to build. Moreover, as the Liberals took power, the country was sliding into an economic depression, and government revenues were falling. The national debt already stood at $134 million and was gobbling up nearly $6 million annually in interest charges.[34]

Mackenzie called a general election early in 1874 and was returned comfortably to power. The scandal-rocked Conservatives were routed in every province except British Columbia, where the populace was as attached as ever to the terms of union and John A. Macdonald.

In British Columbia, the election was an unpleasant affair, with regional rivalries and personal animosities taking their toll. The intense dislike between de Cosmos and Dewdney was a major source of friction. Dewdney felt that de Cosmos's partisan attachment to Vancouver Island interests was jeopardizing the larger interests of the province as a whole. He had a point.

In 1873, de Cosmos was both premier of British Columbia and MP for Victoria, and he tried to use his position to change the terms of union to the advantage of his constituents. The terms committed the Dominion government to guarantee for ten years the interest of a loan not to exceed £100,000 to build a dry dock in Esquimalt. De Cosmos wanted to change this loan to a direct grant so that the work could begin immediately and provide much-needed employment. He secured a grant of £50,000 from the Macdonald government before it fell and another £30,000 from the British Admiralty. But back in Victoria in January 1874, his proposed changes to the terms caused outrage. British Columbians feared that such a move would be a dangerous precedent and would play into the hands of Prime Minister Mackenzie, who was only too willing to modify the terms. After street demonstrations against him, de Cosmos resigned the premiership and his seat in the assembly on 11 February and concentrated on getting re-elected to the House of Commons.[35]

During the campaign, Dewdney and de Cosmos waged relentless campaigns against one another, although they were running in different constituencies. Dewdney posed as the champion of the terms of union and portrayed his rival as the man who would betray them for personal gain. He claimed that during the 1873 parliamentary session, de Cosmos had suggested that the British Columbia MPs demand $75,000 worth of railway stock as the price of their support for Macdonald, but that none of them would agree to such a deal. And he accused de Cosmos of making a secret pact with Mackenzie to modify the terms: "There is not in the Dominion of Canada, a man more double-dealing and deceitful. I know him and have watched him – beware!"[36] Whether there was any truth to these accusations is hard to say, but they showed the growing personal dislike between the politicians.

Both men, it turned out, were re-elected, de Cosmos for Victoria and Dewdney for Yale.[37] Back in the House of Commons at the end of March, sharp exchanges between them aired their bitterness to a wider audience. De Cosmos had come to realize that modifying the terms of union would be politically hazardous for a British Columbian, and he claimed that his intentions had been misunderstood all along.[38]

Even so, the representatives of Yale and Victoria continued to snipe at one another – in a sense, a continuation of the historic rivalry between mainland and island. The issue was no longer the terms of union, which they were seemingly agreed on, but rather the location of the railway terminus on the Pacific coast. There was a lot at stake. The site of the terminus was sure to prosper, unless the country went broke first in building the lines of steel.

By 1874, it was more or less accepted that the railway would penetrate the Rockies through the Yellowhead Pass. Further on, at Tête Jaune Cache, a number of different routes to the sea were possibilities, and two of these, in particular, were likely prospects. One route followed the North Thompson River to Kamloops and then the Fraser River to end at Burrard Inlet. The other went by Fort George, southwest through the Cariboo, and reached the sea at Bute Inlet. From there, a series of bridges to Vancouver Island was envisaged, with the railway terminus at Victoria-Esquimalt.[39]

Dewdney quickly established himself as the leading advocate of the Burrard route and mainland interests while de Cosmos championed Bute and the island. In some ways, their partisan advocacy of these routes overshadowed the broader issue of getting the railway built at all. And getting it built, or even started, was by no means certain, given that Alexander Mackenzie held the reins of power and the purse strings in Ottawa. On the 1874 election trail, the Liberal leader had made clear his intention of modifying the deal with British Columbia and moving forwards with caution. Once returned to office with a comfortable majority, that is exactly what he did. In spite of the terms of union, Mackenzie was determined that no railway construction would begin in British Columbia until the most thorough surveys had been done of the many possible routes. This approach made a lot of sense under the circumstances, but many thought that the prime minister was procrastinating unnecessarily in order to evade the Dominion's obligations to the Pacific province.

Mackenzie's tactics were particularly annoying to de Cosmos, the other

Vancouver Island MPs, and the British Columbia government of George Walkem, which was committed to island interests. This group was pushing for an immediate start to construction, reasoning that with Esquimalt the declared terminus, and most surveys done on the Bute-Yellowhead line, their favoured route was likely to be chosen.

Dewdney, on the other hand, opposed precipitous action and argued persistently for a complete survey of the Fraser-Burrard route before any rails were put in place. Mackenzie's cautious approach appealed to him, and he was able to develop a rapprochement of sorts with the new government. Although still sentimentally attached to the Conservatives, he realized he would have to work with the Liberals to get anything accomplished. At the time, everyone believed that Macdonald and his party were finished and had no hope of a political comeback in the foreseeable future.

In March 1874, Mackenzie sent James D. Edgar, a prominent Liberal, to Victoria to negotiate a compromise with Premier Walkem. Edgar proposed the construction of a wagon road and telegraph line connecting British Columbia to the Prairies, the vigorous undertaking of surveys through the mountains, and an annual expenditure of $1.5 million on rail construction once the surveys were completed. He also offered a railway connecting Esquimalt and Nanaimo, to be built immediately. In May, sensing that these proposals would be unpopular, Walkem brought the negotiations to an abrupt end.[40]

Dewdney, who despised Walkem, described this turn of events as a "disastrous termination to a very friendly overture on behalf of the Dominion Government." He had some concerns about Edgar's proposals, especially the Esquimalt-Nanaimo railway, which he feared might strengthen the case for Bute Inlet. But he favoured the idea of systematic surveys on the mainland, believing that they would work in favour of the Fraser-Burrard route.[41]

Later in the year, Lord Carnarvon, the British colonial secretary, was able to get Victoria and Ottawa to agree to a new set of proposals, not unlike the Edgar terms. This time, a deadline of 31 December 1890 was set for completion of the railway, a sum of $2 million was to be spent annually on construction in British Columbia once surveys were ready, and the Esquimalt-Nanaimo railway was to be built immediately.[42]

Dewdney, a moderate by inclination, thought the Carnarvon terms a useful beginning, and he liked the spirit of compromise they embodied. Nor did he object to the island railway as long as it was simply a local work and not a step towards the adoption of Bute Inlet.[43] He didn't need to worry. In March 1875, a bill to establish the Esquimalt-Nanaimo railway passed in the Commons, but on 6 April, it was defeated in the Senate.

Mackenzie, with his party badly divided on the issue, did not reintroduce the measure.[44]

Meanwhile, Dewdney and de Cosmos were in a war of words in the House of Commons and in the press over the location of the western railway terminus. At times, the exchanges were moderate in tone, but they became increasingly bitter as the months and years went by. Their arguments centred on the strategic and commercial advantages of the two routes, on the relative merits of Esquimalt-Victoria and Burrard Inlet as harbours, and on the engineering challenges posed by the coastal mountains – whether the railway would come down the Homathco Valley into Bute or down the Fraser Canyon on its way to Burrard.

In May 1874, Mackenzie assured Dewdney that no route through the coastal mountains had been selected and that no decision would be made until thorough surveys had been done. Survey work that summer in the Homathco Valley raised serious doubts about the practicality of the Bute Inlet route, and by the fall, Dewdney was assuring his mainland constituents that the Mackenzie government would make "the best decision."[45]

Bute was by no means finished, because that route could count on the unflinching support of Marcus Smith, who was in charge of the railway surveys in British Columbia. Smith, a heavy-drinking slave-driver of a man, had worked so hard to blaze a trail to the Homathco Valley that he was reluctant to abandon it.[46]

By 1875, Dewdney was concerned that Bute had not been entirely written off. The government was also looking seriously at alternative routes farther north along the coast, at North Bentinck Arm or Gardner Channel, for example. The surveys were exasperatingly slow, but he was still confident that when all the information was available, the government would make the right decision.[47]

The slowness was partly due to bad luck, the nature of the terrain, and some of the unavoidable realities of government contract work. In January 1874, the Canadian Pacific Survey offices in Ottawa burned down and much of what had already been done was destroyed. The work itself was difficult and dangerous, and Sandford Fleming could never get enough men with the requisite skills and ruggedness to take it on. Moreover, he was forced to put up with incompetent employees whose political connections rendered them immune to the normal demands of the job. Interestingly, Dewdney's brother, Walter, was in this category. Once, in 1875, when he was supposed to be in charge of transportation for a survey party, Walter was found "blind drunk and making an ass of himself." But because his brother was a prominent member of parliament, he could not be touched.[48]

The Mackenzie government was careful to cultivate Dewdney, who, with the support of James Cunningham, MP for New Westminster, had emerged as a welcome voice of reason in British Columbia and a useful foil to the histrionics of de Cosmos and Walkem. Dewdney felt that the Walkem government was already moving dangerously in the direction of secession from Confederation, and in the provincial election campaign of 1875, he urged voters to elect men who would adopt a "conciliatory manner" towards Ottawa. In a major speech at Cache Creek, he reminded his listeners that Joseph Trutch, one of the British Columbia delegates who had negotiated the terms of union, and now lieutenant governor of the province, had been flexible on the completion date of the railway so as not to bankrupt the Dominion. He, Dewdney, had always agreed with Trutch.[49]

Dewdney was aware, nonetheless, of the widespread dissatisfaction in British Columbia with the delays in commencing construction. To allay this, he proposed to Mackenzie in March 1876 that the government start work on the rail line that season at the Yellowhead Pass, moving westwards to Tête Jaune Cache because that part of the route, at least, had been decided on.[50]

Mackenzie was still unwilling to commit himself, but he and his government appreciated Dewdney's moderate stance and commitment to reconciliation. This was all the more important because Canadian public opinion was growing impatient with the persistent demands of de Cosmos and the others. And an important faction in the Liberal Party led by Edward Blake had had enough of British Columbia. Just before the supply debate scheduled for April, which had become an annual platform for the airing of British Columbia grievances, J.D. Edgar suggested to Dewdney that if he made a speech crediting all parties with a desire to build the railway and cement Confederation, he would help "to cultivate a warm and favourable opinion of British Columbia among Canadians at large."[51]

Dewdney was happy to oblige. In his speech in the Commons on 5 April, he observed that British Columbia had "a good deal of right on its side" as far as the railway dispute was concerned, but he was careful to note that neither the Macdonald nor the Mackenzie administrations had wronged the province.

The fact that construction work had not yet begun was due in large measure, he felt, to the "magnitude of the engineering difficulties encountered." Sectional rivalries in British Columbia had also been a problem, he acknowledged. And he put a good deal of blame on the intransigent attitude of successive provincial governments that had tried to force Ottawa to begin construction before surveys were completed. He considered this pressure evidence of very poor judgment and neither in the interests of the Dominion nor the province.

While he had the floor, Dewdney decided to put in a strong pitch for the Fraser-Burrard route while dismissing the rival route favoured by Vancouver Islanders. He pointed out that from Tête Jaune Cache the distance to Burrard Inlet was 466 miles while the distance to Bute Inlet was 546 miles. With rail construction through British Columbia estimated at between $30,000 and $45,000 per mile, the savings on the shorter route would be considerable. He admitted that the Fraser Canyon presented difficulties, but he noted that grades averaged only eight feet per mile along that route whereas they were 104 feet per mile along the Homathco River. Best of all, Burrard Inlet was a harbour "unequalled in British Columbia" and surrounded by excellent farmland. The other route had nothing comparable.

He concluded the speech by confessing that he was still attached to his "first political love" – John A. Macdonald and the Conservatives – and that this attachment would probably continue. But as long as the Liberal government was pushing forwards with the railway, he would assist the government in the House.[52]

By his own admission, Dewdney was no great public speaker, but this solid performance was calculated to generate goodwill towards British Columbia on both sides of the House. His reasonable position on the railway in general, blended with strong arguments in favour of Burrard Inlet, probably did his favourite route no harm. And his reputation as a pioneer pathfinder and engineer undoubtedly gave weight to his arguments. The declared attachment to John A. Macdonald was evidently sincere, but it may also suggest that Dewdney was a keen observer of political trends. By 1876, the Conservative leader was taking a more active interest in public life and was contemplating a return to power one day – something that was inconceivable just a year earlier.[53]

In the meantime, Mackenzie's position was unassailable, and Dewdney knew that the Liberal leader was still the key to the adoption of the Fraser-Burrard route. A remark by Mackenzie in the House that session to the effect that a line from the Rocky Mountains to Fort George had been "practically located" made him fear that Bute was being favoured once again. But before Dewdney left to spend the summer in British Columbia, the prime minister assured him that no decision would be made until the Fraser Valley had been thoroughly surveyed. On 10 May, the MP for Yale was the guest of honour at a public meeting in New Westminster where he was lauded by the citizenry for his role in promoting the Fraser-Burrard route. Dewdney addressed the gathering at length, expressing confidence that the prime minister would make the right decision. In the course of his speech, he read out a letter he had sent Mackenzie, describing in detail the case for the Fraser Valley and sprinkled with references to the prime minister as a practical man uninfluenced by speculators and political manipulation.[54] He then left for the northern interior to check for himself the route between Tête Jaune Cache and Fort George.

Meanwhile, Governor General Lord Dufferin, alarmed at the rise of separatist sentiment in British Columbia, proposed that he play the role of conciliator, and Mackenzie agreed. Dufferin arrived in Victoria on 16 August and was warmly received. His smooth words had a soothing effect on hotheaded islanders as he appealed for patience on the railway question. He visited Bute and Burrard and took the stagecoach up the old Cariboo Road along the Fraser. Dewdney had come down from the north for the viceregal visit and played a role in organizing His Excellency's trip to the interior. He may also have used the occasion to point out the advantages of a railway along that route.

Dufferin returned to Ottawa convinced that Bute was hopeless and that the only practical railway route was along the Fraser to Burrard. In an interview with the prime minister in November, he persuaded Mackenzie to take a closer look at the Fraser Valley, adding weight to Dewdney's persistent advocacy.[55]

With the matter still undecided, Dewdney and de Cosmos continued their verbal duelling in the 1877 parliamentary sessions. On 14 March, de Cosmos moved for a committee of twelve to inquire into the railway surveys. He accused the government of withholding the engineers' reports, which allegedly favoured the Bute-Esquimalt route. The proposed committee would unearth these facts. But when he said that he had it on the authority of the engineers and members of the House that the Fraser-Burrard route had been surveyed and found impractical, Dewdney interjected, "Who was the authority? Mention the names."

De Cosmos refused to name his informants but agreed to do so once the committee was appointed. The committee, he predicted, would prove that the Bute route would attract more way traffic while the Fraser route would allow traffic to be siphoned off by American lines, and besides, it would not be the best for national defence.

Prime Minister Mackenzie denied that his government was being in any way secretive about the railway terminus. And he went on to remind de Cosmos of the enormous sums already spent on surveys and of the complexity of the issue. His remarks, nonetheless, suggested that he was leaning to Burrard because of its superior navigation.

Dewdney spoke out forcibly against the committee proposed by his rival. He recalled how he had travelled the previous summer between Fort George and Tête Jaune Cache, part of the route towards Bute Inlet, and he found much of it to be very inhospitable country. Way traffic, he believed, would be far superior along the Fraser-Burrard route. And he offered the following explanation for de Cosmos's persistent claim that the Fraser River country was difficult: "The hon. gentleman made a trip through it once, and, when in one of those nervous conditions in which the House often found him, he jumped out of the stage and, had it not been for his coattails, would have rolled over a precipice." The motion was rejected by the House after de Cosmos refused to withdraw it.[56]

The bitterness between the two rivals erupted in the House again in April when de Cosmos complained that the clause in the terms of union requiring regular mail service between San Francisco and Victoria was not being fulfilled to the letter. Dewdney seized the occasion to poke fun at de Cosmos and belittle the anchorage capacity of Victoria harbour.[57]

They were at it once more the following day when the member for Victoria opposed the vote for the British Columbia Indian Reserve Commission – it was a waste of time and money, he said. When he had been premier of the province, he recalled, he had treated the Indians liberally, giving them twenty acres per family, which was enough for their needs. Dewdney pounced on the statement, saying that it would be better to give the Indians the land that they wanted. De Cosmos only opposed the commission because he had no control of patronage appointments to it, he said.[58]

These exchanges showed that differences of opinion between Dewdney and de Cosmos reached beyond the railway question and that the personal animosity that divided them had deepened over the years. The location of the railway terminus remained the major source of contention, however, and it was still far from settled.

A week later, during the annual railway supply debate, Dewdney's speech hinted at a growing impatience with the government. The prime minister himself was sincere, he believed, but the same could not be said for all members of his administration. He accused the government of having made errors of judgment – errors that, if continued, would delay construction of the line in British Columbia for a long time.

Dewdney then quoted triumphantly from a recent report by Sandford Fleming that he claimed favoured the Fraser-Burrard route. It was a selective quotation because the report was indecisive, merely outlining the advantages of each route. He then went on to refute a claim made earlier by de Cosmos that the Bute Inlet route supported a larger population. He assured the House that from the Rocky Mountains to Bute, apart from Hudson's Bay Company posts, not a white man lived within fifty to 100 miles of the proposed route.[59]

The population argument was a new twist in the debate and was linked to earlier claims about which route would generate more way traffic. Both sides readily produced statistics drawn from voters' lists, land titles, and the provincial census in support of their chosen route.[60] It was a curious argument, to say the least, because settlement patterns would follow the rail line rather than precede it.

The 1877 parliamentary session was rough going for Alexander Mackenzie. He had to fight off frequent motions of no confidence while by-elections were eating into his majority. Dewdney could sense power slipping away from the government; he was increasingly pessimistic of its ability to take decisive action on the railway question, and he began to see in his old friend John A. Macdonald the best hope for the future.

By the end of the year, Mackenzie came to a decision on the big question: Burrard Inlet would be the railway terminus on the Pacific. New surveys of the Fraser Valley by Henry Cambie had helped him make up his mind; the arguments of Dewdney and Dufferin had also swayed him.[61]

When Parliament opened in February 1878, de Cosmos was indignant. He moved for a return of all engineers' reports done on the Fraser-Burrard route in 1876 and 1877 so that he could be sure the government was acting on such information. He found it hard to believe. Dewdney countered by moving that all information influencing the government decision, not just engineers' reports, be presented to the House. He knew that his old adversary was on the ropes and landed several telling blows that day during their customary bitter exchanges.[62]

The champions of Bute Inlet were still not ready to throw in the towel. For most of 1877, Sandford Fleming had been on leave of absence, and Marcus Smith was acting as chief engineer. On 28 March, Smith submitted a report supporting Bute. It was too late to influence Mackenzie. The prime minister promptly recalled Fleming from Britain, and Fleming soon produced a report of his own in favour of Burrard.[63]

In May, when Parliament discussed an appropriation of $2,549,700 for the railway, de Cosmos made a last, desperate effort. The Fraser-Burrard route, he railed, was through mountain gorges and barren country with no hope for development. He couldn't believe the government was contemplating such a route – it had to be deception. As usual, Dewdney quickly counterattacked, dismissing his rival's claims, whether strategic, economic, or technical. Burrard Inlet, he proclaimed, had twenty times the capacity of Esquimalt harbour, and he applauded the government's decision.[64]

That month Mackenzie rescinded the order in council naming Esquimalt the railway terminus. And on 12 July, Burrard Inlet became the newly designated end of the line.[65] The battle over the railway routes seemed to be finally over.

A few weeks later, on 17 August, Parliament was dissolved and a federal election called. Tory leader John A. Macdonald, with his National Policy, was confident of defeating the Grits, and with good reason.

Dewdney ran for re-election in Yale, and in doing so, he threw in his lot with Macdonald. He told the voters of the district that the National Policy tariff would protect industries, foster employment, restore confidence in the Dominion, and ultimately enable a government to "carry out in a statesmanlike and expeditious manner our Canadian Pacific Railroad."[66]

It was a landslide for the Conservatives, and Dewdney was returned with ease. Macdonald's great victory was marred, however, when he went down in defeat in his Kingston riding. Almost immediately, the voters of Victoria offered him a seat, and he gladly accepted. This threatened to open up the question of the railway routes once more. The new prime minister, as a mark of gratitude to the city that had adopted him in his hour of need, restored Esquimalt as the terminus before the year was out, but many believed that the gesture was empty.[67]

Even so, agitation by Marcus Smith for Bute Inlet early in 1879 seemed to suggest that the battle was not fully over.[68] Dewdney himself clearly had misgivings, for he wrote a lengthy and detailed defence of the Fraser-Burrard route which he distributed in pamphlet form to senators and members of parliament.[69] He need not have worried. In October, Macdonald's government officially adopted Burrard Inlet as the terminus, settling the matter for good. On 14 May 1880, a dynamite blast at Yale marked the beginning of railway construction through the Fraser Canyon.[70]

It was a sensible decision. The harbours at Victoria and Esquimalt were no match for the enormous capacity of Burrard Inlet, and the success of Vancouver as a rapidly growing metropolis in the latter half of the 1880s is proof of that. And while the engineering problems along the Fraser Canyon were formidable, they paled in comparison with the steep challenges of the Homathco Valley, the cliffs of Bute Inlet, and the long spans of bridge that would have been needed to get the railway to the island.

By the time the blasting started, Dewdney had already moved on to the next episode in his career. And he did so with the satisfaction of knowing that the causes he had championed as MP for Yale had ultimately triumphed. Important, too, was the realization that his voice of moderation over the years had served to soothe the irritation in Central Canada at British Columbia's more petulant politicians and their constant demands.[71]

CHAPTER 3

Indian Commissioner

One evening during the 1878-9 parliamentary session, Dewdney was attending a theatre performance in Ottawa when a niece of the prime minister turned up with a message: Sir John wanted to see him after the show on important business. Dewdney hurried to Parliament Hill to keep the appointment. Macdonald explained that he was in "a serious fix" about the North-West Indians. He needed a man to "take charge of them," but several whom he had approached, including two former Hudson's Bay Company officials, had refused. He would be greatly obliged if Dewdney, who knew the Indians of British Columbia well, would take on the job.

The MP for Yale wasn't exactly thrilled at the offer because it would mean leaving British Columbia, a province to which he and his wife were greatly attached and where they maintained a home. And it would require him to resign his parliamentary seat. At the same time, the job was exactly the kind of sinecure he had long craved, and it paid very well. Besides, he was a loyal devotee of the prime minister and found it hard to refuse him anything. He discussed the matter with Jane that evening, and the next morning, over breakfast with Sir John, he accepted the offer.[1]

Macdonald's "serious fix" had mainly to do with the virtual disappearance of the buffalo from the Canadian Prairies. By 1879 what remained of the once-great herds no longer came north of the international boundary, leaving the Native population starving and destitute. It was unacceptable to allow thousands of people to perish for want of food, especially since they had signed treaties with the Dominion government only a few short years before. Apart from such moral concerns, there was the practical consideration that starving Indians were likely to threaten the fledgling white settlements scattered throughout the Territories.[2] Moreover, there was the possibility of international incidents because Canadian Cree, Blackfoot, and Assiniboine often went south of the border in search of buffalo. And Sitting Bull, fresh from his triumph over General Custer at Little Big Horn, had sought refuge in Canada in 1877 with thousands of his supporters and was camped at Wood Mountain, east of Cypress Hills. Dominion authorities feared that the Sioux leader would cause complications with the Americans or even make common cause with disaffected Canadian Indians who were rallying behind Big Bear and Little Pine. These Cree chiefs had not taken treaty and were agitating for a better deal from their encampments around Fort Walsh.[3]

By this time Ottawa had created a fairly comprehensive administrative system of agencies in what was known as the Manitoba Indian Superintendency.[4] But in the neighbouring North-West Superintendency, only a handful of officials were in place to cater to an estimated 20,000 Indians. David Laird, with his headquarters in Battleford, was both lieutenant governor and Indian superintendent. He had one Indian agent for Treaty 6 (roughly corresponding to central Alberta and Saskatchewan today), M.G. Dickieson, and another for Treaty 4 (southern Saskatchewan), Allan MacDonald. No agent had been appointed for Treaty 7 (southern Alberta).[5] The North-West Mounted Police, from their forts in the region, were often obliged to do the work that otherwise would have been handled by agents.

Laird found his responsibilities tiresome, and in February 1879, he resigned as Indian superintendent while continuing as lieutenant governor. This resignation created the opening that Sir John asked Dewdney to fill. In explaining his choice to the Privy Council, the prime minister said that the job required a man of firmness and tact, mature judgment and experience, and a "knowledge of the Indian character." Dewdney's appointment was as commissioner of Indian affairs for the North-West Territories and was effective 30 May 1879. It paid an annual salary of $3,200 as well as travelling expenses.[6]

Colonel J.S. Dennis, deputy minister of the interior, ordered Dewdney west without delay, giving him elaborate instructions regarding his duties. The new commissioner was to prevent the Indians from starving by distributing food that he would find at Fort Walsh and Fort Macleod. He was to establish fifteen farming agencies and two supply farms that would initially produce foodstuffs, and eventually, they would teach the Indians how to do so themselves because the buffalo were considered finished as a source of sustenance. And he was to visit Sitting Bull, advising him that he would not be molested as long as he and his followers obeyed the law.[7]

Leaving Jane in Ottawa, Dewdney travelled west with Colonel James F. Macleod of the Mounted Police as well as eighty-three new recruits for that force and their horses. The Mounted Police had received special permission to pass through American territory, the fastest route west. Thomas

Wright and J.J. Taylor, the men appointed to run the supply farms for Treaty 7, were also going along. The journey began in Toronto on 19 May 1879 when Dewdney and his companions took the train for Collingwood on Georgian Bay. There, they boarded the steamer *City of Owen Sound* and set sail for Duluth, Minnesota, on the western shore of Lake Superior. Dewdney enjoyed this part of the trip, noting that his stateroom was small but equipped with a comfortable spring mattress. The weather was good most of the time, and in the evening, some of the young policemen entertained the passengers by singing and playing the piano.

At Duluth, he stayed in the best hotel – the Clark – and did some shopping before taking the train west. The train took him as far as Bismarck, North Dakota, which he described as "a small town of 1,600 inhabitants composed mostly of whiskey saloons." The river steamer *Red Cloud* was waiting there to take him and his travelling companions westwards on the Missouri to Fort Benton. After a few days battling against the river currents, the steamer passed into Montana Territory, and there Dewdney saw for the first time herds of buffalo, some of them substantial. But the great herds were in rapid decline, and prairie fires along the border, apparently set deliberately by Americans, discouraged the buffalo from their annual migration to Canadian territory.

They arrived at Fort Benton on 9 June. Dewdney noted that it was a typical western town of square wooden stores and houses. But some impressive brick buildings had already been put up, suggesting an air of prosperity. In truth, the river port had prospered during the decade, first as a key point on the Whoop-Up Trail of the notorious whiskey trade and more recently as a supply depot for the Mounted Police and other Canadian government agencies, such as they were, north of the line. One of the local merchant princes, I.G. Baker, had done very well for himself with such contracts and would continue his profitable arrangements with the new Indian commissioner in the years ahead.

Dewdney stayed in Fort Benton until 23 June, purchasing equipment and supplies and organizing transport for the overland trek to Canadian territory. As he set off northwards, his outfit consisted of twelve horses, two transport wagons, and the wagon with his own effects in which he rode himself. He found this final leg of the journey difficult as he felt unwell throughout – from eating mushrooms, he surmised. There were also discouraging omens. He saw no live buffalo, only rotting carcasses of the great beasts littered the plains. And he continually met hungry Indians.[8]

Hearing that large numbers of Indians were gathering around Fort Walsh, he decided to make that police outpost in the Cypress Hills his first destination.[9] He arrived there on 26 June. After taking a day or two to recover from his illness, he interviewed the various bands of Cree, Assiniboine, and Blackfoot who had come there for that purpose. The encounters followed a pattern that was to be repeated on numerous occasions throughout Dewdney's tour of the North-West. He listened to the chiefs' grievances and then proceeded to lecture them on government policy. The government would help them, he explained, as long as they settled on their reserves and tried to support themselves through agriculture. Instructors were about to arrive who would show them how to do so.

The Indian commissioner cut an impressive figure at these interviews. His tall frame had filled out over the years, and he was rather portly but not fat. Although only forty-three years old, his thick wavy hair had turned grey. So, too, had his beard, which he now wore in the form of bushy, mutton chop whiskers. The Indians immediately dubbed him "Whitebeard," the name by which he was known during his years in the North-West.

The years in Parliament had honed Dewdney's political skills, and he counted on getting his way by persuasion and the judicious application of concession and coercion. There were always gifts of beef, flour, tea, or tobacco for those who cooperated with the government; nothing for those who refused. Following instructions from Ottawa, he was not prepared to renegotiate the treaties, but rather to make them work.

Among the most recalcitrant was Big Bear, who turned up with his followers at Fort Walsh a few days after Dewdney's arrival. The two leaders had several meetings and seemed to reach an understanding of sorts. Big Bear explained that he had not signed Treaty 6 because he found the terms insufficient and wanted to see how it would work out for the others. Dewdney had better luck with Little Pine, who accepted the treaty on behalf of his 272 followers. And when Lucky Man and Thunder Child brought 200 of Big Bear's people into the treaty, Dewdney felt he was undermining the stubborn Cree chief. Even so, he respected his adversary: "I have not formed such a poor opinion of 'Big Bear,' as some appear to have done. He is of a very independent character, self-reliant, and appears to know how to make his living without begging from the Government."[10] He was generous enough to acknowledge a worthy opponent, and his assessment was shrewd: Big Bear was one of the most able Native leaders of his time and would prove a major obstacle to the government agenda.

On 6 July, Dewdney took the trail west to the Treaty 7 area where he met Indians assembled at Blackfoot Crossing, Fort Macleod, and Fort Calgary. Those whom he met at Blackfoot Crossing numbered about 1,300, many of them on the verge of starvation. "Young men," he wrote in his report to Ottawa, "who were known to be stout and hearty fellows some months ago were quite emaciated and so weak they could hardly work"; some had sold their horses, prized possessions, for a few cups of flour, and, after pawning their rifles and eating most of their dogs, "were reduced to [eating] gophers and mice." One of the principal Blackfoot chiefs, Crowfoot, admitted having difficulty restraining his young men from raiding nearby cattle ranches. He promised, however, to cooperate with the government and give agriculture a try. Dewdney issued some immediate relief to the needy and left instructions with the police forts to provide for more if required as long as "the greatest care ... be taken so as not to lead the Indians to believe that regular rations would be issued." And before leaving, he selected the locations of the supply farms Taylor and Wright were to establish at Pincher Creek and Fort Calgary.[11]

The Indian commissioner travelled northwards from there, arriving at Fort Edmonton on 6 August where he met Lieutenant Governor Laird who was visiting settlers in the area. Together, they took a paddlewheeler down the North Saskatchewan to Battleford. The boat made a number of stops along the way, allowing Dewdney to meet Indians assembled at the riverbank. Many of those who had signed Treaty 6 complained of the inferior quality of the cattle and implements given to them. So incessant were these complaints that Dewdney began to believe that they must be well founded, which indeed they were. In such instances, he assured the Indians that with agents coming among them all irregularities would be resolved.

After a day or two at Laird's "ugly house" in Battleford, Dewdney took the trail southwest to Sounding Lake, where a large party of Indians had gathered for the annual treaty payments. Upon his arrival on 19 August, he met Elliot T. Galt, who had been sent west as his secretary.[12] The payments took the best part of four days, interrupted by dancing and speech making, which he felt was unnecessary. He concluded from the experience that it would be better to make the payments on reserves in future to avoid bringing such numbers of Indians together, creating a potential for trouble. He also wanted a better method of identifying Indians so that they couldn't defraud the government by being paid more than once. Back in Battleford, he conferred with Laird, Colonel Macleod, and others, and they agreed that a general famine among the Native population was a real possibility. They proposed a substantial increase in the supplies of flour and meat being requisitioned for the Territories.[13]

Dewdney's itinerary then took him farther down the river to Prince Albert, visiting reserves along the way. By 17 September, he was back in Battleford and about to take the trail south to Fort Walsh. From there, he went west once more to preside at the payments among the Blackfoot early in October. He found satisfactory progress being made on the government farms, and he met Crowfoot once again and was assured by the chief's declared commitment to agriculture and livestock. What with settling accounts, making arrangements for the winter, and listening to ranchers' complaints, the sojourn in Blackfoot country took most of the month.

At the end of October, he set out for Wood Mountain to meet the legendary Sitting Bull. But en route he met a police escort that had accompanied the Reverend Abbott Martin to the Sioux encampment. Hearing that the message borne by the American missionary was substantially the same as his own, he felt that there was no point in continuing and returned to Fort Walsh. Dewdney and his government, like the Americans, wanted Sitting Bull to return to his agency in the United States, and he would be offered no encouragement to stay north of the line.

There was still work to be done before leaving for Ottawa. The fifteen farm instructors appointed to the various agencies had now arrived in the west, and those assigned to Treaty 4 had to be equipped and located in appropriate spots. All was ready by 8 November, and with the first winter snow on the ground, the Indian commissioner set out for Fort Benton. From there, he took a series of stagecoaches south through Montana and Idaho to the railway terminus in Ogden, Utah. A pleasant train journey had him back in Ottawa on 25 November.

Dewdney's tour of the North-West gave him an important first-hand acquaintance with a region with which he would be associated for some years to come. It put him back on the frontier, albeit a new one with challenges quite different from those of his trail-blazing days in British Columbia. He still enjoyed the outdoor life and readily camped out on the prairies when the hospitality of hotels and police forts was not available. But that life was sometimes not to his liking, especially when he was pestered by mosquitoes in the evenings, which happened often enough. He was plagued, too, by back problems and bouts of rheumatism, from which he sought relief in the bottle of brandy hidden in his saddle bag. He also missed Jane, who had stayed in Ottawa, and he wrote frequent letters to her throughout the trip.[14]

He spent a pleasant few months in the nation's capital, dining often with Macdonald and consulting with Lawrence Vankoughnet, deputy superintendent general of Indian affairs. In 1880, the Indian Branch of the Department of the Interior became a department in its own right – the Department of Indian Affairs – but it remained within the purview of the minister of the interior who continued to hold the title of superintendent general of Indian affairs. Macdonald, who held on to the interior portfolio along with the premiership, took an active interest in Native matters, but the everyday running of the department was in the hands of the deputy superintendent, Vankoughnet.[15] The relative powers of the commissioner and the deputy superintendent were by no means clearly defined and would remain a source of difficulty between the two men over the years.

In February 1880, Dewdney's area of jurisdiction was extended to include the Manitoba Superintendency, an area incorporating Treaties 1, 2, 3, and 5. (It encompassed what is now southern Manitoba and some of northwestern Ontario.)[16] And when he went west in April, he did so mainly by rail, travelling via Chicago and St. Paul, making Winnipeg his first destination. He spent several months in Manitoba, reporting positively on reserve conditions, except for St. Peter's, the major Saulteaux settlement near Selkirk, which he found "very unsatisfactory."[17]

In July and August, he was back in the Saskatchewan River country, paying and holding talks with Indians at Duck Lake, Battleford, and other points. Poundmaker and his followers were among those whom he interviewed, and Dewdney sensed a feeling of unease among them but a determination, nonetheless, to work for more assistance. "They must be humoured," he observed, "or trouble will follow – they have no means of living and must be fed."[18]

The Indian commissioner's tour of his domain took him on to Edmonton and Blackfoot country and ended up back at Fort Walsh as in the previous year. It was clear to him wherever he went that the Indians had had a difficult winter, especially those who had not gone south and found buffalo. Many were in a "deplorable state" for want of clothing. The mortality rate had been "greater than usual," which the Indians themselves blamed on the rations they were getting. And Dewdney was inclined to agree: "I have no doubt the sudden change from unlimited meat to the scanty fare they received from the Government has to some extent brought it about."[19]

The agricultural program, launched with such hope the year before, was a disappointment. The farm instructors, mainly patronage appointees from Ontario, were unacquainted with the technical challenges of cultivating the prairies and were unaccustomed to working among Native people. Some of them did not know the first thing about farming, and of those who did, many had arrived too late in the season to get the work of tilling and planting done. By spring 1880, several had resigned, and Dewdney was obliged to recommend that others be fired for incompetence or corruption. He wanted to replace them with local men, and with some difficulty, he persuaded Macdonald to agree.[20]

The Indian commissioner remained cautiously optimistic, however. He observed that many Indians in Treaties 4 and 6 had made credible efforts to produce crops, even though hampered by inadequate equipment and bad weather. And they could be independent of the government in a few years "if properly assisted and instructed in agriculture."[21]

The political situation continued to be tense. Soon after taking treaty in 1879, Little Pine asked for a reserve in the Cypress Hills, not far from Fort Walsh. Piapot asked for one next door, and then other bands, including most of the Assiniboine, selected sites in the same area. In spring 1880, the government agreed to grant these reserves, and surveys began. But as the months went by, officialdom began to question the wisdom of its acquiescence. A large Indian territory near Cypress Hills might be difficult to control. Disturbances around Fort Walsh and assaults on farm instructors were clear warning signals of this potential problem. And it was rumoured that a large Indian council was planned for 1881 at which revisions to the treaties would be discussed. Dewdney's willingness to be more generous with ration distribution was motivated at least in part by a desire to counteract persistent Native militancy.[22]

Sitting Bull remained a source of concern. He was still in Canada, although he made occasional hunting forays south of the border. The Mounted Police were keeping a close eye on him, and he was being encouraged to surrender to American authorities. Denied a reserve and rations, his plight was becoming increasingly desperate, all the more so as his followers gave up and returned to the agency.[23]

On 8 October, Dewdney left for Fort Benton to settle accounts and arranged for the shipment of supplies with I.G. Baker. He returned to Ottawa by stage and rail as he had done the previous year.[24]

The Indian commissioner had been criticized in the opposition press for spending his winters in the nation's capital, and when he went west again in 1881, he had instructions to establish his headquarters at some location. His first choice was an abandoned Mounted Police post at Shoal Lake, but it quickly proved unsatisfactory because it was not connected by telegraph. He then chose Winnipeg, where there was already an Indian office, and Ottawa gave its approval.[25]

In December 1880, during Dewdney's absence in the east, Sitting Bull had finally agreed to hand himself over to the Americans. But before he reached Fort Buford, he learned of a cavalry attack on a Sioux campsite and slipped back into Canada, crossing the border on 24 January 1881. Late in April, he left his encampment at Wood Mountain and travelled to Qu'Appelle, and there on 25 and 26 May, he met Dewdney. The Sioux chief explained that he felt safe in Canada and distrusted the Americans. Dewdney assured him, however, that he would be treated as well as other Indians who had returned to their agencies. In line with his government's policy, he refused Sitting Bull a reserve and would only supply rations for the journey to the United States. Surrender, he believed, could "only be brought about by actual starvation," and he was determined to see it through. The strategy worked. Sitting Bull returned to Wood Mountain, and from there, he made his way to Fort Buford with 187 followers, surrendering on 19 July.[26] Food had proven to be a useful weapon, and it would be used often again as an instrument of Indian policy.

As for Sitting Bull, he spent a number of uneventful years at the Standing Rock Agency. Later in the decade, he toured the U.S. and Eastern Canada as one of the leading attractions in Buffalo Bill's Wild West Show. In 1890, he became caught up in the "Messiah Craze," a movement of Native renewal and militancy. In December, while resisting arrest for his leadership in the movement, he was shot dead in a skirmish with agency police.[27]

In August 1881, Lord Lorne, the governor general, toured the Territories, meeting many Native leaders. Ottawa hoped that the pressure of the representative of the "Great Mother" would mollify Indian militancy and perhaps even persuade Big Bear to take treaty.[28] Big Bear, it turned out, stayed in Montana hunting buffalo, still waiting to see how the treaty would work out. Dewdney, who accompanied His Excellency on the tour, noted with some annoyance that the Indians who did meet Lorne pressed him to improve the treaty terms. The governor general could not oblige, but he did lend an ear to a litany of Native grievances. Dewdney admitted that their demand for more agricultural equipment and work animals was reasonable because the quantities promised in the treaties were inadequate.[29]

The Indian commissioner was well aware that his department did not have the resources to bring about a speedy transition to settled life for its Native charges. Surveys, breaking ground, building fences and houses, and all the other requirements were only slowly being attended to, and in the interim, he did not object to Indians sustaining themselves through buffalo-hunting expeditions. That was better than feeding them in idleness on the reserves. In fact, many went south in 1881 to hunt in Montana. Of course, this journey entailed the danger of them joining forces with Big Bear. If too many left, which happened in some cases, no Indian labour was available to do the work. And when hunters returned, their horses sometimes destroyed crops put in by those who had stayed behind – as on the Blood and Blackfoot reserves.[30] These were some of the problems of a policy that was hastily conceived and being implemented on a tight budget.

Dewdney was also aware by summer 1881 of the potential difficulties inherent in the concentration of a large number of reserves around the Cypress Hills. With so many Indians in proximity and in constant communication, they would be in a better position to resist government policy and demand improvements to the treaty terms. In June, he recommended an increase in the police force and the closure of Fort Walsh and all government operations in the vicinity. Without assistance at that point, he reasoned, the Indians would have to disperse and accept reserves else-where. Although this recommendation violated promises made earlier, Dewdney believed that the dangers of such a reserve cluster warranted his proposed course of action. And he had the rations weapon at his disposal to ensure compliance.[31]

Although dedicated to government policy, Dewdney found the work discouraging and not to his liking. Besides, Jane, who had accompanied him west in 1881, hated the Prairies and longed to return to British Columbia. Dewdney wrote to the prime minister in the summer, suggest-ing that he be relieved of his duties and appointed to the Senate instead. But Macdonald was having none of it. "It will never do for you to throw yourself away on the Senate," the prime minister wrote. "I can do much better for you than that." He promised to make the job more lucrative and expressed full confidence in his Indian commissioner. Dewdney, loyal and dutiful as ever, agreed to carry on, expressing the hope that the work would eventually be successful.[32]

An opportunity arose soon enough for the prime minister to "do much better" for the Indian commissioner. On 3 October 1881, David Laird's term of office as lieutenant governor expired. Macdonald had never been

Edgar Dewdney, lieutenant governor of the North-West Territories, no date (courtesy Glenbow Archives NA-4035-143)

impressed with Laird, saying that he had done little for years besides drawing his salary and issuing liquor permits. He proposed that Dewdney be appointed lieutenant governor of the North-West Territories, retaining his position as Indian commissioner and receiving an annual salary increase of $2,000. And he assured Dewdney that the new position would require little in the way of additional duties. Dewdney agreed, and the appointment took effect on 3 December.[33] Although Laird had held the two posts simultaneously, it was not the normal practice to combine these offices elsewhere in the country. The effect was to make Dewdney a virtual autocrat in the North-West, and his authority in dealing with Indian matters was undoubtedly enhanced.

During 1882, settlement on reserves continued. Canadian Indians hunting for buffalo in the United States were obstructed by American troops and Indians, and they were often obliged to give up. Returning to their reserves, they were forced to submit to a humiliating routine of rations and labour. Many were willing to give agriculture a try, but the conditions were far from ideal. The shortage of equipment and work animals, which Dewdney had acknowledged on several occasions, persisted. And the daily ration of 1 lb. of meat and 1/2 lb. of flour per person was far from adequate. The Blackfoot received their meat ration in the form of beef because they refused to accept anything else and the department felt it wise to accommodate them.[34] Elsewhere, the much cheaper bacon was issued. Even so, Dewdney sometimes authorized the distribution of beef if he thought it would get results – as in the case of the Assiniboine at Indian Head, whom he hoped would stay on their reserve.[35]

Norman Macleod, the agent in Treaty 7, feared that hunger would drive the Blackfoot to kill cattle belonging to the nearby Cochrane Ranch, and he wanted more policemen in the vicinity as a deterrent. Another source of potential trouble was the beef contractors who were supplying the rations. They were a "rough class of Americans" who treated Indians badly. In January, a minor Blackfoot chief, Bull Elk, got into a fight with Charles Daly, one of the contractors, and fired a shot at him during the altercation. A squad of policemen under F.J. Dickens arrested Bull Elk but was forced to release him when surrounded by armed Indians – a major setback for the authority of the Mounted Police. Reinforcements under L.N.F. Crozier were quickly dispatched to the scene and succeeded in taking Bull Elk as a prisoner to Fort Macleod.[36]

Dewdney, fearing that the situation was getting out of hand and that Norman Macleod's age and ill-health impaired his leadership, appointed a second agent for Treaty 7 to take charge of the Blackfoot, Sarcee, and Stoney. His choice for the job was Cecil E. Denny who, until then, had been a mounted policeman stationed at Fort Walsh.[37] Denny was young and energetic and got on well with the Indians. Within a month, by mid-February, Dewdney made him responsible for all of Treaty 7, with William Pocklington as his subagent. Norman Macleod, to his great chagrin, was demoted to the position of clerk in the Winnipeg office.[38]

With Denny as agent and a police force stationed at Blackfoot Crossing, the situation settled down a bit. But the department found it difficult to retain honest and competent men as farm instructors, especially when they could do much better for themselves working on nearby ranches. And farming operations continued to be hampered by lack of equipment.

The department had a roving inspector of agencies in the person of Thomas Page Wadsworth, a native of Ontario. When Wadsworth inspected the agency in July, he found lots to complain about. John Norrish, the instructor on the Blackfoot reserve, was "as lazy as ever" and was having an affair with Calf-Woman's daughter, who was receiving extra rations in return for sex. The inspector fired Norrish, an action approved by the department.[39]

Wadsworth also went after Denny, whom he accused of arrogance, ignorance, drinking, and womanizing: "His breath always smells strong enough of spirits to knock a horse down." But the agent retained Dewdney's confidence, and his job.[40]

Wadsworth was a penny-pincher obsessed with minutiae of expenditure. His inspection visits and the reports that followed were dreaded by agents. He had little sympathy for Indians and was convinced that they were out to swindle the government. When inspecting the Sarcee reserve in August, he observed that the absence of an accurate census and system of identification was allowing some Indians to receive rations twice. He had a solution: "I know of no better way to count these Indians than to drive them into a corral, and allow them to come out by families, then taking their names and classifying them."[41]

The Cypress Hills continued to be a site of potential trouble for Dewdney and the department throughout 1882. About 2,000 Indians were camped there, including Piapot, who refused to accept the reserve he was allocated at Indian Head. Matters became more serious in April when the U.S. cavalry drove the remaining Canadian Indians (including Big Bear) north of the frontier.

When Big Bear arrived at the Cypress Hills, he learned that the government planned to close Fort Walsh and had ordered all Indians to leave the vicinity. Treaty 6 people were to settle at Fort Pitt or Battleford while those of Treaty 4 were to go to Qu'Appelle. Starvation was already forcing many of them to leave.

Big Bear and his followers, as non-treaty Indians, found they would receive no help whatsoever from the government, and as the months passed, their circumstances deteriorated. In mid-October, Fred White, comptroller of the Mounted Police, and physician Augustus Jukes visited the Indian encampments and complained to Dewdney of the appalling circumstances they found. John A. Macdonald was informed and expressed concern, but Dewdney felt that his firm stand was necessary to put an end to the tendency of uncooperative Indians to congregate at the Cypress Hills. He did compromise, however, by allowing – "very much against my inclination" – treaty Indians to receive their payments at Fort Walsh.

Big Bear, of course, received no payments, and as winter came on, the plight of his camp became pitiful. His intransigence on the treaty question was increasingly resented by his family, all the more so because the payments offered included arrears and were substantial. On 8 December, the old chief finally succumbed, signed the treaty, and agreed to accept a reserve in the north.[42]

With the apparent capitulation of Big Bear, Dewdney felt that he could deal more generously and humanely with the Indians camped around Fort Walsh. In January 1883, when the winter weather was at its worst, he ordered presents of tobacco, tea, clothing, and blankets to be delivered to the various chiefs.[43]

Dewdney had wanted the fort closed a year earlier as part of his plan to force the Indians to settle on their reserves away from the frontier. The local commander, Colonel A.G. Irvine, agreed. He considered Fort Walsh an unhealthy "hole" and badly positioned from a military point of view, being surrounded by hills on all sides.[44] But comptroller Fred White decided to keep the fort open over winter 1882-3, after political pressure was brought to bear by the Canadian Pacific Railway, whose construction crews looked to the fort as a source of protection from Indian attacks.[45]

In May 1883, Dewdney finally got his way, and the fort was closed. Several months of difficult negotiations followed, however, before the estimated 3,000 Indians would leave the vicinity. The man who supervised this operation was Hayter Reed, assistant Indian commissioner as of 15 March, upon E.T. Galt's resignation.[46] Reed, working closely with the Mounted Police, used the familiar carrot-and-stick tactics that Dewdney favoured. He cut off rations and promised help to those who settled in the desired areas. By July, the Indian encampments had broken up, and the chiefs were leading their peoples under police escort to their reserves.[47]

For Dewdney, this turn of events was a major triumph, for it symbolized the end of the hunting way of life: "It is a matter of no wonder that such a strong stand should have been made against our repeated efforts to cause them to leave their own haunts, places associated with thoughts of freedom and plenty, whilst the buffalo roamed the Plains in countless numbers. Leaving these hills behind them dashed to the ground the last hope to which they had so strenuously and fondly clung, of once more being able to live by the chase."[48]

Equally important in his eyes was the practical benefit from an administrative point of view of securing control over Native lives, a control epitomized by the work and ration routines of the reserves:

> I look upon the removal of some 3,000 Indians from Cypress and scattering them through the country as a solution of one of our main difficulties, as it was found impossible at times to have such control as was desirable over such a large number of worthless and lazy Indians, the concourse of malcontents and reckless Indians from all the bands in the Territories. Indians already on their reserves will now be more settled, as no place of rendezvous will be found where food can be had without a return of work being exacted, a fact which lended materially to create much discontent among those who were willing to remain on their reserves, as well as to increase the laborious duty of our agents.[49]

Getting the "worthless and lazy Indians" to settle on their reserves only served to draw attention to the inadequacies of one of the cornerstones of the department's policies – its agricultural program. This program had already come in for public criticism. The *Saskatchewan Herald* claimed that the government was doing too much to help Indians and was undermining their self-reliance. And in the House of Commons, Liberal spokesman David Mills, a former minister of the interior, attacked the program as expensive and unproductive.[50]

Whatever his partisan motivations, and he had a solid track record in such matters, Mills had a point. When Inspector Wadsworth visited the Pincher Creek supply farm in May 1882, he found the most astonishing waste and neglect. The place had excellent land and was equipped with an abundance of the finest implements and work animals. And yet, little was being done. The man in charge, Samuel Bruce, rarely bothered to supervise his labourers, and they, in turn, put in short hours while collecting good wages and rations estimated at 13 lbs. of flour, meat, and potatoes per person daily. Wadsworth fired most of the employees, hired new men, and took over operations temporarily.[51]

The contrast between the resources provided the white men on the supply farm and those available to Indians on their reserves was striking. Department officials were aware of this difference, but were reluctant to effect a radical redistribution. Just as Wadsworth was reporting on the dismal state of affairs at Pincher Creek, Deputy Superintendent Vankough-net was admitting to Dewdney that they would probably have to provide more work animals to reserves to get cultivation going. It would be best, he said, if the Indians would buy their own with their annuities, but failing that, the department could supply them on loan.[52]

The strategy was the same for such equipment as mechanical mowers, rakes, and grist mills, now recognized as essential for successful agricultural operations on the prairies. The department refused to supply them to reserves but encouraged bands to pool resources to buy their own. A few successful bands did so.[53]

By 1882, the supply and home farms were recognized as expensive fail-ures, and in the following year, they were gradually given up. The land was either sold or leased. Farm instructors were moved on to reserves and were required to provide direct supervision of Native agriculture efforts. In 1884, this process was completed.[54]

Although he had been appointed lieutenant governor of the North-West Territories in December 1881, Dewdney spent little time in Battleford, the territorial capital. Given the primacy of his role as Indian commissioner, his usual headquarters were in Winnipeg. By 1883, however, he had relo-cated himself in Regina, the new capital city being built on the Canadian Pacific Railway. And on 14 June of that year, the Indian office was officially placed there, becoming part of the complex of government buildings.[55]

Ned and Jane, seated outside Government House, Regina, N.W.T., 1885 (courtesy Glenbow Archives NA-3205-1)

Dewdney's dual role and the developing apparatus of state enhanced his authority in the Territories. But his discretionary power in dealing with Native issues was often challenged or even undermined by Lawrence Vankoughnet, the deputy superintendent general of Indian affairs. In September 1883, Vankoughnet spent a few weeks touring the West, and upon his return to Ottawa, he recommended changes in practice and personnel in the interests of economy. Several storekeepers and clerks were to be dismissed and their work done by agents. The agents were to restrict their visits to reserves because too much time and money was being spent on these tours. Farm instructors were to reside on reserves and ought to be married men if possible. Indian labour was to be used on all reserve farming operations, and the work-for-rations rule applied strictly.[56]

On 23 November, telegrams were sent to North-West Indian agents listing the personnel who were to be dismissed as of 31 December.[57] A week or so later, Vankoughnet informed Dewdney of the changes he had initiated, which had been approved by the superintendent general.[58] The Indian commissioner, although he agreed with some of the changes, was furious at not having been consulted, and he objected to many details of the plan that he believed would result in hardship for Indians and department employees alike. In a series of lengthy letters to the superintendent general in December, he described his objections in full.

Dewdney pointed out that in agencies such as Battleford and Pitt, where there were large numbers of newly settled Indians, agents could not do their work properly without the assistance of clerks and storekeepers. Nor did he deem it appropriate for agents to do the work of lesser officials: "I do not consider that our agents should be called on to handle greasy bacon, and carry flour or other supplies in and out of the storehouse."[59]

Indians would suffer unduly, he argued, if provisions were completely cut off, which Vankoughnet had recommended in the case of the Stoney at Morley:

> I regret to notice the views, which on several occasions lately, have been expressed by the Deputy of the Superintendent General in regard to our Indians – "Let them suffer." Our Indians *are* suffering and although the hurried visit made through the Territories by the Deputy last season might have led him to believe that a harsh treatment could be safely adopted by the Government towards the Indians, I am of a different opinion and take this opportunity of warning the Government that the feeling among the Indians is such that they will not suffer without an effort to obtain what they consider is their right.[60]

Dewdney himself had been ready to employ harsh measures when he felt they were warranted – as, for instance, when he wanted Sitting Bull to leave Canada and the Cree and Assiniboine to leave the Cypress Hills. But now, with the Indians more or less cooperating, he believed that the punitive approach was ill-advised and only likely to cause further trouble.

He wasn't alone. Throughout January 1884, the agents in the field sent a litany of protests to the Indian commissioner's office over the dismissals and economy measures. And C.E. Denny, agent to the Blood and Peigan, resigned his position rather than carry on under impossible circumstances.[61]

The protests did bring some immediate results. Vankoughnet was forced to compromise on many of the details of his plan, and several dismissals were either suspended or postponed.[62]

Meanwhile, Dewdney drew up his own blueprint of administrative change, which he submitted to the superintendent general on 11 January. It was optimistic in tone and anticipated a new role for Indian agents. Before this time, he argued, agents had been mainly concerned with distributing supplies to their destitute charges. But the day was fast approaching when Indians would produce large crops for themselves. Because they were "utterly useless" when it came to disposing of such crops, he foresaw agents taking on this role. Therefore, men with good business ability should be appointed agents on all large reserves. This requirement would mean hiring an additional eight agents for the Territories who would be provided with comfortable quarters on the reserves. The change, he estimated, would actually save the department $4,000 per year, because with more agents on the spot, farm instructors could be laid off. His plan was approved by the superintendent general, and even Vankoughnet, perhaps chastened by the howls of protest his proposals had generated, went along with it.[63]

Dewdney triumphed in this jurisdictional skirmish, but he sought further clarification on the limits of his authority that summer in private correspondence with the prime minister. Macdonald was as supportive as ever, noting that while Vankoughnet was "a zealous officer," he could hardly be expected to "run the North-West from Ottawa." General regulations would continue to emanate from headquarters, he explained, but Dewdney would have "discretionary power to alter them for the occasion." Except for extraordinary circumstances, agents would receive their instructions through the Indian commissioner's office.[64]

The adjustments to policy in 1883-4 – closing the supply and home farms, moving instructors onto reserves, subdividing agencies – were realistic responses to initiatives that had failed. They also represented economy measures in a certain sense. The concern was not so much to save money, but rather to reallocate it where it might produce better results. Officials such as Dewdney were of the view that the older generation of Indians would make the transition to settled life with difficulty, but the younger generation, if properly trained, would accept it as natural. Investment in education, therefore, had to be a keystone of policy.

As a result of the western treaties, the government was obliged to provide schools and teachers for the Indians when they settled on their reserves. Just as with the promise to provide the wherewithal to engage in agriculture, this obligation was only slowly and unevenly fulfilled. According to regulations adopted in 1881, teachers in Indian schools in the West were remunerated at the annual rate of $12 for each pupil in attendance for up to a total salary of $504. In schools supported by a religious denomination, the department's annual contribution to a teacher's salary was limited to $300. Low and irregular attendance meant that few teachers could survive on the per capita salaries. In practice, most reserve schools were sponsored by the Christian churches, and the teachers were men and women motivated by missionary zeal.

Because of Dewdney's initiative, these regulations were changed in April 1882 so that teachers in non-denominational schools were guaranteed a minimum annual salary of $300 with an additional $12 grant for each student beyond an enrolment of twenty-five and up to a maximum of forty-two. The new rules also allowed the Indian commissioner to take the initiative in establishing schools on reserves with a minimum of twenty-five students between the ages of six and seventeen years. And he or his designates were authorized to examine teaching applicants on their suitability.[65]

Dewdney soon found that these new arrangements were inadequate to stimulate the growth of schools on reserves. Parental opposition and indifference continued to be a problem, and only rarely were the requisite twenty-five students available for the establishment of a school. In December 1883, he put forward a comprehensive proposal incorporating his carrot-and-stick philosophy, which he felt would make a difference. It included the following requirements: twenty children between six and fourteen years of age for the establishment of a school; teachers' annual salaries of $500; public school inspectors to include Indian schools in their inspections; parents who send their children to school to be rewarded; midday meals and clothing for children to encourage attendance; school attendance eventually to become compulsory and assistance withdrawn from parents who refused to cooperate; the school day to last for six hours, one-third of which to be spent in field or garden; the Native tongue should not be taught; $200 rather than $100 to be spent on the construction of schoolhouses, and at least two rooms adjoining the school to be built to accommodate the teacher.

Vankoughnet and Macdonald agreed with Dewdney's proposals in principle but asked for an estimate of what they would cost. It turned out that the annual expenditure on education in the North-West Territories was $4,780 while the proposed scheme would cost a total of $16,165.[66]

The Indian commissioner's plan to expand and improve reserve schools lingered in limbo except for some minor details mainly because the department had decided to focus its educational energies in another direction – in the sponsorship of a network of industrial schools. Dewdney supported this initiative, but he tended to view these new institutions as part of a larger educational system that included day schools on reserves, rather than as a system unto themselves.

Industrial schools such as the Mount Elgin and Mohawk Institutes already existed for Indians in Ontario, and there were similar experiments in the United States. As the word "industrial" implied, the schools provided a mixture of academic and manual learning. The program was based on the idea that Indians were better suited to working with their hands than with their brains. The schools were residential, had a strong religious ethos, and were modelled closely on similar institutions designed for the moral reform of delinquent and neglected children in mainstream society.

A close partnership was envisaged between the department and the missionary churches in establishing and operating the industrial schools in the Prairies. It was hoped that this partnership would keep costs down and attract personnel with the religious fervour to make the experiment work. The supplementary estimates for 1883-4 allocated $44,000 for three industrial schools: at Qu'Appelle and High River under Roman Catholic management and at Battleford under the Anglican Church. The Battleford school opened its doors before the end of 1883, and the two others were ready the following year.[67]

In December 1883, Assistant Commissioner Reed was recruiting boys for Battleford when he discovered that parents objected to the place, fearing that they would lose their children's treaty money as well as their company and help around the home.[68] Parental hostility would plague this ill-fated educational experiment throughout its existence.

In his report for 1884, Dewdney acknowledged the initial problems faced by the industrial schools while proclaiming that he had "every confidence in their ultimate success." Even so, he was clearly exasperated by the Native attitude towards these expensive new institutions and found it hard to believe that they could not readily see the advantages of what was being offered, a view shared by his colleagues and collaborators in government and church: "As was at first premised, no little difficulty is met with in prevailing upon Indians to part with their children; and even after the latter have been cared for in the kindest manner, some parents, prompted by unaccountable freaks of the most childish nature, demand a return of their children to their own shanties to suffer from cold and hunger."[69]

The cold and hunger to which Dewdney referred were real enough, especially over the harsh 1883-4 winter. Low temperatures, deep snow, and a shortage of game animals meant that the Indians could not supplement their meagre resources with the products of the chase. Hayter Reed, after touring the Saskatchewan District, predicted trouble in the spring because Big Bear and his followers were planning a large gathering near Battleford "to test their powers with the authorities." He suggested that the police in the district be augmented and that they patrol the country before the Indians got moving in order to frustrate their efforts.[70]

Reed was right: 1884 proved to be a year of dangerous confrontations between Indians and the authorities. Genuine hardship among Natives and a tightfisted rations policy administered by insensitive officials were often the direct causes of such problems. Agitation by Big Bear and others was also a contributing cause.

Bloodshed was narrowly avoided on Yellow Calf's reserve at Crooked Lakes in February. When the farm instructor refused to distribute rations on request, armed Indians overpowered him and seized the storehouse. A police patrol was unable to secure their surrender, and only after difficult negotiations mediated by Reed did the Indians agree to submit to a trial. They explained that if they were to die, it was better to do so quickly in battle rather than slowly through starvation.[71]

In March, news arrived in Regina that the government intended to increase the number of Mounted Police in the North-West and that at least 150 would be stationed in the Saskatchewan District to assist the Department of Indian Affairs in keeping the peace. Hayter Reed, temporarily in charge of the commissioner's office during a visit by Dewdney to British Columbia, readily endorsed this move. He suggested that if the Indians tried to organize large gatherings, the "ringleaders" ought to be arrested even if it meant stretching the letter of the law.[72]

When Dewdney returned in April, he set off immediately on a tour of Treaty 4 reserves. He found that most of the bands had suffered greatly from illness over the winter and that there had been many deaths. Several bands were working hard at agricultural operations but were hampered as usual by a shortage of equipment. Piapot, however, still refused to submit to department wishes. He blamed the deaths among his people on bacon rations and demanded a new reserve where they could catch fish. Dewdney interpreted these complaints as an excuse to avoid work.[73]

The local agent, Allan MacDonald, was initially sympathetic. Early in May, he slaughtered an ox for Piapot's people, sent a doctor among them, and pressed on Dewdney the need to supply more than bacon. But when the chief left his reserve at Indian Head, and his young men became "very forward and bold," the agent urged police intervention. Piapot admitted that he was leading his people to Pasquah's reserve in the Qu'Appelle Valley, where he hoped to fish and hold a thirst dance.[74] Colonel Irvine and a force of over fifty Mounted Police caught up with them en route, and another dangerous confrontation ensued. But Piapot stood his ground, and rather than provoke a fight, the department agreed to let him have the reserve of his choice – on a site adjoining Muscowpetung's on the Qu'Appelle River with woodlands, arable land, and running water.[75]

Dewdney followed his tour of the Treaty 4 reserves with a visit to the Battleford area in May, believing that his presence turned Native despondency into hope. His report to the prime minister was optimistic. He noted that many of the Indians were working diligently, and he proposed giving them additional equipment to encourage them in agriculture. Big Bear's agitation for one large reserve, he believed, was getting nowhere. He was a bit concerned that the St. Laurent Metis, whom he described as "very touchy," had sent messages to Louis Riel in Montana, although they appeared to be satisfied after discussing their grievances with Dewdney.[76]

He was no sooner back in Regina when more than 2,000 Cree were gathering on Poundmaker's reserve for a council and thirst dance sponsored by Big Bear, developments that alarmed local settlers. On 17 June, as preparations were under way, an Indian named Kawechetwemot assaulted farm instructor John Craig, who had denied him rations. Agent John Rae demanded immediate retribution; otherwise, department authority would be undermined. A police force under Superintendent L. Crozier arrived to enforce the law, but he thought it wise to wait until the thirst dance ended before making a move. Even then, several days of difficult and dangerous negotiations followed before the police were able to seize the assailant. During this tense confrontation, in which a number of Mounted Police were roughed up by armed Indians, one shot could have sparked open warfare.

Kawechetwemot received a relatively light sentence of one week in jail. Dewdney conceded that Craig was not entirely blameless in the incident because he could be "too overbearing in his manner towards the Indians." Agent Rae, who until then had advocated a strong police presence and the arrest of troublemakers, now urged that department officials have greater discretion in the use of rations.

Dewdney agreed. While he wanted to uphold the principle of the work-for-rations rule, he could see that a too rigid application could precipitate an Indian war, as almost had happened in the Yellow Calf and Kawechetwemot incidents. He told the prime minister that an element of flexibility was necessary at the local level: "The time often arrives when this rule must be of an elastic nature and the Indian humoured but under cover of a pretext which will lead him to the belief that the rule is not being broken."[77]

Vankoughnet, with obvious reluctance, gave his consent to the greater discretionary power for officials in the field, but he warned against a repetition of the Fort Walsh situation – "a big camp composed of all the idle Indians in the country being fed at large expense."[78]

Dewdney was well aware that Indian leaders were pushing at the limits of department policy to see where they could make gains. This dangerous game of bluff and bravado on both sides could easily explode at any moment. He was concerned, however, to assuage the fears of the settler population, and his public pronouncements continued to echo a reassuring optimism. At the opening of the North-West council on 3 July, he described recent press reports of Indian difficulties as "exaggerated." From his own tours of the Territories, he was able to state unequivocally that the Indians were more contented than ever since signing the treaties and that there was no cause for alarm.[79]

In truth, he was constantly dealing with crises, either real or anticipated. Aware that pressure was being brought to bear on the Treaty 7 Indians to join the resistance to the government, he invited Crowfoot to Regina in July to talk matters over. The chief turned up with his brother, Three Bulls, along with Red Crow of the Blood and Eagle Tail of the Peigan. Realizing that they believed most whites had already arrived in their country, Dewdney arranged for them to visit Winnipeg, a growing urban centre. The trip had a most beneficial effect on their minds, he surmised, and they would return and inform their followers of "the supremacy of the white man and the utter impossibility of contending against his power."[80]

While the Indian commissioner was attempting to overawe the Treaty 7 chiefs, an alarming development took place that convinced him more than ever that the Saskatchewan District was the real powder keg in his domains. On 5 July, Louis Riel turned up at the St. Laurent Metis settlement, declaring his intention of leading his people in the campaign for the redress of their grievances – which mainly had to do with title to their lands. Riel had been living in Montana for some years, a fugitive from the wrath of the Canadian state since the Red River Resistance of 1869-70. The authorities now feared that the Metis and Indians would unite in pressing their demands on the government, and such an alliance might be a force difficult to contain. The prime minister even gave credence to a rumoured insurrection involving not just the Indians and Metis, but also the dreaded Fenians![81]

Joint action on the part of the two Native groups was a real enough possibility. In July, Beardy, a leading chief in the Saskatchewan District, decided to hold a council of the Carlton-area Cree at his Duck Lake reserve and invited Big Bear to attend. Before the council opened, the chiefs met with Riel, who assured them they had rights that he could help get recognized.[82] The Duck Lake council began on 31 July, and a few days later, some of Beardy's men went to Fort Carlton to ask Subagent J. Ansdell Macrae for provisions. Macrae knew that to accede to this request would create a troublesome precedent, yet he had no desire to provoke a confrontation such as the Kawechetwemot-Craig incident. Using the new discretionary powers granted to officials in the field, he sought a compromise. He proposed to supply provisions if the council was moved to Fort Carlton, he was invited to attend, and the working men were returned to their reserves. These terms were agreed to. Later, Macrae reported to Dewdney on the demands made at the council. The chiefs outlined eight treaty promises that they believed had been inadequately fulfilled, and as a result, they felt that they had sold the country for nothing. They said that they would wait until the following summer to see if the government was sincere or not, and only then would they act.[83] They didn't specify what action they would take, but the threat was enough to warrant a closer look at the situation.

Dewdney sent Judge Charles Rouleau and Assistant Commissioner Reed to the Saskatchewan District to investigate, and they reported early in September. Rouleau played down the danger of a Metis-Indian alliance. He urged, however, that Metis claims be settled as soon as possible, or else Riel, who was peaceably disposed, could do a lot of harm. He also urged that the government provide generous assistance to the Indians in the coming winter. Otherwise, he predicted misery and starvation because crops had failed on most reserves.[84]

Reed anticipated difficulties the following spring when the Metis would be "much harder up" and the Indians would try to organize large gatherings. He did not advocate concessions or compromise; he rarely thought in such terms. A large police presence in the district was the best antidote to trouble, he believed, and a close eye should be kept on Big Bear and Poundmaker, the leading agitators.[85]

Dewdney favoured a middle ground between these positions, and he was assured by the prime minister that the government would endeavour to settle the Metis claims that winter and at the same time increase the Mounted Police force by 100 men.[86] It was also arranged that, in an emergency, the police would take their orders directly from Dewdney in his role as lieutenant governor.[87]

The Indian commissioner believed that the situation was serious enough, but that he had it under control. There was no imminent danger, and if any should occur, he had the wherewithal to deal with it. As an added precaution, however, he hired Peter Ballendine in November for "special service" in the Saskatchewan District. Ballendine was a Metis who spoke Cree and was respected by the Indians. His role was to discover the feelings of the Indians and their intentions in the spring. Ballendine reported that there was no danger of a Metis-Indian alliance. All the same, the Indians were profoundly dissatisfied and critical of the department and its officials. These feelings even applied to Mistawawsis and Ahtakakoop, chiefs who until recently had cooperated with the government.[88]

All would be fine, Dewdney believed, as long as Ottawa cooperated with him and accepted his advice. But on 5 December, Vankoughnet wrote telling him to reduce rations to Big Bear's band because too many band members were being fed without working in return. The deputy superintendent also objected to the practice of feeding Indians during meetings with them. This objection was exactly the sort of interference that Dewdney strongly resented, and he replied on 12 December sharply attacking the instructions. He explained that he was dealing with an explosive situation and that any false move could set the whole thing off.[89]

That 1884 ended on a peaceful note was itself a minor miracle. Violence had been prevented by judicious compromise and sheer good luck. Dewdney was confident that his patient and cautious approach would ultimately yield results. Whether patience and caution would be enough to contain the situation the following spring was another matter. Much would depend on whether Ottawa would allow him the authority and resources to solve problems as he saw fit.

CHAPTER 4

Rebellion

Dewdney knew that spring 1885 would present government Indian policy with its greatest challenge to date. The Indian and Metis agitation continued to simmer and the reports that reached him in January all predicted trouble in the coming months, especially in the Saskatchewan District. Informants such as Peter Ballendine and Superintendent Crozier passed word of plans afoot for a large Indian gathering in the district where the Blackfoot had been invited. Little Pine, Little Poplar, and Big Bear appeared to be the principal instigators.[1]

With sufficient power and trustworthy personnel at his disposal, Dewdney felt that he could prevail, regardless of the challenge. But he lacked confidence in some Indian agents and their subordinates and wanted them supervised more carefully. One agency inspector, he believed, could not adequately cover such a broad territory. To make matters worse, he didn't completely trust the department's roving inspector, T.P. Wadsworth, whom he knew reported directly to Vankoughnet behind his back. On 9 January, he proposed the appointment of a second inspector to the prime minister, while complaining of Wadsworth's tendency to bypass him in the chain of command.

Vankoughnet, while agreeing with the need for a second inspector, defended Wadsworth and his activities, which only exasperated Dewdney. In a lengthy report on policy to the prime minister in February, the commissioner argued forcefully that Indians could not be managed except by people with the intimate knowledge of their character and circumstance that could only be acquired with prolonged experience. Wadsworth on his hurried trips around the country had often shown a lack of understanding, yet he had the ear of the deputy superintendent. This connection was undermining the authority of the commissioner's office, and he, Dewdney, had been written to over Vankoughnet's signature as if he had no experience in the country: "His directions are issued in the most trivial affairs and the conclusion I have arrived at is that Mr. Vankoughnet is placing all the power he can in the hands of the Inspector without any regard to me." He demanded discretionary power to act in the management of the Indians and to act swiftly as circumstances required.[2] His anger at the deputy superintendent had been building for a number of years, and the orders he received in December to reduce rations to Big Bear's band were just too much – especially because these orders had been based on Wadsworth's inspection report.

Dewdney's immediate concern was to prod Ottawa into action on outstanding Native grievances – Indian and Metis – so that the disaffected would have little to complain of when the spring came. An immediate concern was the list of alleged broken treaty promises presented to J.A. Macrae at the Duck Lake council in July and August. Hayter Reed, who was spending the winter months in the Saskatchewan District, reported on the matter on 25 January.

Reed admitted that many of the original cattle and horses given to the Indians in the district were wild and unmanageable. But they had been killed or replaced with the commissioner's permission. Some implements were also of inferior quality, but this problem tended to be exceptional. All tools and equipment promised in the treaty had not been handed over, but that was in accordance with department policy: Indians only received such materials when they were ready to use them. Schools were operating in the district as regularly as possible, in Reed's opinion. On some reserves, however, it was not possible to keep teachers, and missionary societies had not come forward to do the job. The medicine chest, as stipulated in the treaty, was not being kept at the agency. In spite of these shortcomings, Reed claimed that the Indians had no real ground for complaint. He believed that their agitation was being stirred up by Louis Riel.

Dewdney, who usually found it necessary to modify his assistant's harsh dictums, did so once more, and he urged that the treaty terms be fulfilled to the letter and that rations be increased. This time he was supported by Vankoughnet, who was finally coming to accept the gravity of the situation.[3]

Meanwhile, the commissioner's office was receiving numerous letters from settlers, clergymen, and the like, stressing the need for a swift resolution to the Metis land claims question. Dewdney, who had wanted the matter resolved for some time, sent this correspondence on to Macdonald on 2 February, urging that action be taken. Although he had been receiving mixed messages regarding Riel's intentions and the possibilities of a Metis-Indian alliance, the dangers were now far too great, in his opinion, for further foot-dragging.[4]

Native issues rarely received the priority they deserved in the corridors of power. Ottawa did act, but in its own unhurried way. A government measure of 28 January allowed the minister of the interior to appoint a three-person commission to draw up a list of Metis entitled to claims in the West. Dewdney felt that it was inadequate because it made no reference to river-lot titles or other grievances. Moreover, he thought the list would only annoy the Metis, who would likely interpret it as another delaying tactic. And even though he modified the message somewhat to make it seem more purposeful before passing it on, his fears were well founded. Riel was furious at receiving it.[5]

Dewdney's primary preoccupation remained with the Indians, and his men in the field were constantly vigilant for signs of trouble. In February, Vankoughnet suggested throwing the instigators of agitation in jail. Dewdney liked the idea, but he pointed out that it hadn't worked very well in the past, mainly because magistrates rarely handed down sufficiently lengthy jail sentences to act as a deterrent or to keep troublemakers out of the way when their presence was least desired. He proposed that he, as commissioner, be given the power to depose chiefs and that this power would greatly strengthen his hand when meting out swift punishment. But the prime minister thought that such power was unnecessary because the governor general would act on the commissioner's recommendations where it came to deposing chiefs. Macdonald supported the proposal to arrest troublemakers as long as a sufficient force was on hand to succeed. And he encouraged Dewdney to use his personal influence on magistrates to secure their cooperation on the question of sentencing.[6]

Throughout February, the men in the field – department officials, Mounted Police, and the like – were sending reports to the commissioner's office on the state of Indian military preparedness. There were assessments of the numbers of horses and weapons and the quantities of ammunition at hand. As a precaution in such matters, the government had banned the sale of fixed ammunition (that is, used for rifles rather than shotguns) to Indians under Section 2, Chapter 27, of the Indian Act in 1884. But the prohibition had not been all that effective because notices proclaiming the law had not been distributed in the North-West. Police reports showed that some traders were still supplying Indians with ammunition and concern was growing.[7]

By mid-March, the reports reaching Dewdney from the Saskatchewan District made him so alarmed that he felt an immediate stand should be taken against all agitation – Indian and Metis alike. And he made preparations to send a force of 100 policemen into the district.[8] Amid the bad news, however, was one note of cheer. Word came via Peter Ballendine and Subagent Thomas Quinn that Big Bear had finally selected his reserve at

Dog Rump Creek about twenty-five miles west of Frog Lake. The old agitator was settling down after pressure from his followers and family.[9]

By this time, the Metis were the major source of concern as the potential instigators of trouble – trouble that might provoke what every white person in the North-West feared most, a full-scale Indian war. On 8 March at a large meeting in St. Laurent, Riel announced his intention of forming a provisional government, just as he had at Red River fifteen years earlier. At the meeting, a ten-point Revolutionary Bill of Rights was adopted that demanded, among other things, land titles and government by the people instead of "the despotism of Mr. Dewdney."

On the evening of 18 March, as Colonel Irvine was marching north from Regina with 100 policemen, Riel and his supporters began to take prisoners and seize property around Batoche. The next day, he established his provisional government and organized his men into fighting units. The Metis were taking direct control of the land they claimed as their own around the south branch of the Saskatchewan River.[10]

Almost at once, frantic telegrams from officials and settlers in the district began to arrive in the commissioner's office, demanding that men and weapons be sent in. And there were disturbing reports that the Indians were being "tampered with," meaning that Riel was seeking support on reserves. It wasn't clear at first if the Metis would fight or not. In any case, Dewdney decided, in consultation with the Mounted Police comptroller, to allow Irvine and his 100 men to proceed northwards.[11] Their presence would at least serve to calm settler fears and protect stores and armaments in the district.

But just before Irvine was on the scene, a force of policemen and settler volunteers under Crozier was confronted and defeated by Gabriel Dumont and Metis marksmen at Duck Lake on 26 March. Riel's defiance of the government was now open rebellion and there was no turning back.

Major-General F.D. Middleton, commander of the Canadian militia, happened to be in Winnipeg when news of the Duck Lake skirmish arrived, and he immediately took charge of military operations against the insurgents. He began to organize a force of local volunteers, policemen, and militia units while reinforcements were being assembled in Central Canada.[12]

On 31 March, the general met Dewdney in Qu'Appelle to discuss the situation. Dewdney surmised that the rebellion was a local affair totally dependent on Riel's leadership. He feared, however, that it might spread to include the Indians, especially if government forces suffered further setbacks at the hands of the rebels. Middleton decided, therefore, that the best plan was to march on Riel's headquarters at Batoche as quickly as possible to snuff out the affair.[13] In the meantime, Dewdney would devote himself to preventing Indians from joining the fray, calming settler fears, and keeping in close touch with Ottawa and with developments throughout the North-West.

Dewdney's principal tactic for preventing the spread of fighting was the authorization of a policy of unprecedented generosity in the distribution of food and goods to Indians who stayed on their reserves and worked. He also supported the idea, clamoured for by settlers, of stationing troops throughout the Territories. Settler panic, especially after the sack of Battleford by Poundmaker and Little Pine at the end of March and the Frog Lake massacre by some of Big Bear's band on 2 April, dictated that the troops be spread around, even though this strategy weakened Middleton's plan of a swift assault on Batoche. The military presence throughout the country was supposed to intimidate Indians, but sometimes it only served to agitate them. In at least one case, it almost led to disaster.

On 24 April, a militia column under Colonel D.O. Otter came to the relief of Battleford, where the residents had been huddling in the Mounted Police fort for weeks, fearing an Indian attack. Because Middleton's orders to him were slightly ambiguous, Otter wired Dewdney, suggesting that he be authorized to go after Poundmaker, whose men had been pillaging surrounding homesteads. Dewdney agreed, and the soldiers set out on their mission on 1 May. The next day, they stumbled into Poundmaker's camp at Cutknife Creek and quickly got themselves in trouble. Otter only managed to withdraw his force from the scene of battle with difficulty.[14]

Dewdney's leadership was more successful when he confined himself to familiar aspects of Indian administration. As soon as hostilities broke out, he toured the reserves in the Qu'Appelle area, consulting with the chiefs on their concerns. The Indians took advantage of officialdom's nervousness to press for better treatment, and the commissioner saw the expediency of giving way. He agreed to an increase in flour and bacon rations and ordered an additional 800 lbs. of tea and 200 lbs. of bacon for all bands in the district. He reasoned that the expense would be worthwhile if Indians were kept busy and contented on their reserves. Before leaving on 8 April to visit the Treaty 7 reserves, Dewdney also authorized the purchase of more cattle for Piapot, who was regarded by the department as potentially the most troublesome chief in the district.[15]

The approximately 5,000 Indians of Treaty 4 were the responsibility of two agents, Lawrence W. Herchmer at Birtle and Allan MacDonald at Indian Head, assisted by six farm instructors. Throughout the disturbances, the agents carried on Dewdney's policy of appeasement, making frequent tours of their reserves and reporting regularly to the Regina office.

The policy worked. The department discovered that when the Indians were treated well and supplied with food and equipment, they stayed on their reserves and worked hard. And several chiefs, including Pasquah, Muscowpetung, and Piapot, went out of their way to express their loyalty to the government while all the time asking for more equipment so that they might keep working.[16]

To some extent, the department was counting on chiefs to keep their young men in check. The warriors were likely to be tempted into action by messengers from Riel, and this danger was real enough. Ironically, the greatest source of conflict came from troops passing through the district.

Early in May, Agent MacDonald rushed to Touchwood Hills on learning that the Day Star and Poor Man bands had left their reserves and were camped on Gordon's. The Indians explained that they had moved to avoid soldiers who were nearby. MacDonald, who initially feared that some trouble was afoot, accepted the explanation. He discovered that teamsters with General Middleton's troops had vandalized property on Poor Man's reserve, and this action had precipitated the flight to Gordon's.[17]

Apparently, news of military reverses for government forces in the north was reaching soldiers on their way to the battlefront, and they were taking out their frustrations on Native communities along the way. Indian patience and the policy of careful diplomacy and generosity instigated by Dewdney kept the fighting from spreading. For example, when the File Hills Indians were annoyed by soldiers, they left their reserve and seized some property of local settlers. Agent MacDonald calmed matters by withholding the usual punishment for such infractions on the condition that the Indians return to their reserves.[18]

The same policy of conciliation with a helping of generosity was applied in the Treaty 7 area to keep the much-feared Blackfoot Confederation out of the fight. With the outbreak of hostilities, the prime minister wired Father Albert Lacombe, asking him to visit the Blackfoot chiefs to secure promises of loyalty. The well-known missionary was happy to oblige – any excuse would do to get away from Dunbow Industrial School where he was floundering as principal. By the end of March, Lacombe had seen all the chiefs and was able to assure the prime minister of their support for the government.[19]

Meanwhile, Dewdney was taking several initiatives of his own, including ordering an immediate increase in rations and tobacco. At the time, the 6,000 Treaty 7 Indians had two agents and five farm instructors working with them. The commissioner lacked confidence in the agents, William Pocklington at Fort Macleod and Magnus Begg at Blackfoot Crossing. Besides, Begg was temporarily indisposed, and his job was being done by an acting agent, W. Sherwood. Dewdney, therefore, called on the services of former agent C.E. Denny, who was ranching near Calgary since his resignation from the department a year earlier. Denny agreed to serve as a special agent to the Blackfoot for the duration of the trouble. He would spend the next few months touring the various reserves, taking measures to ensure that the Indians were content, and reporting regularly to the commissioner's office.[20]

After his tour of Qu'Appelle, Dewdney hurried on to Blackfoot Crossing, arriving there on 9 April. He spent several days in council with Crowfoot and other chiefs, lavishing them with tea and tobacco. His gift-giving and soothing words had the right effect, and he went away happy with the expressions of loyalty offered by the Indians. They were so loyal, he assured the prime minister, that they would even fight on the side of the government if called on.[21]

Such a notion had already occurred to Sir John A. He believed that the Cree feared the Blackfoot "like the devil" and that assembling a force under Crowfoot might "panic the rebels." He proposed this idea several times in April to Dewdney and Middleton, but neither of them liked the notion. It would only cause even greater alarm among settlers.[22]

The residents of Calgary were already petrified at the prospect of an Indian war and petitioned the government for military protection. To this end, Adolphe Caron, minister of militia and defence, persuaded Major-General Thomas Bland Strange, then ranching south of the city, to come out of retirement and take command of local operations. Strange immediately began to organize his Alberta Field Force from volunteers, policemen, and militia units sent to him by Middleton. Within a few weeks, the force was large enough for something more ambitious than garrison duty; it was ready to march northwards to take on the rebels.[23]

But as the soldiers assembled in Calgary, their presence had an unsettling effect on the Indians. This fact was reported to Dewdney by Denny as he toured the Treaty 7 reserves. The Indians were satisfied and working for the most part, he wrote, especially when he increased their rations. In one case, the ration increase had even dissuaded some young Peigan men from going off to join the rebels. The real danger, however, did not centre on messengers from the Cree or Metis, but on General Strange's men, who were in the habit of threatening the Indians with their revolvers. Denny was also concerned about an unsigned notice posted throughout the district, allowing anyone to shoot someone killing cattle or running off horses. He felt it put public safety in the "hands of a few cowboys who would shoot an Indian on sight."[24]

The erratic and self-important General Strange was far from helpful.

Responding to a rumour that some Blackfoot had tried to steal some of his horses, he sent threatening telegrams to Crowfoot, holding him responsible for the actions of his people. A major row was only avoided by the shrewd judgment of the interpreter, who did not read the messages to the chief. Dewdney was furious on hearing of the incident and described Strange as "utterly unfit to handle Indians." He told Ottawa that the general should be instructed to have no dealings with Indians without consultation with his office. Happily for peace in Treaty 7, Strange led most of his force north on 20 April en route to Edmonton and eventually the field of battle.[25]

Throughout May, Denny and other department officials in the district continued their careful monitoring of the situation. Early in the month, Denny reported some Cree among the Blackfoot, but that didn't concern Dewdney so long as they were not hostile. Agent Pocklington, who tended to be more alarmist, passed on a story that he thought might be true about Crowfoot sending tobacco to Red Crow, chief of the Blood, and asking him to make common cause with the Cree. Dewdney did not believe it.

Rumours and wild stories were always going around, and officials were kept busy limiting the unsettling effect they had in both Native and white communities. Such was the case on 25 May when the *Fort Macleod Gazette* announced that 150 Blood had gone north, presumably to join the Cree. The story was untrue, as it turned out. And officials did not hesitate to embroider the truth themselves, if it served the interest of keeping the peace. Pocklington, for instance, told Red Crow that Colonel Otter's defeat at Cutknife Creek was in fact a victory. By the end of the month, with hostilities winding down and the situation calm throughout Treaty 7, Dewdney was able to dispense with Denny's services.[26] Denny, whom the Indians much preferred to Pocklington and others, had played a critical role in keeping the peace in the district. He was anxious to return to his ranch in the aftermath of the troubles but would be called on soon to again help out the department.

Dewdney was less successful in preventing the spread of unrest to the Edmonton area. The Edmonton agency was originally the large western segment of Treaty 6 and had an Indian population of around 2,600, mainly Cree. Just before the rebellion, the department was subdividing the agency into three smaller units in line with reforms originating with Dewdney. One of these new agencies, Peace Hills (Hobbema today), was in the hands of Samuel B. Lucas as acting agent, while the other, Victoria (St. Paul area), was under farm instructor C. Carson. The agent in Edmonton, William Anderson, remained the department's principal officer in the area and the commissioner's main contact during the insurrection.

The Indians at Saddle Lake in the Victoria agency were the first to respond to the excitement. On 2 April, they received an invitation from Riel to join him for a council at Frog Lake. Spurred on by this message and various encouraging rumours from the battlefront, they assaulted their instructor, Carson. The next day, they helped themselves to agency supplies and prepared to leave for the Saskatchewan District. Carson, fearing for his life, fled during the night with his assistant, arriving in Edmonton on 7 April.[27]

News of these depredations reached the Peace Hills bands a few days later, and it was even rumoured that the Saddle Lake Indians, supported by a couple of other bands, were marching on Edmonton. When a messenger arrived from Big Bear asking for assistance, a war tent was set up on 8 April. Lucas, the acting agent, lost his nerve and moved with his family to the safety of Edmonton. The Methodist missionaries and other whites on the reserves also joined the exodus. The only exception was Father Constantine Scollen, a Catholic missionary, who stayed at his post. At this point, the Indians raided the Hudson's Bay store and the abandoned missions at Peace Hills.[28]

Dewdney learned of these alarming developments when a messenger from Edmonton met him in Calgary on 9 April. Further details were filled in by Agent Anderson in subsequent correspondence. Anderson reported that the settlers in and around Edmonton were in a state of panic, had raised a volunteer force, and were fortifying the Hudson's Bay Company fort in anticipation of an Indian attack.

At once, Dewdney sent a message of good will to the Peace Hills Indians, which was read to them by Father Scollen on 13 April. The chiefs, Bobtail, Ermineskin, Samson, and Muddy Bull, came out in support of the government, and the war camp was broken up. In the following days, much of the plundered property was given up. A number of young men, however, rejected the overtures of the commissioner and went off to join Big Bear.

By now, Agent Anderson had moved his office into Fort Edmonton and was urging Dewdney to send in a strong force as soon as possible to prevent a wholesale Indian rising. The chiefs generally supported the government, he noted, but they were not confident of controlling their young men. He had taken the initiative in supplying extra oxen to some bands and planned to increase rations generally as a measure of appeasement.[29]

Shortly afterwards, Anderson was relieved to learn that Pacan (also known as James Seenum) had rejected Big Bear's overtures and would remain loyal. Pacan was chief of the Whitefish Lake Cree, the largest band in the Victoria agency, and was earlier reported to be with the rebels. He subsequently took a leadership role in encouraging loyalty among other bands, including Saddle Lake, and demanded provisions and equipment in return. Anderson acted promptly to reward him, authorizing Pacan to kill government or band cattle if his people were hungry, a move that Dewdney approved.[30]

When General Strange and his men marched through the district early in May leaving garrisons in their wake, settler and government confidence revived somewhat, and department officials were able to venture back to their posts. Anderson remained apprehensive nonetheless, because he felt that the soldiers stationed in Edmonton by the general were not sufficient for the defence of the community. He was worried about the numerous "strange Indians prowling about the settlement" and ill omens such as the organization of a sun dance at Rivière-qui-barre. He continued to treat the Indians generously, with Dewdney's full support, until Big Bear's surrender brought the rebellion to an end early in June.[31]

Dewdney's policies of generosity and appeasement had little effect in the Saskatchewan District. There, the entire system of Indian administration virtually collapsed. The approximately 3,700 Indians of the district were signatories of Treaty 6 and were divided for administrative purposes into the three agencies of Battleford, Carlton, and Fort Pitt.[32] J.M. Rae, the Battleford agent and the department's principal officer in the district, spent the rebellion cringing behind the walls of the Mounted Police fort, pleading for reinforcements. Tom Quinn, the subagent at Fort Pitt, was killed in the Frog Lake massacre. And J.A. Macrae, subagent at Carlton, left his post when the police abandoned that fort after the Duck Lake fight.

Small wonder then that so many bands, left to themselves, engaged in activities considered disloyal. By department definition, disloyalty could mean such things as killing cattle, raiding agency stores, or simply leaving one's reserve.[33] Of course, it could also mean taking on the military in battle, but this engagement rarely happened except when initiated by government forces. Some Indians did participate in the defence of Batoche, the Metis stronghold, but they were the exception.

General Middleton finally reached Batoche on 9 May, and his army overran the Metis position on 12 May. Gabriel Dumont fled to the United States, where he continued to be a concern to the government. Riel surrendered on 15 May without even trying to cross the border. In the weeks that followed, the various Indian bands and individuals who had been in arms gave themselves up, a process culminating in the surrender of Big Bear on 2 June. Some Indians thought it prudent to slip south of the border, Little Poplar being the most notable among the fugitives.[34]

As the locus of governmental authority in the North-West, Dewdney was constantly on the alert during the disturbances. His first act was to tour

the Qu'Appelle reserves, instituting his policy of generosity and appeasement. Immediately afterwards, he was off to Blackfoot territory on the
same mission. He spent most of the remaining weeks in Regina, maintaining telegram contact as best he could with his agents in the field, with
Middleton, and with Macdonald. In the end, he received much of the
direct blame for the rebellion at the hands of the Liberal opposition. The
government and its policies were the real source of the abuse, of course, but
as the man on the spot, he was the logical and easiest target. For his part, he
readily defended his department, absolving it of responsibility for the outbreak. In June, he sent documents to the prime minister, allegedly showing
that just before the outbreak, there "was no reason to believe that our Indians were even dissatisfied, much less that they contemplated violence."[35]

Dewdney blamed Riel for the entire affair and believed that had it not
been for the Metis agitation, Indians would never have resorted to arms.
He recognized that the arrival of Big Bear and "those wandering Cree dis-
contents" in the Saskatchewan District had introduced a "dangerous element" with "mischievous propensities" among "settled and well-disposed
Indians." Even so, the government would have been able to control these
malcontents had not "unfortunate circumstances" drawn them into action
with "the misguided half-breeds." When young, "ill-disposed" Indians
committed "overt acts," they often had a disturbing effect on loyal members
of their bands who, fearing the government would be indiscriminate in
meting out punishment, joined in the depredations. And when some
Indian Department officers were taken captive by the Metis, the Indians
under their charge, now no longer supplied for their wants, gathered
around rebel headquarters and became inadvertently caught up in the
fighting. The spread of the rebellion to Indian reserves, then, was the result
of a certain configuration of circumstances rather than of "universal race
hatred" or of "the existence of grievances, discontent or general malignity."
He claimed: "We may rest assured, I think, that the past policy of the Government was not to blame, as none of the Indians, when spoken to of their
conduct on the reserves, have pleaded grievances in extenuation of it."[36]

Dewdney's assessment was fair in one respect: Indian involvement in the
rebellion had been sporadic and circumstantial. In other respects, however,
his attempt to exonerate government policy was hardly honest, even if
understandable for someone in his position. Although, like most officials,
he believed Indians to be chronic complainers, he knew too well of the
hardships of reserve life. His sudden generosity with rations and other supplies during the disturbances was a sure sign of this awareness. And his
several disputes with Vankoughnet showed that he challenged the more
mean-spirited details of policy emanating from Ottawa while supporting

its general contours. There could be no question, of course, of airing such differences in public. The government's Indian policy was under attack and everyone implicated in some way closed ranks in its defence.

But what was to be done with those Indians who had taken up arms, and how would their actions affect policy in general in the aftermath of the rebellion? These were the most pressing issues that Dewdney and his department faced in the remainder of the year.

There was no shortage of calls for revenge, especially from officials in areas caught up in the troubles. In June, Agent Anderson complained to Dewdney of reports in the Edmonton area that rebel Indians were to be treated leniently. This practice was causing those who had not joined the fray to behave in "a saucy and independent manner." They seemed to regret not having shared in the plunder, knowing that the whites were afraid to punish the rebels. The mild policy, according to Anderson, was putting agents and instructors in danger, because "nothing can be done with them [Indians] unless terror is struck into them." Moreover, settlers were indignant at the government's lack of resolve and might even take the law into their own hands by shooting Indians.

Agent Rae reported a similar state of affairs in Battleford. Indians who had been let off easily thought the whole thing a joke and would probably resort to crime again unless swiftly punished. He was taking the initiative, touring reserves with a body of armed men, searching for stolen property, and making arrests.

The government was certainly prepared to act, but its immediate preoccupation was with the rebel leaders and those who had killed in cold blood. Cattle killing and robbery did not merit the same urgency as treason and murder. In the meantime, Dewdney was advised by Ottawa to gather evidence against all criminals that they might ultimately be brought to justice.[37] He was also asked to report on the status of property on reserves and on the willingness of Indians to get back to work after the excitement.

Mid-June was too soon after the end of hostilities to have ready information at hand, and Dewdney asked his men in the field to investigate fully local conditions before initiatives could be taken. But with some discouraging data filtering into his office daily, he was prepared to make a couple of recommendations concerning retribution. He proposed that annuities be withheld from rebel Indians until such time as the government recovered the cost of damaged or destroyed property. And he proposed breaking up bands implicated in the troubles and amalgamating them with others.[38] These ideas ultimately formed part of a broader punitive package discussed and refined in the department during the following months.

Getting accurate information on property damage by rebel Indians was frustrating because department records were sometimes destroyed during the disturbances. This was the case, for instance, in the Victoria agency where depredations had been carried out by young men from the Saddle Lake reserve. But after investigating the matter, the new acting agent J.A. Mitchell found that some of the pillage had been the work of teamsters attached to General Strange's column.[39] This finding lowered even further Dewdney's grim assessment of the general's character.

At Carlton, on the other hand, the new agent J.B. Lash was able to provide a detailed account of the property losses sustained at the hands of Indians. The total came to $11,657.88. The four bands responsible for these losses, One Arrow, Beardy, Okemasis, and Petequakey, received annual treaty payments amounting to $2,610.[40] If annuities were withheld until this property was paid for, as suggested by Dewdney, these Indians would not receive their treaty money for almost five years.

While this sort of information was being compiled by his men in the field, Dewdney asked Assistant Commissioner Reed to prepare a series of recommendations regarding the future management of Indians in the North-West in light of the recent troubles. Reed's report was ready late in July, and Dewdney sent it on to Ottawa on 1 August, having made his own comments in the margins. Vankoughnet and John A. Macdonald made further refinements to it, and the report became the basis of the more restrictive and repressive system of administration that emerged in subsequent years.[41]

An immediate aim of the new departure was to make a conspicuous distinction between the loyal and disloyal, and the harshest measures in the document were reserved for the latter. Rebels lost their annuities until the damage they had caused had been paid for. By 1888, some of them were returned to the pay list, and the rest were gradually restored within a few years.[42]

Some bands considered particularly disloyal were broken up and amalgamated with others nearby. One Arrow's band was amalgamated with that of Beardy, while Petequakey's was distributed among those of Ahtakakoop and Mastowawsis. Lucky Man's band was spread among others in the Battleford and Peace Hills agencies. Big Bear's band was also broken up, some members going to Thunder Child's, the rest to other bands in Battleford and Fort Pitt.[43]

Reed, who was always pushing for strong measures, wanted to confiscate rebel horses and replace them with cattle; to confiscate the rebels' rifles and loan them fowling pieces during the hunting season instead; and to prohibit rebels from leaving their reserves without a pass from their agent. Dewdney, Vankoughnet, and Macdonald agreed in principle, but they shared some concerns about the practicality of the proposed measures. They decided that it would be better to persuade the Indians to exchange their horses for cattle and their rifles for shotguns whenever possible. Besides, if the law against selling fixed ammunition were properly enforced, Indian rifles would soon become useless. The pass system was to be used to discourage Indians from leaving their reserves and to keep track of them when they did so. But, as the prime minister pointed out, Indians could not be confined to their reserves according to the treaties, and therefore, no penalties could be imposed on those leaving without a pass.[44]

In their correspondence that summer, Dewdney and Macdonald agreed that Indians conspicuous for their loyalty to the government during the rebellion should be appropriately rewarded. The commissioner's office began to compile a list of those to be so recognized as well as the gifts they were to receive.[45]

The Blackfoot were considered a special case and were the first to be rewarded. When Dewdney attended the Treaty 7 payments towards the end of September, he found that the chiefs expected unprecedented generosity in return for their loyalty. Crowfoot asked for cash because, unlike goods, he wouldn't have to share it with others. Dewdney gave him $100. Red Crow received $50. The total value of goods given to the Blackfoot was $1,640.[46]

For the other loyal Indians in the North-West, the reward bill came to $11,433. The rewards were mainly in the form of livestock, farm implements, and items for the home – gifts designed to encourage agriculture and sedentary living. These goods were welcomed because the Indians had always complained about the inadequacy of their farming equipment and supplies.[47]

Meanwhile, the leaders of the unrest who had either surrendered or been captured in its denouement were receiving the full force of the law. Louis Riel was charged with treason and was brought to trial on 20 July in the Regina courthouse, one of the new government buildings in the territorial capital. On 1 August, he was found guilty and sentenced to hang.[48] Dewdney approved the decision, noting to Macdonald, "I hope sincerely that he will be hanged; he is too dangerous a man to have a chance of being loose on society." Macdonald described the verdict as "satisfactory," but he noted without undue alarm that there was an attempt "to pump up patriotic feeling about him" in Quebec.[49]

Appeals delayed the execution, which was originally scheduled for 18 September. Dewdney went to Ottawa late in October, where he apparently discussed with the prime minister the political implications of carrying out the sentence. Upon returning to Regina, he discussed the matter further with western politicians, including John Norquay, premier of Manitoba, and A.C. Larivière, an MP for that province. He concluded that it would be best to hang Riel while granting clemency to the Indians and Metis in the penitentiary, with the exception of murderers. That was how he advised Macdonald.[50]

On 15 November, Dewdney received a despatch from the secretary of state containing the governor general's wish that the law take its course in the case of Louis Riel.[51] The Metis leader was hanged the next morning. Dewdney reported to Macdonald that the hanging had taken place without a hitch. He was relieved that it was all over, and he believed that the execution would "do an immense amount of good."[52]

Meanwhile, a number of Indians who had participated in the rebellion were put on trial in Regina and Battleford. Many of these, including Chiefs Poundmaker and Big Bear, received jail sentences from the courts; others, eleven in all, were condemned to death for their part in various killings.[53] The prime minister believed that the execution of these men, as well as of Riel, would have a good effect on the Indians by convincing them "that the White Man governs."[54] When the condemned men were hanged in Battleford, Dewdney arranged for twenty Indians to witness the event.[55] This arrangement showed a spirit of vindictiveness towards those who had defied them. Macdonald and Dewdney were already well aware of the political difficulties that the rebellion had caused for themselves and the Conservative government, and they were not inclined to be lenient with those responsible. In fact, the jail sentences and executions marked the beginning of an even harsher North-West Indian policy.

One of Dewdney's more immediate concerns was the possibility of renewed violence. Stories in some North-West newspapers suggested restlessness among certain elements of the Metis and Indian populations, and there were reports of arms and whiskey traders among them. The newspapers tended to exaggerate, prompting Dewdney to remonstrate with them on occasion for unduly alarming settlers.[56] His men in the field, especially the Indian agents and Hayter Reed, were his principal sources of information, and he hired others on special assignment as circumstances dictated to keep him informed about the situation.

In November 1885, Dewdney re-engaged C.E. Denny as a special agent among the Treaty 7 Indians, some of whom were arousing suspicion by their excursions south of the border to trade with their American relatives. The Indian commissioner also had some doubts about Crowfoot's loyalty.[57] Denny remained in service until the following year and was able to reassure his employer that the Blackfoot would not cause trouble.[58]

Another potential source of trouble lay in Montana, where Metis led by

Gabriel Dumont and Indians led by Little Poplar had sought refuge as the rebellion collapsed. It was rumoured that they would return in spring 1886 to lead another Native rising against the government. In November 1885, Dewdney employed James Anderson as a secret agent to investigate and report on the activities of these men. Anderson spent a month south of the border on his fact-finding mission. In his frequent letters to the Indian commissioner, he was able to reassure him that there was little sympathy for the rebellion in the American Metis settlements and that there were no plans afoot for another outbreak. As a precaution, he proposed pardoning those at Turtle Mountain and inducing them to return to Canada so that they might not be misguided once more by their leaders.[59] Dewdney acted on this suggestion the following March, with the prime minister's agreement.[60]

Spring 1886 passed without mishap. By July, Dewdney was able to assure Macdonald that there was nothing exciting to report. The Indians were contented, he said, and the Metis had "had enough."[61]

As security matters were brought under control, Dewdney's department took measures to ensure that life on the reserves was more carefully supervised. The subdivision of agencies, begun before the rebellion, now intensified. The Treaty 4 area, for instance, became five agencies: Assiniboine, Crooked Lakes, File Hills, Muscowpetung's, and Touchwood Hills. Agents were more readily available to keep an eye on things, and Indians had fewer excuses, as Dewdney noted, "to wander about at times when they should be at work." The appointment of a second agency inspector in the North-West Territories, Alexander McGibbon, allowed for closer monitoring of activities at the local level and attempted to ensure that department supplies and equipment were fully accounted for and put to efficient use.[62]

Greater control of Native lives was also sought by expanding another aspect of the department's mandate: education. Dewdney, like other senior officials in the service, believed that the ultimate triumph of Indian policy hinged on the younger generation, provided they were subjected to the transformative powers of schooling. But he had little faith in day schools as instruments of change. Indeed, he now advocated closing some of them and concentrating department funds and efforts on boarding and industrial schools whose residential nature secured "separation from the retarding influences of the daily return to the home."[63] Besides, the churches were anxious to assist with this work and would "contribute largely to maintaining the schools."[64] In other words, boarding and industrial schools would achieve better results but without substantial outlay because of missionary involvement.

In keeping with this initiative, Dewdney proposed in spring 1886 the appointment of J.A. Macrae as inspector of Indian schools in Manitoba and the North-West Territories. This proposal was agreed to. Before taking up his appointment, Macrae spent a few months visiting the Mohawk and Mount Elgin Institutes in Ontario and the Carlisle Indian School in Pennsylvania. On 18 December, he submitted a fifty-six-page report to Dewdney setting forth his proposals for Indian education based on his observations at those institutions.

Macrae envisaged an elaborate and comprehensive program that would have children begin their studies in day schools, move on to boarding schools, and culminate in three or four years of practical training in industrial schools. He advised that new industrial schools, like existing ones, be located in centres of white settlement so that "the school's surroundings can be made educational in nearly every impression that they make upon the young minds of the pupils ... the example of a thriving, healthy civilization may be ever before them." And a further reason for so locating them was that it was "unlikely that any Tribe or Tribes would give trouble of a serious nature to the Government whose members had children completely under Government control."[65]

In the context of the post-rebellion concern with security, the schools were to take on a custodial role, holding children hostage to guarantee the good behaviour of their parents. Dewdney was fully supportive, and in 1887, arrangements were made to establish new industrial schools in Regina and in Elkhorn, Manitoba, in partnership with the Presbyterian and Anglican Churches respectively. Within a few years, there were ten of these institutions on the Prairies – expensive experiments in accelerated assimilation.[66]

On 17 January 1888, Big Bear died at his reserve.[67] His death was symbolic of the passing of an age. He was one of the last to lead his people in war and hunting parties, and he had only succumbed to the indignities of the reserve system when desperation drove him to it. In some ways, his demise marked the triumph of Dewdney and of an Indian policy that sought to subdue and marginalize Natives.

Dewdney left the department that year to re-enter federal politics. He had served as Indian commissioner for nine years. It was a turbulent era that saw him avert mass starvation, force settlement on reserves, promote agriculture through work for rations, fight a rebellion, reassert department control in its aftermath, and establish a system of schooling aimed at rapid cultural transformation.

In the end, he boasted that Indians were becoming progressively "more fully alive to the benefits which they receive under the humane and wise policy of the Government."[68] It is doubtful that many Natives would have agreed, and in the years that followed, their resistance to official policy aims manifested itself in their refusal to send their children to school and in their attachment to traditional ceremonies.

Many non-Natives, too, were unimpressed with the much-vaunted progress of the North-West, although often for partisan reasons. Dewdney was painfully aware that he and his department were the subject of much complaint by the press and the parliamentary opposition. Some of this criticism centred on the fact that he was both Indian commissioner and lieutenant governor, which put an excessive source of patronage and power at his disposal. These questions are considered in the next chapter, which looks at specific aspects of Dewdney's role as lieutenant governor.

CHAPTER 5

Lieutenant Governor

The North-West Territories never appealed to Edgar Dewdney. He found the land bleak and inhospitable, the climate harsh and unforgiving. His duties as Indian commissioner were onerous and tiresome. Apart from difficult negotiations and dangerous confrontations, he was obliged to travel constantly by buckboard or on horseback, often camping out along the way. In spite of the robust image he liked to cultivate in Ottawa, he was no longer the rugged young trailblazer of the gold colony. He was portly, middle-aged, and subject to bouts of rheumatism and back problems. Jane shared his dislike of the Prairies, and they both longed to return to British Columbia, the land of forests and mountains that had enchanted them as young immigrants.

It was mainly to entice Dewdney to stay on the job that the prime minister offered him the additional post of lieutenant governor of the North-West Territories in fall 1881. The attractions of the offer were an annual stipend of $2,000 and Macdonald's assurance that there would be "no material increase" in his duties.[1] Dewdney, ever loyal to the old chieftain, accepted.

Being lieutenant governor brought a certain prestige. Dewdney was now addressed as "Governor" or "Your Honour." But, unlike similar positions in the provinces, his position also brought real political power, control of patronage appointments, and access to avenues of personal enrichment that proved too tempting to resist.

Because of the undeveloped state of the Territories, they were administered in a quasi-colonial manner by the federal government through the person of the lieutenant governor. The details of this arrangement were set out in the North-West Territories Act of 1875 and in subsequent amendments to it. The Act stipulated the creation of an appointed council with both legislative and executive powers presided over by the lieutenant governor. When an area of 1,000 square miles (twenty-eight townships) acquired a population of 1,000 adults (excluding Indians and aliens), it could become an electoral district and elect a member to the council for a two-year term. As soon as twenty-one members were elected in this manner, the council would be transformed into the legislative assembly of the North-West Territories. Democratic constitutional evolution was thereby allowed for and envisaged.[2] It was not until 1881 that the first electoral district was formed and returned a member to the council. The district in question was called Lorne and included the settlements of Prince Albert and St. Laurent.[3]

The inadequate local tax base meant that the expenses of running the government came from a parliamentary appropriation administered through the Department of the Interior. The federal grant, which grew substantially in the 1880s, was at the disposal of the lieutenant governor, not the council.

Dewdney, in his role as governor, controlled most expenditures, but he also had various other powers that, considered as a whole, made him a virtual autocrat. He appointed people to all sorts of offices – game wardens, health officers, justices of the peace, and so forth; he issued licences for operations such as ferries, auctions, and billiard halls; he determined when and where electoral districts would be established; and he granted permits for the import and sale of liquor in the Territories.[4] The concentration of authority in his hands was to his liking because his views on the superior claim of the well-born to high office and his antipathy to the levelling effects of democracy had not changed since he had first expressed them during the British Columbia debates on Confederation. In exercising these powers, often in close consultation with Ottawa, he could hardly please everyone – and he didn't. The Grits were a constant source of annoyance, and so were those who, although Tory in sympathy, balked at the slow pace of political development.

The autocratic structures were considered necessary while the non-Native population of the region remained small and dispersed. Although Canada attracted 886,000 immigrants during the 1880s, only 40,000 of them chose to settle in the North-West. This fact was at least partly due to hostile accounts of the region published in American, British, and central Canadian newspapers. The country's leading Grit paper, the *Globe*, was consistently negative in its reports and commented frequently on the harsh climate, poor agricultural potential, and the communication and transportation difficulties that faced those who headed west.

There was truth to this. Agriculture on the prairies was still experimental in nature, with no guarantees of its success. Falling wheat prices in the early 1880s were a discouraging sign, and the returns to farmers fell even further when an early frost damaged crops in September 1883. In the same year, the Macdonald government raised duties on imported farm machinery to protect central Canadian manufacturers from American competition, provoking outrage from the already beleaguered western farmer.[5] It seemed that the federal government, whose authority Dewdney represented in the North-West, was adopting policies at variance with local interests.

Most of the arriving settlers were of Anglo-Saxon origin and were impatient with the existing political structures and their relative inability to influence decisions affecting the region's future. Above all, they wanted a voice in government, and they made their views known through a vigorous regional press. Indeed, some of the newspaper editors (Frank Oliver of the *Edmonton Bulletin* and N.F. Davin of the *Regina Leader*) used their positions to launch political careers.[6]

One of Dewdney's principal challenges as lieutenant governor, then, was accommodating local concerns while acting as the principal agent of Macdonald's National Policy. This policy, while ostensibly serving the nation as a whole, treated the North-West as a hinterland of the central Canadian provinces.

The new lieutenant governor became embroiled in controversy right from the start when he played a role in selecting a new capital for the Territories. This choice was made necessary when the Canadian Pacific Railway abandoned the northern route west of Winnipeg through Battleford, Edmonton, and the Yellowhead Pass. The capital would have to be on the railway, somewhere along the new route through the southern part of the prairies. Because the project was a joint venture between the government and the railway, the location of the capital was chosen by Dewdney and William C. Van Horne, general manager of the CPR. In June 1882, they picked the spot where the tracks were to cross Pile o' Bones (Wascana) Creek, and the lieutenant governor reserved land in the vicinity for the townsite. The townsite ultimately embraced sections 19 and 30 in range 19, and 24 and 25 in range 20. As it turned out, section 26 in range 20, just west of section 25, had been bought earlier by Dewdney from the Hudson's Bay Company.[7]

Speculators had been buying land and paying squatters to occupy sections on their behalf at likely locations along the projected line, hoping that their properties would be in or near the capital. Naturally, many were disappointed when the selection of Pile o' Bones was announced. They were quick to accuse Dewdney of having made the choice simply to increase the value of his own land holdings and railed against Pile o' Bones for its lack of wood and water and its general unsuitability. These accusations were published in the Winnipeg newspapers, much to the lieutenant governor's embarrassment.[8]

Although motivated by spite and political partisanship, the charges could not easily be denied. Dewdney was as concerned as ever with achieving his "competency" and could not resist the "land fever" that gripped the Prairies in anticipation of the railway. In fact, more than a month before he and Van Horne made the journey to select the capital, he had admitted his preference for Pile o' Bones to the prime minister. The site of the capital was undoubtedly chosen with personal gain in mind. He tried to explain to Macdonald that he would have done a lot better for himself had he selected instead the Bell Farm at Qu'Appelle, where he had a much more substantial interest – a rather lame excuse under the circumstances.[9]

The new capital was named Regina, a dull, unimaginative choice considering the colourful original, Pile o' Bones. In an interview with the *Winnipeg Times* published on 19 September 1882, Dewdney praised its location as having the best soil, drainage, and volume of water of any place between the Assiniboine and Swift Current Creek. And he defended his role in its selection by pointing out that he had done so in consultation with the CPR, which would hardly have approved had he been mistaken.[10]

Dewdney apparently expected the railway station to be built in range 20, section 24, which would have greatly increased the value of his nearby land. He was disappointed to learn, however, that Van Horne had decided to put it on range 19, section 19, a half-mile farther east. But he could still get a good return on his investment if he could shift the town centre away from the railway station towards his section. This he tried to do by locating the lieutenant governor's residence, the North-West council building, and the North-West Mounted Police barracks farther to the west.[11]

George Stephen, president of the CPR, immediately complained to the prime minister that Dewdney's action would adversely affect the sale of lots near the station. W.B. Scarth, one of the managing directors of the Canada North-West Land Company, which was selling lots in the townsite that it had purchased from the CPR, lodged a similar complaint. Macdonald only partly supported Dewdney, advising him that it was best to locate the governor's residence and the police barracks away from the centre, while putting other government buildings near the station.[12] This was done, and the town grew up around the railway, which was to be expected.

Dewdney profited from his role in the founding of Regina, but his reputation suffered. The Liberal opposition in Parliament sought to depict him not just as the personification of Tory mismanagement in the North-West, but also as an unprincipled carpetbagger adept at exploiting his position for personal gain. In the House of Commons on 7 May 1883, in response to Edward Blake's suggestion that the lieutenant governor be fired, Macdonald offered a ringing endorsement: "I never made a better selection of a better man or a better officer than I did in selecting Mr. Dewdney."[13] Exchanges of this nature became almost a regular feature of parliamentary debates on North-West issues in the following years.

It wasn't just the selection of Regina that cast a shadow over Dewdney's reputation. It was generally known that he was involved in numerous other speculative ventures as well. The loose moral code of frontier capitalism encouraged such activity, but there was a growing suspicion that men in public office held an unfair advantage in the game. In Dewdney's case, the results were mixed.

He did well in the Winnipeg land boom of 1881, boasting to Macdonald that he was offered $1,300 more than what he had paid for the three city lots the previous fall.[14] He also had a hand in the feverish speculation surrounding the location of the western terminus of the CPR. In 1884, Port Moody was considered to be the end of the line, but it was widely believed that the tracks would be extended farther west along Burrard Inlet. In anticipation of this extension, Dewdney, in partnership with his old friend Peter O'Reilly, had bought a parcel of land at Coal Harbour, believing it would greatly increase in value if the railway terminus was located nearby. All the land in the vicinity was being held by other speculators with similar hopes. In August, acting on a tip that the terminus would probably be at English Bay, about five miles from his land, Dewdney sold half of his holdings – 16.75 acres at $600 per acre, realizing $9,547 after his agent's commission.[15]

For every investment that succeeded, there was another that failed. Dewdney was a shareholder in the Bell Farm, a major agricultural enterprise begun in 1882 under the auspices of a joint stock company known as the Qu'Appelle Valley Farming Company. With 53,000 acres of land and initial capitalization of $600,000, the company hoped to wrest profits from the prairie soil by employing the latest equipment and sound business practices. But by 1885, the operation was in financial trouble. When Dewdney resigned from the directorate in February of the following year, he was informed that the company could not pay cash for his shares.[16]

Another losing proposition was the Qu'Appelle, Long Lake and Saskatchewan Railway and Steamboat Company, in which Dewdney was a director. It proposed to build a rail and steam line connecting Regina with Battleford. At the time, the federal government was counting on branch lines to encourage settlement north of the CPR and provided land grants of 6,400 acres per mile of track to such companies. Construction began in 1885, but a year later only twenty miles of track had been laid. Few settlers took up land along the route, and with the company experiencing cash flow problems, operations ground to a halt.[17]

If some of his business ventures soured, Dewdney always had his salary to fall back on. And it was substantial, reaching $7,200 per year when another increase was forthcoming from a grateful prime minister in summer 1883.[18]

The choice of Regina as territorial capital continued as a matter of controversy that summer. The *Globe* kept up its attacks on Dewdney, and he felt powerless to respond. At one point, he vented his frustration to the prime minister, vowing that were he free for a few weeks, he "would make them eat some of these slanderous letters and articles."[19]

Regina was now taking on the appearance of a permanent settlement. Wooden structures were going up to house the lieutenant governor, the North-West council, the Mounted Police, and the Indian Department – all fairly close to one another, at Dewdney's insistence.[20]

As this work was under way, preparations were being made for elections to the council. In June 1883, Dewdney decided to create new electoral districts at Broadview, Qu'Appelle, and Regina so that more people would be represented. This step was allowed for and was indeed required under the North-West Territories Act.[21] It was the first of several small and hesitating steps to be taken in the direction of democracy. Under prevailing circumstances, the council was poorly positioned to play a meaningful role in territorial administration. The difficulty and expense of regular attendance meant that it sat for less than two months in the year. The lieutenant governor had a free hand most of the time in conducting the business of his "Crown colony."

True as ever to his conservative principles on constitutional development, Dewdney had no intention of allowing the council to become a forum for opposition to the Macdonald government, whose power he represented. To ensure that men favourable to his views were elected, he was prepared to manipulate the process or at least attempt to do so. He wanted his friend and business partner in the farm, Major M.R. Bell, returned for the Qu'Appelle District. He wrote, therefore, to Sir Hector Langevin, asking him to persuade Archbishop Taché to secure the Metis vote for Bell. Taché, apparently, failed to act. The Metis supported Bell's opponent, T.W. Jackson, who was a Conservative and a supporter of John A. Macdonald, and who held a personal grudge against the lieutenant governor. Even so, Dewdney was reasonably pleased with the 1883 election, noting to the prime minister that the people had chosen "all pretty good men." The only exception was Frank Oliver, an incorrigible Grit returned for Edmonton.[22]

The North-West council of 1883 consisted of six elected members, five appointed members, and the lieutenant governor. With such an arrangement, Dewdney was confident that he could get his legislative program adopted without complications or delay. The appointed members would cooperate, he believed, because he made them understand the position that they should occupy. And he thought that his personal charm should be sufficient to get most of the elected members on side.[23]

In his speech at the opening of council on 22 August, Dewdney, after praising the selection of Regina as territorial capital, outlined the matters on which he wanted the members to legislate. Law-making was to be the major task of the council over the following years, because the Territories had few ordinances on the books at the time.

A select committee was appointed to reply to the lieutenant governor's speech, and it did so on 28 August. The reply was boosterish in tone and in keeping with the optimism of a fledgling frontier community. It was full of praise for the government's railway policy and the Mounted Police, making rosy predictions of future growth and prosperity. It also asked for a revision of electoral boundaries to give broader representation to the people in council.[24] This request was the first hint of resentment among the elected members at what was perceived as the undemocratic privileges of the appointed members. While most members identified themselves as Conservatives and supporters of the Macdonald government, they didn't hesitate to agitate for a more representative council and greater autonomy for the territorial government. Dewdney was determined to obstruct these tendencies, in keeping with the wishes of his masters in Ottawa.

The council already held some executive functions. Most important here, perhaps, was its control of the general revenue fund – money raised locally through licences, permits, and the like. This fund was divided evenly among the electoral districts and was spent under the guidance of each local member. But they wanted more. In the 1883 session, a committee of all the elected members demanded council control of the parliamentary appropriation. Dewdney's position, maintained throughout his term of office, was that he should retain control of these funds because he was responsible for all the North-West, not just the electoral districts, which, in any case, only comprised a small portion of the whole.[25] His resolve on this issue was reinforced by his sense that the elected members were all too anxious to spend money on themselves rather than on their constituents. Some of them were demanding payment of $1,000 for their council attendance, to be taken from the parliamentary appropriation. This Dewdney refused. After some negotiation, he agreed to let them have $400 each.[26]

The control of liquor was a question that engaged the council during the session and revealed deep differences of opinion. Liquor had had a troublesome history in the North-West since the notorious whiskey trade of the early 1870s. Preventing its sale to Natives had been the principal reasoning behind the prohibition clause inserted into the North-West Territories Act. The clause banned the import, sale, or possession of liquor except with a permit from the lieutenant governor. Settlers who were granted permits could import liquor for their personal use only, usually from Manitoba. The system was seriously flawed. Not only was there widespread smuggling, but the permit system was open to abuse. It was impossible to tell, for instance, if a bottle accompanied by a permit had been refilled or not.[27] A major annoyance for Dewdney throughout his term of office was the resentment of those who were denied permits and the accusation that he granted them in a partisan manner.

In August, the council received a petition requesting that the brewing of ale be permitted in the Territories. Dewdney supported the idea on the grounds that it would counteract smuggling, illicit manufacturing, and permit system manipulation. The council was divided on the issue, reflecting divisions among the settler population as a whole. Oliver and three of the appointed members, Richardson, Macleod, and Irvine, opposed Dewdney's position, showing that they didn't always support the governor. But in spite of majority council support, Ottawa refused to budge on the prohibition question and wouldn't do so until 1891.[28]

The council session ended early in October with passing and signing of the various ordinances agreed to. These included measures for preventing profanity on the Lord's Day, disposing of found or stolen horses, destroying noxious weeds, and licensing billiard tables – a range of measures one would expect on the frontier.[29]

Dewdney was reasonably happy with the session. He had held his own, he reported to the prime minister, and the elected members were generally pleased with his leadership. Of course, relations with Oliver had been difficult, and he had had to give Jackson a bit of his mind on one occasion. With the exception of Hayter Reed, he had found the performance of the appointed members less than satisfactory. Irvine was "no good," Richardson had "no backbone," and Macleod was only anxious to see him, Dewdney, in difficulties.[30]

Dewdney accepted the inevitability of democratic structures but was clearly uneasy about them. In December, he told Macdonald that he had received petitions for five new elected seats in council from districts either unrepresented or underrepresented, and he could see no option but to concede. He observed: "I can foresee that under the present arrangement with a large majority of elected members difficulties will arise." He simply didn't want to be around to face such a challenge and suggested once more to Sir John that he was ready to return to British Columbia whenever his return was advantageous to the government. In the meantime, to slow the advance of representative institutions, he proposed dividing the Territories into twenty-one electoral districts eligible for a seat in council on achieving an adult population of 5,000 rather than the current 1,000.[31] This proposal was not approved.

For some time, he had longed to visit England, where he had not been since 1859. He realized, of course, that with his various responsibilities, such a lengthy journey was out of the question. Nevertheless, both he and his wife wanted some relief from the tedium of the prairie winter, and in January 1884, he asked the prime minister for a month's leave to visit British Columbia, which he still regarded as home. He had some investments he wished to attend to there, and Jane wanted to spend time with her mother. Besides, travel was increasingly convenient, and Victoria was now only a week's journey away by connecting with the Northern Pacific Railroad south of Winnipeg. The leave was granted, and they departed on 17 February, to Mrs. Dewdney's great delight.[32]

In Victoria, the couple stayed with their old friends, the O'Reillys, at their elegant house on the Gorge. And they toured the lower mainland, and then visited Jane's mother at Hope. Dewdney was impressed by what he saw. The old land speculator noted that some farms in the Fraser Valley that had been virtually worthless in 1879 were now selling for up to $100 per acre. "BC is very prosperous," he told Macdonald. "Everyone is happy and making money."[33]

Quite apart from the obvious natural attractions of British Columbia and the presence there of friends and family, a sense that he was not fully capitalizing on BC's economic growth made Dewdney's return to Regina early in April somewhat distressing. And all the more so because the outlook in the Territories was anything but bright. The land boom of 1882 had collapsed, and agricultural prospects were dimmed by frost, low prices, and declining immigration. Moreover, Indian and Metis discontent was posing a serious challenge to the authorities. The settler population was also aggrieved. Old irritants such as the Canadian Pacific Railway monopoly and the tariff remained, and the autocratic structure of the territorial government magnified their sense of powerlessness.[34]

Under these difficult circumstances, Dewdney was even less enthusiastic about advancing the representative nature of the council. A year earlier, he had indicated his intention of creating five new elected seats; he now settled for two – Calgary and Moose Mountain.[35]

The North-West council that met on 3 July had eight elected members, a majority for the first time. There were three appointed members and three stipendiary magistrates. The latter included a newcomer, Charles B. Rouleau. In Dewdney's address to the council, he outlined his legislative program, which contained, among other matters, ordinances on munici- palities and education. He discussed the controversial liquor question. A fee for permits had been introduced the previous year, he noted, but the anticipated decline in applications hadn't taken place. He still hoped that Ottawa would approve his proposal to establish breweries in more heavily settled districts to reduce smuggling and illicit manufacturing.[36] On the reports of Indian restlessness found in the press, he assured the council that they were exaggerated: "That there is any cause for alarm I deny."[37] There was more to this claim than just an attempt to calm settler fears. He genuinely believed at the time that his Department of Indian Affairs had the situation under control.

It was a controversial and contentious session of council, confirming Dewdney's worst fears about democracy. The lieutenant governor's posi- tion on the liquor question was again challenged, and there was open criti- cism of Ottawa's inaction on Metis grievances. Frank Oliver and J.H. Ross proved particularly difficult. They proposed political reforms that would give council greater financial control, lead to the expulsion of the official members, and create a legislative assembly. Some of these ideas found their way into a memorial of the council adopted on 2 August for the federal government's consideration. Dewdney informed the prime minister that he opposed the idea of giving council control of the federal grant. He also opposed an increase in representation. In fact, he favoured increasing the population requirement for representation from 1,000 adults to 2,000 to slow the pace of democratization.[38]

Educational legislation was also potentially difficult because of its reli- gious dimension. Section II of the North-West Territories Act allowed for publicly funded separate schools, and this alternative partly reassured Catholics who feared for the future as their population lost ground to the increasingly numerous Protestants. Even so, there was much lobbying behind the scenes by Bishop Vital Grandin and others to ensure that Catholic interests were protected.[39] Dewdney expected trouble on the issue, with Rouleau championing the Catholic cause and Oliver opposed. "I suppose it is the old fight," he remarked to Macdonald.[40]

The lieutenant governor sought a compromise acceptable to both sides, and after much debate in committee, such a formula emerged. The school ordinance adopted on 6 August gave the North-West a dual educational system similar to those in Quebec and Manitoba. It allowed for an administrative structure comprising a board of education appointed by the lieutenant governor in council and divided into Catholic and Protestant sections, each responsible for its own schools. When the board came into being the following year, it had two Catholic members and two Protestants, with the lieutenant governor as chair.[41]

The council came to an end on 6 August, much to Dewdney's relief. He blamed Oliver for most of the trouble and hoped it had been the man's last session.[42] His long-standing antipathy to representative government was only confirmed and strengthened by the experience.

John A. Macdonald's prediction that the lieutenant governorship would not add substantially to Dewdney's duties was proving correct in most respects. The council only met for about a month each year, and in the remaining months, there was not much business to attend to beyond ceremonial and social events, which Dewdney usually enjoyed. Routine administrative matters were conducted by Council Clerk Amedée E. Forget while legislation was prepared by the appointed legal experts. The position of Indian commissioner continued to be Dewdney's principal responsibility and the most demanding on his time.

In spring 1885, the rebellion was his major preoccupation, understandably enough. In Ottawa, too, this issue was the main concern, and there could be no attention to the constitutional matters raised by the North-West council until the violence came to an end. In May, Interior Minister David Macpherson replied to the memorial of 1884. He rejected council's demand to control the federal grant and insisted that increased representation should await a census. He did agree, however, to increase the federal grant from $32,000 to $65,450. This agreement was a complete endorsement of Dewdney's position.[43]

A census was held that summer that resulted in greater representation. In the council elections held in September, there were five new seats in all. Dewdney was confident that loyal Conservatives would be returned in most of them, and this belief mitigated his apprehension at the advance of democracy. If, however, a district elected a man opposed to the government, he was prepared for retribution. In the case of Prince Albert, for instance, he had this to say: "I don't expect much from that place – and if they send a ruffian they should not have the headquarters of the Police there." He anticipated that, within another year, there would be enough elected members to form a legislative assembly. He didn't want to be around for that development and asked Macdonald once more for the lieutenant governorship of British Columbia, which would be available the following June.[44] But the prime minister already had someone lined up for that job and couldn't oblige.[45]

The September elections did return government supporters to the council, but their political allegiance did not inhibit them from demanding constitutional reforms or criticizing the administration. Dewdney was generally pleased with the results and especially with the rejection of Frank Oliver by the voters of Edmonton.

By now, there was a new minister of the interior, Thomas White, who took a more active interest in the North-West than his predecessor, David Macpherson. Influential in cabinet, White was able to accelerate the pace of political change by his energetic leadership. He came west after the September elections and received several petitions demanding provincial status and representation in Parliament for the region. He declared his support for the latter and for a simplified form of provincial government as a transitional measure.[46]

Buoyed by White's assurances, the council that met on 5 November was in an ambitious mood. Dewdney tried to set the tone in his opening speech by defending government policy, exonerating the administration of all blame for the rebellion, and generally praising progress in such matters as the establishment of school districts and the completion of the railway, the last spike of which was about to be driven.

It didn't work. The reply to the lieutenant governor's speech was more disagreeable than ever, even without Oliver's guiding hand. The councillors demanded some of the usual things, such as greater representation and control of the federal grant. But they were critical, too. They regretted policies that hindered settlement, such as reserving odd-numbered sections for railway companies and allowing other companies to hold large tracts of land for speculation purposes. This remark was particularly stinging because it was well known that Dewdney had interests in both railway and land companies. They also regretted inaction on Metis claims in spite of their representations on the matter, implying that the government bore some responsibility for the rebellion.[47]

Dewdney's involvement in land speculation and his handling of Indian and Metis grievances made him the object of much less muted criticism on the national stage around this time. The first salvo in this assault had been fired a year earlier in a House of Commons debate on the North-West "disturbances." In the July 1885 debate, the opposition roasted the government on its policies which, it claimed, had caused the rebellion. Malcolm C. Cameron, Liberal MP for West Huron, took matters much further in what amounted to a blistering, personal attack on Dewdney. Here is some of what he had to say about the lieutenant governor: "He is domineering, arrogant, tyrannical, brusque in his manner towards them [Indians]. His reputation is such that it has become proverbial in the North-West

Territories, where he is known among the Indians as 'the man with four tongues' ... His self-seeking, his brusque and uncourteous manner, his business transactions and relations in the North-West – all render him a man exceedingly dangerous to be kept in such an important position as that of Lieutenant-Governor of the North-West Territories and Commissioner of Indian Affairs."[48]

Cameron, who had built a political career on protecting Canadian salt mines from foreign competition, was motivated by more than just the usual partisan spirit. He, too, had investments in western lands that led him to take a special interest in the administration of the Territories and in their constitutional evolution.[49]

Almost a year later, in April 1886, Cameron renewed his attack in the Commons, denouncing Indian Affairs officials in the North-West from Dewdney downwards as incompetent and untrustworthy. In the absence of the prime minister, Hector Langevin came to Dewdney's defence and accused the Liberal MP of manipulating the evidence.[50]

Dewdney considered the matter serious enough to warrant preparing an elaborate fifty-two-page response to the allegations, which he sent to the interior minister on 1 May. In the response, he described Cameron's speech as "one of the most unfair dishonest and malignant attacks ever made by a public man." He made a vigorous defence of the Department of Indian Affairs, quoting newspaper articles and the letters of various missionaries to refute the charges of corruption. Some of this material was later incorporated into a pamphlet that was distributed to Indian agents across the country.[51]

The issue was raised again in the Commons (in June), this time by John A. Macdonald. The prime minister was concerned that Cameron had published his speech and distributed it widely with damaging results. He praised Dewdney as a good officer who faithfully carried out a difficult policy of forcing Indians on to reserves and compelling them to work.

When Richard Cartwright responded for the opposition, he switched the focus to Dewdney's "various speculative transactions in the North West," which he considered inappropriate for a senior officer of the Crown. This theme was also taken up by Edward Blake when he alluded to the profiteering associated with the Regina townsite selection.

Macdonald again defended Dewdney while admitting that the lieutenant governor "would be exercising a wise discretion in not buying any land directly or indirectly from the Government." He blamed Dewdney's unpopularity in some quarters on the difficulty of administering the liquor permit system, and he promised an inquiry into Cameron's allegations.[52]

Dewdney was concerned at the prospect of such an inquiry and urged that those chosen to conduct it be carefully selected for their knowledge of "the Indian character" and the difficulties faced on reserves. He proposed Father Lacombe, D.H. Macdowall, and a number of his other associates.[53] The inquiry was never held. In the February 1887 federal election, Cameron was defeated. With Dewdney's most virulent critic removed from the political arena, Macdonald felt no urgency to act on his promise. He explained in the Commons that the Department of Indian Affairs pamphlet had shown him the falsity of Cameron's charges.[54]

Meanwhile, the North-West council met between 13 October and 19 November 1886 in a much more amicable mood than a year earlier. Ottawa had agreed to several demands made after the previous session, and this decision was the major cause of satisfaction. The North-West was to have its own supreme court, representation in the House of Commons, and the power to incorporate certain companies and to impose direct taxation. The government did not concede to council the right to control the federal grant as demanded, perhaps in deference to Dewdney. This issue was no longer a major irritant, however. Even critics of Dewdney agreed that his willingness to consult the council on spending matters lessened the annoyance over his control of the money. Besides, it was now believed that provincial status would soon be granted, and this status would automatically change the financial arrangements.[55]

For purposes of representation in Parliament, the Territories were divided into four federal constituencies: Alberta, Saskatchewan, Western Assiniboia, and Eastern Assiniboia. In October 1886, Macdonald asked Dewdney to make discreet arrangements for the nomination of candidates.[56] He didn't care who they turned out to be as long as they were loyal supporters of the government. Dewdney now took on a new role – that of Conservative Party boss in the North-West. He assured the prime minister that he could "depend on all four seats."[57]

The initial plan apparently was to hold by-elections before the opposition could get organized. But the Conservative nomination process took longer than expected. Several credible candidates were identified in Alberta and Saskatchewan, and much negotiation and deal-making took place behind the scenes to ensure united support for one man in each case.[58]

Dewdney realized that the Metis vote would be critical in several areas, especially in Saskatchewan. He had a number of ploys to get them onside. In October, hearing of destitution in Prince Albert, he decided to send in 300 sacks of flour. By using the Qu'Appelle Metis to freight it in, he hoped to get the votes of both groups.[59] Other ideas, which he discussed with Macdonald, were to get missionaries and Hudson's Bay Company officials to bring influence to bear on behalf of the government.[60] In one letter to the prime minister, he asked if Metis who had just left treaty would have a vote and made the following suggestion: "A man who lives in a teepee should not be considered a householder unless he is a Conservative."[61]

The lieutenant governor was probably being serious. The phrase may be a curious one, but it sums up the virulent partisanship of politics at the time and is indicative of Dewdney's determination to use whatever resources at his disposal to serve the party and its leader.

The North-West went to the polls in February 1887 as part of the general election. Antagonism over the treatment of Riel caused the Conservatives serious losses in Quebec, but Macdonald held on to his majority and comfortably secured all four seats in the North-West.[62] Dewdney had served his master well.

Representation in Parliament complicated the Territories' constitutional question because all the men elected could not be relied on to march at the slow pace favoured by Dewdney and Macdonald. This was especially so in the case of Nicholas Flood Davin, the Irish-born journalist who was returned for Western Assiniboia. Davin was no sooner in the House of Commons than he introduced a measure to give the North-West a legislative assembly of twenty-four members and an executive council – in effect, provincial status. The government was not prepared to move on this measure, but Davin's initiative added to a momentum that was increasingly difficult to ignore.[63]

When he opened the next North-West council session on 14 October 1887, Dewdney acknowledged the trend but was clearly still trying to apply the brakes. He invited the councillors to suggest "some inexpensive form of Government, which (would) give the people a greater control over the management of their affairs." A committee considered the matter and proposed an arrangement with the following features: a legislative assembly of twenty-five members chosen for a four-year term presided over by one of the members; an executive council made up of the lieutenant governor and three elected members; abolition of the householder franchise qualification; expulsion of the appointed members; and assembly control of the federal grant.[64]

The proposal was short of provincial status but was a major step in that direction. It was too much for Dewdney, who took every opportunity to denigrate it to Macdonald in the months that followed.[65] He argued that there was no support for it in many parts of the Territories for the following reason: "A strong fear is expressed that the establishment of a purely representative form of government will lead to direct taxation and thus impose on the settlers burdens which they are at present unable to bear."[66] It is improbable that he had any evidence for this assertion.

Potentially far more problematic during that council session was a bill to amend and consolidate the school ordinance. Proposed changes to the language of classroom instruction, the composition of the Board of Education, and the procedure for certifying teachers alarmed the Catholic Church and provoked vigorous lobbying in Regina by Father Lacombe and others.[67] With shrewd diplomacy, Dewdney succeeded in allaying clerical fears and working out compromises on these issues that avoided major controversy. As usual, his main concern was to prevent matters from getting out of hand, spilling on to the national stage and causing embarrassment to the government. And yet personally, he had little sympathy for French and Catholic concerns. As he said to Macdonald: "This French business of domination won't work in the Territories – it is taking root already."[68] As a true conservative, he favoured the gradual and incremental evolution of institutions and practice to reflect changing realities, and this stance can be seen in the solutions he worked out on the education question.[69] He had little time for the politics of confrontation being pursued on the same question by the Liberal Party in neighbouring Manitoba, and he predicted, with foresight, that it would not turn out well there.[70] In his own small way, he thus contributed to the survival of public funding for Catholic schools in the North-West and subsequently in Alberta and Saskatchewan.

There was movement on the constitutional question early in 1888 in the government's North-West Territories Act. It provided for an assembly of twenty-two elected members and three appointed legal experts presided over by a speaker. There was no allowance for an executive council, but the lieutenant governor could choose four members as an advisory council on financial matters. The lieutenant governor retained control of the federal grant. It was not everything asked for by the North-West council and represented the gradual devolution of powers favoured by Dewdney and Macdonald.[71]

Dewdney would not be around to deal with the new assembly. His term as lieutenant governor was supposed to have ended in December 1886, but the prime minister decided to keep him on the spot at least until the 1887 federal election took place and a suitable successor was found. Dewdney, of course, had wanted to leave long before his term was up, but he agreed to stay out of loyalty to the old chieftain. Naturally enough, he was concerned about his future and, having been rebuffed for the lieutenant governorship of British Columbia, proposed instead that he might become a senator for that province. Macdonald was not opposed to the idea but pointed out that there would be no vacancy for a while.[72]

Although anxious to leave Regina, Dewdney took an active interest in the question of his successor. Early in 1886, a rumour reached his ears that

Joseph Royal would be the man. Royal was a well-known French Canadian politician who represented the Manitoba riding of Provencher in the House of Commons. The rumour started when Royal's son, a clerk in the land office, got drunk in Regina and boasted of his father's imminent appointment. Moreover, he claimed that the French Canadian members of Macdonald's cabinet were threatening to resign unless Dewdney were got rid of. Dewdney, who tended to dislike French Canadians, was quick to pronounce on Royal's unsuitability while informing the prime minister of a strong feeling in the North-West against such a move.[73] In fact, no decision had yet been made. Royal was, however, actively canvassing for the job, claiming that he would conciliate the Metis and that he deserved a sinecure after years of service to the party.[74]

Macdonald was in no hurry to make the appointment. After serious losses in Quebec in the 1887 general election, however, he admitted to Dewdney that he was under pressure to choose a French Canadian and mentioned Royal as a possibility.[75] The news was no surprise to Dewdney, but he still found it hard to accept: "Well I shall be sorry to see a Frenchman here and it will create a very bad feeling. Royal is despised by those who know him and when it is known that he was conspiring with Riel in '79 when he was in exile from here it will make things worse."[76]

In the end, the prime minister had to overlook his friend's misgivings and consider the more important issue of appeasing the various factions that made up his government. In August 1887, he let Royal know that he would get the viceregal job in Regina. Royal was anxious to take up his duties right away before opposition to the appointment could be organized.[77] But again, Macdonald was in no hurry. He wanted Dewdney to preside at the North-West council session that fall and to remain at his post well into the new year.[78]

In the meantime, the question of Dewdney's future had to be considered. The North-West was already represented in the Commons, and plans were afoot to give it a couple of seats in the Senate. In January 1888, Macdonald let Dewdney know that he had him in mind for one of them, a suggestion that was well received.[79]

Everything seemed to be set when an unexpected tragedy occurred. On 21 April, Thomas White, the energetic interior minister and close friend of the prime minister, died of pneumonia.[80] It was a major blow to the administration and much speculation ensued about who would inherit the increasingly important interior portfolio.

It occurred to Macdonald that Dewdney might be "the man for the place." Early in May, he made a tentative offer of the portfolio to the lieutenant governor, noting that the matter was still "in the clouds" and had not been discussed in cabinet. Dewdney, with his customary sense of duty, agreed to serve: "I will do my part to the best of my ability." By the end of the month, it was more or less settled. It was arranged that W.D. Perley would resign his Assiniboine East riding to open up a Commons seat for him. Perley, in turn, became one of the North-West's senators.[81]

Meanwhile, even though the prime minister's intentions were not made public, a spontaneous campaign of support for Dewdney's appointment emerged in much of the North-West press. The *Calgary Herald* and the *Saskatchewan Herald* endorsed him unequivocally, noting his unsurpassed knowledge and experience of the west. Even the *Regina Journal*, a Liberal organ, was in favour, although critical of his "partisan proclivities." It admitted that he was "certainly head and shoulders above the other poor sticks who aspire to the position, such as Davin et al."[82] The campaign was a tribute to Dewdney's personal popularity in the North-West, but it was more than that. Territorial leaders rallied behind him, realizing that he was the region's best chance for representation in the cabinet. Of the local MPs, only N.F. Davin was opposed, because he wanted the job for himself.[83]

In June, when Macdonald's candidate for interior minister became known, howls of protest arose in Central Canada. The reaction of the rouge element (a radically democratic party) in Quebec was predictable, explained the prime minister. They had been denouncing Dewdney ever since 1885 as "the Hangman of Riel." The opposition of the Ontario Grits was also to be expected, but Macdonald was annoyed to discover that they were supported by some ambitious Conservative MPs who felt they had a claim on the position.[84] The *Globe* quoted one of them as saying that Dewdney's appointment "would be like giving the key of a house to a robber and the combination of the safe to a burglar."[85] Macdonald had to meet with them and explain firmly that the job had to go to a westerner. He also wrote to Dewdney and other close associates in the West, urging that they forward him newspaper articles, petitions, and the like favourable to the appointment so that he would better quell the opposition.[86] It was done.

Early in June, Dewdney moved out of Government House and rented a place nearby. He continued to fulfil his duties as Indian commissioner and lieutenant governor – visiting reserves, organizing elections for the legislative assembly, and so forth. His duties in the latter capacity ended in July when Royal was sworn in, but Dewdney remained in charge of the Indian Department until 3 August when he was succeeded by Hayter Reed. A few days later, he learned that the governor general had approved his appointment as interior minister.[87]

The only thing left to do now was to secure a seat in the Commons. He had been approached to run in New Westminster and seriously toyed with the idea. But in the end, he accepted Macdonald's advice and stood for Eastern Assiniboia, made vacant by W.D. Perley, who was only too willing to step aside and go to the Senate. Early in August, he hit the campaign trail, making himself known to new settlers in the outlying districts. "I do not think there is any chance of a contest," he reported to the prime minister. "If there is, it will be a fiasco."[88] His confidence was well placed. A few Liberal associations met and realized there was no point in opposing him. On 12 September, he was elected by acclamation.[89]

The Grits were resentful at a process they considered blatantly unfair: Dewdney's offer of a cabinet post virtually ensured his return. His old adversary, Frank Oliver, while bowing to the inevitable a month before the poll, took the occasion to vent the rage of those affronted by the patronage system, the liquor permits, the slow pace of constitutional reform, and all the other Dewdney grievances in the pages of his *Edmonton Bulletin:*

> The appointment of this gentleman to the position of lieutenant-governor and Indian commissioner of the North west was a huge and costly mistake, history is proof, and there can be no doubt that the present appointment is a still greater mistake. What was the cause of Mr. Dewdney's appointment to the lieutenant governorship was always a mystery, and the reason for his present appointment is a still greater mystery. That it was obnoxious to the people of eastern Canada of both political parties is notorious, and that it was not to meet the wishes of the people of the North west is plain.[90]

The move to Ottawa in mid-September closed a long and difficult chapter in Dewdney's career. He was glad to leave. The creation of the legislative assembly and the gradual whittling away of the lieutenant governor's powers made that job increasingly unattractive. He had little stomach to face the ever assertive voice of the people's representatives. Moreover, the rheumatism and back problems that continued to plague him made the constant travel required in his dual roles a test of painful endurance.[91] He had never liked the North-West and had often reminded Macdonald of his desire to return to British Columbia. Ottawa and a place in the cabinet would not have been his first choice, but at least it would afford him the opportunity, as he put it, to confront his defamers.[92]

His wife, Jane, was even more delighted to be going. An avid gardener and nature lover who was enthralled with British Columbia's extravagant foliage and rugged beauty, she despised the Prairies – "this dreary waste of snow" – with "nothing" in every direction. In June 1886, on a visit to Ottawa, she "feasted" her eyes on trees. As chatelaine at Government House, she had complained of only having one woman servant and was run off her feet with the constant dinner parties. To make matters worse, the stores rarely had what she needed. If Ned was away on official business, which was often enough, she had to attend tedious functions in his place, not to mention endure the annoyance of his spoilt dogs, one of which slept under the bed.[93]

Most of all, Jane suffered from loneliness. She missed her friends and family in British Columbia and those new friends she had made in Ottawa in the 1870s, most notably Agnes Macdonald, the prime minister's wife.[94] Matters improved greatly with the completion of the railway. The Dewdneys could travel with greater ease, and there were frequent visitors from east and west. Mrs. Glennie came to stay, and so did the O'Reillys. The Macdonalds came, too, and on one occasion left their handicapped daughter, Mary, under the Dewdneys' care for a month.[95] Even so, Regina had been a trial for both of them – Ottawa could only be better. It was not British Columbia, but it had trees and more of the sort of people with whom they felt an affinity.

CHAPTER 6

Minister
of the Interior

The government that Dewdney entered in 1888 was dispirited and in decline. John A. Macdonald was worn out and not in the best of health. He had led his Conservatives to victory in the election of February 1887 but with serious losses in Quebec. Although his majority of around thirty was secure for the moment, a peculiar constellation of circumstances threatened to bring the government down. Canada was badly divided on linguistic and religious grounds. Quebec nationalism was on the rise, spurred on by the Riel affair. The Jesuits Estates controversy didn't help, and the schools crisis being stirred up in Manitoba would prove almost impossible to resolve.

The Liberals, under their new leader, Wilfrid Laurier, were confident and aggressive and believed they had the government on the run. They advocated unrestricted reciprocity or free trade with the United States, an idea that was anathema to the prime minister. Yet the ongoing economic recession suggested flaws in the National Policy, and Macdonald was willing to consider lower tariffs if the terms were right.[1]

Many of the old chieftain's most trusted colleagues were now absent from the cabinet table. Cartier was dead, and Sir Charles Tupper was in London as high commissioner. In search of new blood, Macdonald had brought John S.D. Thompson from Nova Scotia to serve as justice minister and considered him his most valuable associate.[2] Thompson and Dewdney became good friends, and their wives, Sally and Jane, also became intimates.[3]

Dewdney's cabinet responsibilities, if not the most prestigious, were complicated and diverse. In fact, it could be said that he held a number of portfolios. As superintendent general of Indian affairs, he was in charge of a department for which he had worked for many years. He knew the Department of Indian Affairs and its modus operandi well, although its machinations in Central and Eastern Canada were unfamiliar to him. The long-serving deputy superintendent, Lawrence Vankoughnet, was an old adversary, but the two men found it possible to work together under these new arrangements.

The Department of the Interior had been established on 1 July 1873 to oversee the evolution of the North-West Territories. It was mainly concerned with surveying lands and granting them to homesteaders. Other responsibilities included the development of natural resources (the Mines Branch) and the administration of Banff National Park, the first entity of this sort in the country.[4] Since 1883, A.M. Burgess, a dull, conscientious bureaucrat, had served as deputy minister.[5] The Geological Survey came under the department as well, but it usually functioned as a department unto itself. Indeed, the director of the survey, A.R.C. Selwyn, a prickly and self-important Englishman, strongly resented any suggestion that Burgess was his superior.[6] As minister, Dewdney was also in charge of constitutional change in the North-West Territories – very familiar terrain for him.

He had wanted a sinecure – an appointment either to the Senate or to the lieutenant governorship of British Columbia – something with a good salary, social prestige, and not too much work. The cabinet post, while it paid well and had many advantages, was very demanding. Jane soon observed that her husband was so busy, she saw him even less than in Regina. "It seems to me the older he grows the harder he has to work," she complained to Caroline O'Reilly.[7]

Much of the work was routine administration – correspondence, meetings, and the like. And then there were the annual parliamentary sessions that Dewdney disliked. But being minister opened up enormous possibilities for patronage, and he did not flinch at helping friends and supporters of the party with the resources at his disposal.[8] Most important from his point of view was the prime minister's approval, and that was never in doubt. Within a few short months of his taking the job, Macdonald told Joseph Schultz that "Dewdney has justified all that was expected of him by me and his friends when he assumed office."[9]

When Parliament opened in spring 1889, Dewdney took his seat on the front benches. He had been away from the House for a decade, but he knew its routines, and many familiar faces were still around from the old days. Even so, his new role was very different. No longer an outsider championing the cause of distant British Columbia and his favourite railway route, he was now in the spotlight and the target of opposition attacks. Spontaneous debate did not come easily to him, and he rarely spoke on matters other than those directly affecting his own departments. Even there, he sometimes took a minor role, allowing Macdonald and Thompson, who were much better speakers, to respond to opposition taunts.

The Liberals had no shortage of powerful speakers, David Mills, Richard Cartwright, and Wilfrid Laurier being particularly effective in their assaults on the government benches. Extravagance, mismanagement, and patronage were their usual charges. They argued for a smaller, more frugal government and an end to state subsidies. The Departments of the Interior and Indian Affairs came in for their fair share of scrutiny when estimates were brought down, and Dewdney was often thrown on the defensive as he tried to justify expenditures. His inexperience served him poorly in these exchanges in the 1889 session. In April, he made the mistake of reading a lengthy speech full of statistics designed to show that the Department of the Interior was less costly under the Conservatives than it had been under the Liberals in the 1870s. The Liberals immediately launched a vigorous counteroffensive, denouncing him for having read the speech, which was against House practice. And the remarks of one of the speakers, James Lister, showed that the opposition would not hesitate to open old wounds if a few points could be scored: "For what did they make him Minister of the Interior? Was it on account of his vast parliamentary experience, was it because he had served his country faithfully, honestly, and heroically in the past, or was it because he was the primary cause of the rebellion which has cost this country nearly $7,000,000?"[10]

These kinds of attacks were to be expected from the opposition, and Dewdney became more adept at responding to them as the years passed. But he also had to contend with criticism from within his own party, especially from those who resented his sudden prominence and who had coveted the interior portfolio for themselves. Most noteworthy in this regard was Nicholas Flood Davin, Conservative MP for Regina and proprietor of that city's newspaper, the *Leader*. Davin was vain and ambitious, and he was bitter at being overlooked for a cabinet post. He disliked Dewdney and was jealous of his success in politics and business. In Parliament, he sought to portray himself as the champion of North-West interests while castigating Dewdney for his indifference.

One of the issues used by Davin to this end was second homesteads. According to Section 38 of the Dominion Lands Act of 1883, a settler who received patent to his land after three years was entitled to a second homestead. The idea was to encourage settlement, which was slow enough at the time. But Thomas White, the previous interior minister, discovered that the policy was only resulting in large sections of land being claimed and left undeveloped. Consequently, legislation in 1886 abolished the right to a second homestead. Davin said repeatedly in the House that this change was unjust to those who had taken up land under the original legislation because some had not had time to qualify for the second homestead before the law was amended. He argued that the cut-off date should be extended until May 1889 so that all legitimate claimants would have a chance to fulfil the requirements and take up the extra land they had been promised.[11]

Dewdney had always opposed second homesteads, and during his 1888 election campaign, he had come out openly against them.[12] As minister, his position was the same. He rejected Davin's overtures, saying he would not perpetuate a system that had "been a very great injury to the country."[13] The question caused sharp exchanges between the two of them in the House in 1889 and 1890. When Davin raised it once more in June 1891, he found support on the opposition benches. Wilfrid Laurier argued the point on the grounds of justice and fairness, and he said that only a couple of dozen cases were involved. Dewdney was prepared to compromise if such was the case so long as the principle of second homesteads was not revived. He expressed a willingness to entertain amendments to the Dominion Lands Act when it next came up for revision.[14] In March 1892, such an amendment was accepted. It allowed second homesteads to be claimed by those eligible until 2 June 1889.[15]

Another of Davin's obsessions led to more bitter exchanges with the interior minister. In the past, the editor of the *Leader* had run afoul of Commissioner Lawrence Herchmer, commanding officer of the Mounted Police in the North-West, and he was determined to have the policeman disciplined. He denounced Herchmer regularly in the pages of the *Leader*, and in Parliament, he demanded an inquiry into Herchmer's conduct, which he described as "Russian tyranny."[16]

While the Mounted Police were not part of Dewdney's portfolio, he felt obliged to defend Herchmer whom he had recommended for the position of commissioner. He praised him for bringing much-needed order and discipline to the force, while admitting that he had "a little fault with regard to his temper." In making these remarks, he poked fun at Davin, describing how he had once interfered with Herchmer's and the governor general's review of the troops in Regina by passing by "in a buckboard driven by a cayuse, a spotted old horse."

These comments drew an outburst from Davin in which he aired his long-simmering resentments against Dewdney: "I am not at all surprised that he should regard a cayuse and a buckboard with contempt. I cannot afford to flaunt in a carriage and pair as he can; I did not have his advantages, and if I had had his advantages I might not have made the use of these advantages that he has made. I was not for ten years trying to pick the eyes out of the country; I was not for ten years occupying a high position, and the whole time, with my eyes open, watching how I could fatten my own purse." At this point, the deputy speaker and Dewdney protested, and

Davin was forced to withdraw his remarks.[17] The motion for an investigation of Herchmer was defeated.[18] All the same, it was clear from this minor
fracas that Dewdney carried the stigma of someone on the take and that his
antagonists would not hesitate to remind him of this fact on occasion.

Personal squabbles and differences on policy matters were not unusual
in both national political parties, and the leaders often had to use diplomacy to keep the members working in harmony, especially on such divisive
issues as the Manitoba schools crisis. The Davin-Dewdney feud was a
minor affair by comparison and was sometimes a subject of mirth in the
Commons.

The Department of Indian Affairs was a favourite object of Liberal
wrath in the House. Expenditure was excessively high, they claimed; too
much was being spent on supplies and implements and officials' salaries.
And when they noticed a budgetary reduction from a previous year, they
were quick to praise even when praise was hardly appropriate. On more
than one occasion Dewdney was obliged to explain that costs had been
reduced because of population decline. In 1891, for instance, he informed
the House that the Blood Indians, 2,041 in all, had experienced fifty-nine
births and 180 deaths in the previous year.[19] The government took little
satisfaction in such figures, because it had proclaimed that its policies
were successful and that the Native population was progressing under its
guiding hand.

When it came to expenditure, nothing raised the ire of the opposition
like the estimates for Indian industrial schools in the west. David Mills
once argued that they were a waste of time and money because the best
education for Indians was to put them to work next to farm instructors.[20]
Richard Cartwright complained that the schools were "very extravagant"
and cost more per capita than what was being spent on whites.[21] Dewdney
was always ready to spring to the defence. The institutions were necessary,
he argued, because day schools offered little chance of improving children
when they had to return to their "wigwams" at night.[22] In truth, however,
he and his department were having second thoughts about the rising costs
of industrial schools. In 1891, the schools were put on a per capita funding
basis to keep expenditure under control.[23] Missionaries still eagerly agi-
tated for the creation of new schools, but they were less likely to have their
wishes granted. The government was turning more and more to cheaper
boarding schools, institutions where the churches paid a greater proportion
of the bills.[24]

The close collaboration between the Department of Indian Affairs and
the churches in the enterprise of education drew regular criticism in Parliament from some Liberal members. Mills and James McMullen questioned

the principle of state subsidies to denominational institutions, a contro-versial issue in the context of the 1890 Manitoba schools crisis. Dewdney defended the practice because the Indian Act required that Indians be given schools in accordance with their Christian affiliation. While Dewd-ney had no ideological commitment to the separation of church and state, his experience in the North-West had shown him the problems arising from denominational rivalry. In other words, he could appreciate the contri-butions churches made to education, but he wished they would cooperate more and not encroach on one another's territory.[25]

As far as this part of his portfolio was concerned, Dewdney's major legislative program comprised a series of amendments to the Indian Act assented to in May 1890. The new clauses forbade the removal of timber and other resources from reserves, gave Indian agents magisterial power under the act, applied the game laws of Manitoba and the North-West Territories to Indians, and forbade federal employees, missionaries, and teachers from trading with Indians except with the superintendent general's permission. These measures increased bureaucratic control of Indians' lives in the prevailing spirit of protective paternalism. At the same time, another clause allowed Indians in Manitoba, Keewatin, and the North-West Territories to acquire a certificate of occupancy to a piece of reserve land not larger than 160 acres.[26] This clause reflected an idea strongly favoured by Dewdney and Commissioner Hayter Reed – the need to replace communal notions of property with individual ones.

As usual, Indian policy exhibited an interesting contradiction. Some measures were clearly designed to encourage individual initiative and self-sufficiency; but officialdom feared where the spirit of independence might lead, and therefore it created checks and controls that ultimately induced either apathy or resistance. A good illustration of this tendency was Dewd-ney's attempt to extend the Indian Advancement Act to Caughnawaga in 1889. This legislation allowed for elected band councils to have some minor regulatory powers. The plan was to extend these powers gradually so that the councils could evolve into a form of municipal government. In this way, democratic notions of citizenship would be fostered, and traditional forms of authority undermined. Of course, any by-laws made by band councils were subject to approval by the superintendent general.

When the Advancement Act was applied to Caughnawaga, the newly elected council tested its powers by adopting a resolution to fire the local constable and to replace him with two men of its own choosing. Dewdney refused to sanction the change on the grounds that the proposed appointees were "unreliable." Some councillors responded to this refusal by disrupting council business. Cyrille Doyon, MP for Laprairie, was approached, and in the 1890 parliamentary session, he proposed an amendment to the act that would have exempted Caughnawaga council by-laws from the need for the superintendent general's approval. Laurier and Mills strongly supported the bill and suggested it be applied to all bands. As the Liberal leader pointed out, powers under the act were extremely limited anyway. But Dewdney was adamantly opposed to giving up control and even produced a petition from the principal property owners on the reserve who feared for their position should Doyon's measure go through.[27] That is, the superintendent general could not relinquish his authority; otherwise, wealthy Indians would lose their place in a local political power struggle.

The Jesuits Estates brouhaha and the question of language and denominational schools in Manitoba were two divisive issues at this time that both major federal parties would have preferred to avoid. Dalton McCarthy, Conservative MP for North Simcoe, had played a pivotal role in stirring up both controversies and was looking for further arenas in which to continue his agitation. He found such an arena in one of Dewdney's domains. In January 1890, shortly after Parliament opened, McCarthy introduced a measure to modify Clause 110 of the North-West Territories Act, the clause that guaranteed the use of English and French in the territorial assembly, courts, and official documents. He wanted the use of French eliminated.

French Canadian MPs on both sides of the House adamantly opposed the bill and acrimonious debate followed. Macdonald came up with a compromise he hoped would satisfy opinion in Ontario and Quebec. Thompson presented the compromise to the House. He proposed that after the next territorial election, the North-West assembly would have power to decide the language of its proceedings, written and oral. The use of French would, however, continue in the courts and ordinances would still be printed in both languages.[28]

Dewdney entered the debate to add a note of moderation and to clarify a few matters. He pointed out that when he had been lieutenant governor, he ensured that ordinances and journals of the North-West council were printed in both languages. The average annual cost for printing in French was only between $400 and $500, and no one had ever seriously objected to it. The only reason he had not read his opening speeches to council in French was his poor command of that language. Fair play demanded that francophones should have documents available in their own language, and he could not see why European settlers should not have school ordinances and other important laws in their languages, too. He wanted to stamp out the spark that might ignite the conflagration forever, he said, and the amendment proposed by the justice minister might do it. The people of the

North-West did not want controversy, he assured the House, only peace and prosperity.[29]

Dewdney's remarks were consistent with his distrust of extremism. He was all too aware of the passions aroused by the religious and linguistic divide, and he believed that the average citizen was fundamentally tolerant, if not led astray by inflammatory demagogues. Although distrusted by French Canadians because of the Riel affair, he was eminently fair to them when it came to their linguistic rights in the West.

The government's compromise on the language question was incorporated into the North-West Territories bill of 1890. But with McCarthy threatening to continue his agitation at the committee stage, the bill was dropped. A general election was coming up, and Macdonald apparently did not want the annoyance of dealing with this issue.[30]

The language question, although it aroused passions in the national Parliament, was really a minor footnote in the ongoing struggle of the North-West assembly to wrest greater autonomy from Ottawa in the regulation of territorial affairs. The assembly, elected around the time of Dewdney's departure from Regina, was vigorously assertive in demanding full responsible government from the start. Lieutenant Governor Royal, perhaps in an attempt to court popularity, made a major concession in this direction by allowing his advisory council to determine the expenditure of the federal grant.[31]

When Dewdney had been lieutenant governor, he had always resisted such a move. He was no more enamoured of it now, and his views were shared by his colleagues in cabinet. Pressure was brought to bear on Royal, and when his advisory council resigned in October 1889, he ensured that its successor did not exercise such financial prerogatives. Relations between the lieutenant governor and the assembly were difficult after that, especially because his new advisory council did not have the backing of a majority of elected members, an affront to the principles of parliamentary democracy.[32]

In response to a request from Royal, Dewdney clarified his position on the money question in September 1890. Federal funds for public works should be spent in accordance with the wishes of the assembly and advisory council as much as possible, he said. Funds for education, care of the insane, and payment of officials should remain under the lieutenant governor's control. On other matters of expenditure, it was up to Royal to decide the degree of consultation.[33]

In summer 1891, two delegates from the advisory council, J.F. Betts and R.G. Brett, went to Ottawa to make representations to Dewdney on certain North-West issues. They recommended that the assembly control the greater part of the federal grant rather than the lieutenant governor. They also wanted a responsible executive and assembly control of liquor legislation, education, and the use of French. And they suggested replacing the legal experts with three elected members. These views represented those of the majority in the assembly. In the negotiations that followed, the government indicated a willingness to make substantial concessions.[34]

The North-West Territories Amendment Act, which Dewdney introduced in July 1891, reflected this willingness. It permitted the assembly to legislate on some aspects of property law, on liquor, on the use of French in its proceedings, and on its own elections. Dewdney explained, for instance, that it would be possible to introduce the secret ballot, a reform he had long supported. The three legal experts were eliminated – the last vestiges of the original appointed system – and the assembly was increased from twenty-two to twenty-six elected members. The Act moved in the direction of democratic financial control by suggesting that federal funds could be spent by the lieutenant governor "with the advice of the Legislative Assembly or of any committee thereof." Justice Minister Thompson was careful to point out that such a committee would not constitute a responsible executive. In keeping with long-standing tradition, the government was moving slowly and cautiously. There could be no chance of creating a powerful executive dominated by "agitators."[35]

Dewdney spent a few days in Regina in December to get a sense of the situation. He spoke to several members of the assembly and noticed a disposition to work harmoniously. Royal seemed to be the problem. If he "had any tact he could get along very well," Dewdney noted to Thompson, but the members could not forget his earlier mistakes promising them everything and then going back on his word. He felt that the assembly had the wherewithal to exercise real power, but the members were not quite aware of it. He urged them to be patient, to put the machinery in place, and not to waste time "in dickering with the Governor."[36] Relations between Royal and the assembly nonetheless remained difficult during the remainder of Dewdney's term of office.

Dewdney recognized the inevitability of responsible government for the North-West. He wanted it to be achieved in small incremental stages while being assured that the new powers were exercised judiciously and prudently. This approach was in keeping with his conservative political philosophy, which had not changed since his days in the British Columbia assembly. But there was also a pragmatic side to these democratic concessions. As MP for Assiniboia East, he could not be indifferent to the wishes of his constituents, and public opinion in the North-West was strongly in favour of greater autonomy for the regional government.

The Geological Survey was arguably the least potentially troublesome component in Dewdney's portfolio. Or so one might have expected. The survey was the first scientific arm of the federal government and was respected for its pioneer work in identifying and mapping the country's resources. The director, A.R.C. Selwyn, saw the work primarily in scientific terms, but in the 1880s, his unit came under increasing pressure from government and industry to focus on commercially useful explorations.

Selwyn himself was a bit of a problem. He was not the most meticulous of administrators, and his accounts often attracted criticism from the auditor general. His low opinion of Canadians was hardly disguised, and many of his staff found him "aloof, overbearing, lacking in tact, stubborn, autocratic, and unwilling to explain his policies."[37] Nonetheless, Dewdney had confidence in the man and generally left the work of the survey in his hands. He was, of course, aware of Selwyn's shortcomings and acknowledged them in Parliament: "Every man has his failings, and probably the Director has his. Although I have had no difficulty with him, I know that he is a man who has opinions of his own, and a gentleman who likes to stick to his opinions."[38]

Selwyn liked to hire university graduates in the sciences, especially geology, for the survey. This practice made sense, but under the Civil Service Act, these highly qualified professionals were classified as clerks and received salaries that were inadequate to their level of education. Many were soon tempted away to more lucrative posts in universities or in the private sector.[39] One such departure caused a minor embarrassment for the government in 1890.

The case involved Eugene Coste, a graduate of the Ecole des Mines in Paris, who had been with the survey since 1883. While surveying in Essex County, Ontario, he discovered gas and suddenly resigned from the public service. Shortly afterwards, he was managing a company exploiting the gas in partnership with John Haggart, the postmaster general. When the issue was raised by the Liberals in the 1890 parliamentary session, Haggart openly admitted his involvement but told the House it was none of its business.

The opposition made the point that publicly funded research should be made available equally to all. In this case, however, Coste and Haggart had apparently acted on information before it was made public. These allegations put Dewdney in an awkward spot because he had the reputation of one who had profitably mixed his public role with private business. He made a few lame excuses about not knowing the details of the case. At the same time, he implied that there was nothing wrong with capitalists investing money on the strength of Geological Survey reports. But his weak defence was an acknowledgment that Coste and Haggart had taken undue advantage of their positions.[40]

The government was clearly embarrassed by the revelations, and some measures were quickly put into place to prevent recurrences, presumably with the minister's support. New legislation that year forbade officers of the survey from engaging in business ventures related to their work, purchasing Crown land, or doing private contract work in their spare time. And all reports on scientific work had to be submitted exclusively to their superiors in the service.[41]

These measures showed a growing awareness of the need for ethical guidelines for those who would combine public and private enterprise. A tangential issue was that of state subsidies for private business, a tradition with a long lineage in the country's history.

The best known example of this sort of arrangement was the grant of 25 million acres of land to the Canadian Pacific Railway for the construction of its line to the West Coast. This grant followed an American precedent, but the Canadian terms were more generous. Unlike in the United States, the company was only obliged to select land that was "fairly fit for settlement." In practice, that meant these lands would be selected on the Prairies.[42] This result may have made a certain amount of sense in view of the urgency in finishing the national project, and in fairness to the CPR, it did fulfil its side of the bargain.

In the 1880s, however, the Conservative government extended similar terms to what were known as colonization railways – smaller companies that pledged to build lines connecting various parts of the Prairies to encourage settlement. The usual deal was 6,400 acres of land "fairly fit for settlement" in return for the construction of each mile of track. Unfortunately, such government largesse attracted companies of dubious reputation, many of which just wanted the land but had no intention of either building or operating railways.[43] These lands were administered by the Department of the Interior, and by the time Dewdney took the portfolio, there was growing scepticism in the opposition ranks about the motives of the colonization companies.

There were so many of these charters that they became an annual topic of debate in Parliament. The opposition attacked the practice, with Cartwright once describing it as "a scandalous and shameful waste of our resources." The Liberals demanded guarantees that railways would indeed be built and operated. They pointed to the case of the North-West Central Railway which, almost twelve years after receiving its charter and land grant, had only built fifty miles of track and still had no rolling stock.

These exchanges put Dewdney on the defensive. While he was forced to acknowledge the abuses, he defended the railway policy on the grounds that it was necessary to develop the country. And he opposed placing restrictions in the charters that might have obliged the companies to sell their land to settlers on reasonable terms. There should be no discouragement to investment, he claimed.[44]

Dewdney's position was more than an automatic defence of government policy. He firmly believed in that curious conservative approach to economic development: state subsidies without state controls. Speculation was good, but it was best done with the money of others. The close relationship between investors and the state was underlined even more by the interior minister's personal friendship with many of them. He was on good terms, for instance, with Edmund B. Osler and Hubert C. Hammond, major players in the Calgary and Edmonton Railway. Both men had also been involved in one of the earlier colonization lines, the Qu'Appelle, Long Lake and Saskatchewan Railway and Steamboat Company, which, it will be recalled, numbered Dewdney among its investors. The minister had long endorsed speculative ventures even before he acquired his portfolio; his commitment to the colonization companies remained until the end of his term of office, in spite of the easy target this policy afforded the opposition. The Liberals were able to pose as the champions of the struggling homesteaders while portraying the government as an ally of the railway tycoons.

Dewdney was uncomfortable with the cut and thrust of parliamentary debate, especially when issues came close to touching on his own reputation as a speculator. But the job had its compensations. One of these was the opportunity of working closely with John A. Macdonald, a man whom he continued to admire without reservation. The two men not only worked together, they socialized as well. In July 1889, the Dewdneys spent two weeks at Macdonald's summer home in Rivière du Loup, a time of relaxation and conviviality spoilt only by the cool weather and the prime minister's toothache.[45]

Another compensation was travel. The nature of his portfolio justified at least one extensive visit to the West Coast each year. These were occasions to mix business with pleasure. Business meant consulting with officials in his various departments along the way and promoting the interests of the government and the Conservative Party. Pleasure came in getting together with old friends and acquaintances at the elaborate banquets to which he was treated at major locations.

He commenced the first of these western tours in August 1889 after his vacation with the Macdonalds. The reception in Regina was rapturous, and Mrs. Dewdney officiated at the sod-turning ceremony that marked an extension to the Long Lake Railway. Before continuing westwards, the minister traversed part of his constituency via the Manitoba and North-West Railway, to remind the electorate of his work on their behalf.[46]

At New Westminster, Dewdney was the guest of honour at a banquet at the Colonial Hotel attended by the city's most prominent men. Several speakers acclaimed him as a true pioneer and a champion of British Columbia and of the Fraser Valley railway route. In his remarks in response to the toasts and eulogies, he reminisced on his days as a rugged frontiers-man and Indian fighter. Describing the Indians of the North-West as wild and warlike, he boasted of how they were now confined to reserves and learning to live like the whites. The speech, punctuated by rounds of applause, was the sort of fare loved by the boosterish businessmen of settler communities.[47]

At a similar event at Victoria's Hotel Delmonico on 16 September, there was more praise for Dewdney, but also a sense that he should help British Columbia now that he was in the cabinet. Mayor John Grant suggested that the province should control minerals in the railway belt and that fed-eral assistance would be welcomed in the development of railway branch lines. In replying, Dewdney chose his words carefully and avoided making any promises that might embarrass the government. Instead, he regaled his listeners with tales of the pioneer days, which at least had entertainment value.[48]

During his week at the provincial capital, he spent time consulting with local politicians and power-brokers in the government's interests. In these discussions, he let it be known that should Victoria ever return a Grit to the House of Commons, the government's attitude to the city would be affected.[49] Helping supporters and penalizing opponents was integral to the clientelist tradition of national politics. And Dewdney's tours were occa-sions to remind communities of the consequences of their political choices.

His trip west in July and August 1890 was very much a repeat of the ear-lier one. In Winnipeg, he visited the land office and found ways to reduce its operating expenses, a matter for which the opposition had been pressing in Parliament for some time.[50] In Calgary, he turned the first sod of the railway to Edmonton, an event attended by thousands of enthusiastic spec-tators.[51] In British Columbia, he was taken on a tour of the lower Fraser Valley by local politicians, and after being shown erosion of the river bank, he promised to consult the cabinet about deepening and widening the channel.[52] He reported regularly to the prime minister in his usual opti-mistic way, noting signs of growth and development and stressing the great future that lay ahead for the West. He was most impressed with Victoria's prospects – its new buildings, new enterprises, and thriving tourist trade.[53]

The minister of the interior turning the first sod of the Calgary-Edmonton Railway, Calgary, N.W.T., July 1890 (courtesy Glenbow Archives NA-3320-8)

For many years now, Dewdney had longed to pay a return visit to the land of his birth, but his duties had prevented him from doing so. Neither he nor Jane had been to England since leaving over thirty years earlier. In August 1890, while vacationing with the Macdonalds at Rivière du Loup, he prevailed on the prime minister to allow him five weeks to make the trip. John Thompson agreed to look after his portfolio in his absence.[54]

On 10 September, the Dewdneys embarked from New York on a White Star Line steamer on this long-anticipated voyage. Their fellow passengers were mainly Britons returning from trips to the United States, and Dewdney was astonished at their "ignorance of our Canada," a problem he tried to rectify during the voyage. The couple spent most of their sojourn in Devonshire by the seaside and visiting family places. He observed that railways had worked great changes since his youth and little fishing villages were now flourishing towns – "but not half as interesting as of old." They travelled to Wales and to London and were overwhelmed everywhere by invitations to stay with old friends. So great was their enjoyment that Dewdney asked the prime minister by telegram to allow him a few more weeks. Being apprised that the work of the Department of the Interior was in good shape, Macdonald agreed. They returned to Canada in mid-November.[55]

A few months later, on 21 January 1891, Macdonald decided to call a general election, the vote being scheduled for 5 March. Reciprocity, or free trade with the United States, was the central issue in the campaign, with the Conservatives opposed and the Liberals in favour. Macdonald raised the spectre of American political and economic domination and accused the opposition of leading the country to annexation. The government won, but with a reduced majority.[56]

All four Conservative MPs were returned in the North-West Territories, including Dewdney. During the campaign, he issued a vague statement to the electorate reminding them of how hard he had worked for their interests and asked for their support once again. His opponent, J.G. Turiff, tried to stir up resentment by focusing on the issue of control of the federal grant, but to no avail. Dewdney's personal popularity and the importance of territorial representation in the cabinet were enough for him to retain his seat.[57]

Macdonald, worn out from the campaign, faced new problems early in his mandate. Parliament opened at the end of April and shortly afterwards it was disclosed that Thomas McGreevy, MP for Quebec West, had been receiving kickbacks from a contracting firm in return for cementing deals with the Department of Public Works, which just happened to be the responsibility of Hector Langevin, McGreevy's brother-in-law. Meanwhile, the country was embroiled in a bitter dispute with the United States over the seal hunt in the Bering Sea, a dispute the prime minister feared would lead to hostilities.[58]

While struggling to cope with all of this, Macdonald suffered an incapacitating stroke on 27 May. His condition deteriorated in the days that followed, and it was clear to family and friends that he had little time left. Dewdney and his wife were frequent visitors to his bedside from then on, sending reports to John Thompson who was managing the government. On 6 June, Dewdney realized that the end was near and stayed at Earnscliffe, the prime minister's residence, rather than attend the regular cabinet meeting. He and Jane were present that evening at 10:15 when Macdonald died.[59]

The old chieftain's death was a personal tragedy for Dewdney. Whether as Indian commissioner, lieutenant governor, or interior minister, his career in public service had always hinged on loyalty to Macdonald. With Sir John gone, Dewdney no longer felt the same incentive to carry on. His search for a comfortable sinecure would now be renewed, but his tenure in charge of the Department of the Interior still had some episodes to be played out.

Macdonald's passing left the Conservative Party in disarray. John Thompson was his logical successor, but he did not want the job. A compromise candidate, Senator John J.C. Abbott, was prevailed on to lead the government, with Thompson in charge of matters in the Commons. When Parliament resumed on 16 June, each minister retained his old portfolio in order to provide continuity. All summer, the government wrestled with the Public Works scandal while the opposition hoped that Conservative defectors would bring the regime down. With Langevin's resignation in September, the crisis faded and Abbott shuffled his cabinet in November to make a fresh start.[60] In the shuffle, Dewdney retained the interior portfolio, news warmly welcomed by influential elements in the West.[61]

One unpleasant development for the minister was the re-election that year of Malcolm C. Cameron in Huron. In 1885-6, Cameron had made a name for himself as an uncompromising critic of Indian policy in the West. Defeated in the 1886-7 election by what he claimed had been a concerted campaign of vilification by the Conservative Party establishment, he was now back and out for revenge. On 30 June, he took the occasion in the House to denounce those who had allegedly sabotaged his career and to refute the defence of Indian policy that Dewdney had prepared in pamphlet form in 1886. The minister defended the government – and himself, of course – by accusing Cameron of misrepresentation and rejecting the need for a detailed reply. He offered instead a general statement similar to that which he had made in countless speeches on the subject across the land. Indian administration in the North-West in the 1880s, he claimed, had been difficult and dangerous, but it had achieved its goal: "These Indians, who were then as wild and savage as they ever had been in their lives, are now settled on their reserves, and a great many of them are making their living independently."[62] Further unpleasant exchanges took place between the two adversaries in August and September over expenditure on Indian education and on staff at the legislative assembly and Government House at Regina.[63] In both instances, it was clear that Cameron was motivated not just by his oppositional role but by a deep personal animosity towards the minister. From Dewdney's point of view, these clashes, disagreeable as they were, allowed him to confront one of his major detractors, which had been impossible to do during his Regina days.

In its search for points of weakness in an already vulnerable government, the opposition unearthed a minor scandal in the Department of the Interior that gave Dewdney some moments of discomfort. When the Public Accounts Committee examined the department's operations in 1891, it discovered that some employees were accepting compensation for overtime work in violation of the Civil Service Act of 1882. The officials did not deny the practice and defended it, as did Deputy Minister A.M. Burgess, on the grounds that the government received a good return for the money, which, in any account, totalled less than $2,000.[64] Their arguments were in vain. As a consequence of the irregularities, Burgess was demoted for several months to the rank of chief clerk while continuing to act as deputy minister. His salary was reduced from $3,000 to $2,800 for the duration of his demotion. Other civil servants partaking of the overtime had their salaries "docked" for a couple of months.

During the 1892 parliamentary session, the opposition made as much of this as they could, demanding to know what would happen to Burgess and suggesting that the Public Accounts Committee had been a bit of a "whitewash" and had not brought all the facts to light. They drew particular attention to the activities of L.C. Pereira, secretary of the Department of the Interior and formerly Dewdney's personal secretary in the North-West Territories. Pereira had been in the habit of assigning work to his wife, Lizzie Evans, while claiming that it had been done by a fictional Ellen Berry so as to avoid that taint of nepotism. Dewdney was clearly annoyed by all of this, and when William Mulock suggested that he was wholly to blame for the irregularities as head of the department, he could no longer contain himself. In an angry outburst, he called Mulock a "blackguard," a remark he was forced to withdraw and apologize for.[65]

A far more aggravating problem for the minister around this time was his government's cozy relationship with western cattle barons. It was a source of much negative publicity in press and Parliament and required of Dewdney the most astute application of diplomatic skills to at once appease public opinion and protect powerful interests connected with the regime.

The District of Alberta was the centre of the cattle industry. The area south of Calgary was considered by the Department of the Interior to be too arid for agriculture but ideal for cattle raising. Agitation by well-connected investors who hoped to get into the business resulted in legislation in December 1881 that allowed for twenty-one-year grazing leases on swaths of land up to 100,000 acres at an annual rent of one cent per acre. Leaseholders were required to stock their land with one animal per ten acres. These generous terms resulted in a rush to participate, and soon several enormous ranches were in operation, capitalized by elements of the central Canadian and British financial and political elites. Many prominent Canadian Conservatives were involved, including Senator M.H. Cochrane and D.W. Davis, MP for Calgary. The business was a huge success and soon controlled the lucrative British beef market. Some of the better-managed ranches returned more than 20 percent dividends to their investors during the 1880s. The cattlemen were a powerful lobby group and succeeded in improving their lease terms and holdings as time went by. In 1886, for example, the Department of the Interior created water reserves – tracts of land near rivers and ponds that could not be settled lest cattle be denied access to water. And in 1888, the stocking requirements were reduced from one beast per ten acres to one per twenty. All the while, the ranchers enjoyed the benefits of a substantial police presence, protecting their herds from Indians and rustlers at no cost to themselves.[66]

The major threat to the cattle kingdom came from "sodbusters" – settlers who sought homesteads on the vast tracts of land leased to the ranchers. With the completion of the railway in 1885, these newcomers appeared in greater numbers and often squatted on the leaseholds. Relations between settlers and ranchers, always tense, had reached a point of almost open warfare by the end of the decade. This was particularly so at the British-owned Walrond Ranch, a 287,000-acre operation managed by the abrasive Duncan McEachran, who also happened to be the chief veterinary inspector for Canada. McEachran's harsh eviction tactics had settlers spoiling for a fight, a situation widely reported in the press.[67]

This was a difficult dilemma for the government. It could not abandon the cattlemen, many of whom were faithful Conservatives. At the same time, settlement had to proceed for the nation's long-term prosperity. Besides, other powerful interests, the Canadian Pacific Railway, for instance, needed settlement to dispose of its grant lands profitably. In other words, two of the Department of the Interior's western land policies were in direct conflict.

The opposition pounced on this issue in the fall 1891 parliamentary session, championing the settlers while denouncing the government's graze-leasing terms. A number of Liberals used the eviction of the Dunbar family from the Walrond Ranch lands as a glaring example of injustice. The Dunbars had occupied their farm long before Walrond was given a lease to the area and had even had their homestead entry approved. Subsequently, however, the Department of the Interior cancelled their entry, apparently through the influence of the ranchers, and Walrond was able to evict them legally.

In response, Dewdney made a reasonably spirited defence of his government's policy. He pointed out that investors had put more money into cattle ranching than into any other enterprise in the North-West. These investments had to be protected because they had been undertaken in good faith. The grazing leases were no carte blanche, he explained, and when terms were not fulfilled, they were cancelled. And in a remark that caused a frisson of anxiety in cattlemen circles, he acknowledged that changes in the leasing arrangements would probably take place if an influx of settlers followed the completion of the southern part of the Calgary-Edmonton Railway.

As far as the Dunbar family was concerned, he disputed the facts as presented by the opposition and offered an unconvincing legalistic justification for the eviction. And he accused squatters such as the Dunbars of opportunism – of occupying prime tracts of land near water and later demanding exorbitant compensation from leaseholders for the improvements made.[68] Later, however, with several opposition members pressing the case privately, a settlement was negotiated for the Dunbars. They were offered land elsewhere and compensation for their original improvements by the Department of the Interior.[69] This action was a clear recognition that the family had been wronged and that the government was unwilling to stand up to the bullying tactics of powerful ranchers.

Even so, with public opinion so strongly on the side of settlers, the status quo could not continue indefinitely. In view of this, and in the context of potential violence between ranchers and settlers, a meeting was arranged in Ottawa in February 1892 between Dewdney and representatives of the cattlemen. Dewdney reiterated his government's support for such an important industry but explained that some lands would have to be released to provide a promised subsidy for the Calgary-Edmonton Railway. The cattlemen balked at any loss of privilege, but the minister's personal charm and persuasive powers induced them to accept an agreement, the terms of which were as follows: all leases that did not allow for homesteads or railway grants would be cancelled by 31 December 1896; ranchers had the option of purchasing one-tenth of their leases at $2 per acre, a sum subsequently reduced by 50 percent after vigorous lobbying; and ranchers were promised a large increase in the region's stock-watering reserves.[70]

The deal was a victory for Dewdney and the government. New lands became available for settlers and railway grants, and at the same time, the ranching industry was not undermined. In fact, the cattlemen continued to retain huge holdings and herds and remained a potent economic and political force for decades to come.

If settlement was to be encouraged, and it was, then something would have to be done about Canadian immigration policy. Canada had simply not been able to compete with the United States as a desirable destination for land-hungry Europeans. In the hope of breathing new life into this policy, immigration was transferred from Agriculture to Interior in April 1892, a move welcomed in the West. In June, Dewdney was able to announce a bonus scheme of $10 for each adult immigrant and $5 for each child over twelve years when they settled in Canada, these incentives being widely advertised in Europe. The minister was optimistic for the future, noting that restrictions were being placed on immigration to the United States.[71]

He was wrong. In fact, immigration to Canada plunged from 82,165 in 1891 to 30,996 in 1892, the very year of the bonus, and it continued to decline in the four subsequent years. The transfer of responsibility to the Department of the Interior may have simply been another measure of economy. Dominions Land agents were now expected to double as immigration agents.[72] Whether Dewdney's leadership would have made a difference is difficult to say. He left office before any real changes could be made.

With Hugh Nelson's term as lieutenant governor of British Columbia due to end in fall 1892, it was widely rumoured throughout the spring and summer that Dewdney would replace him. The only problem was that John Robson, premier of the Pacific province, was also interested in the job, and the Victoria *Times* came out in favour of him. But Robson died unexpectedly that summer, and the problem of a rival contender disappeared. Dewdney, of course, had his own cadre of supporters, in British Columbia and in Ottawa, who made no secret that he was their choice for the appointment in Victoria. And there were other supporters, such as Thomas Cunningham, MP for New Westminster, who urged him to remain in cabinet where his services were greatly valued.[73]

Dewdney had long wanted the lieutenant governorship of his adopted province, and he pressed his case with Prime Minister Abbott on several occasions.[74] A cabinet meeting early in October approved the appointment, and the decision was announced in the press in the middle of the month.[75]

The news was well received, especially in the West where Dewdney had acquired an almost legendary status. Indeed, his years in cabinet had only served to augment that status. As one of the most prominent pioneer figures in both British Columbia and the North-West Territories, he was constantly receiving invitations to visit communities, to preside at official functions, and to be the guest of honour at banquets. Of course, he was also the only westerner in the cabinet and was in charge of departments that dealt primarily with western concerns. With the patronage and influence at his disposal, it is small wonder that he was feted lavishly on his tours of duty. The trail-blazing, Indian-fighting frontiersman had been transformed into an influential power-broker and confidant of the prime minister.

He had made enemies to be sure, and they were often uncompromising in their attacks on him, but they were usually motivated by partisan spite, personal jealousy, or moral self-righteousness. His legions of friends and supporters more than compensated for these inconveniences.[76] The Victoria *Daily Colonist*, while welcoming his appointment as provincial viceroy, noted the widespread regret in Ottawa at his departure from cabinet: "As a departmental administrator he is acknowledged to be one of the best, and his social, genial, nature gained him hosts of friends."[77]

CHAPTER 7

Semi-Retirement

Dewdney's career was winding down, but several episodes were still to be played out. By a curious irony, what remained was almost an uncanny parody of what had gone before. A middle-aged man was back at the scene of his youth to relive the challenges of his early career, although he was waning in energy and fading in hope. Once again, there would be public office, speculative ventures, a gold rush, a survey contract, a political campaign, and a romance – strange echoes of those first encounters with a frontier land.

On 9 November 1892, at a brief ceremony at the Supreme Court in Victoria, Dewdney was sworn in as the new lieutenant governor of British Columbia by an old friend, Judge Matthew Baillie Begbie. He declined to give a speech, preferring to hurry off to Government House in the company of a coterie of intimates that included the O'Reillys and Agnes Macdonald, the widow of Sir John A., who had settled for a time on the West Coast.[1]

Cary Castle, an odd architectural conglomeration on a rocky hillside, had served as the lieutenant governor's residence since Arthur Kennedy's days in the 1860s.[2] Agnes Macdonald thought it would be quite suitable for its new occupants, or at least for Jane: "The Government House is quite charming – such an English-looking place – and dear old house, just the place Mrs. Dewdney will enjoy with a capital big garden and orchard – a pretty conservatory and above all a first rate poultry yard!"[3] In fact, the place was in a poor state of repair and required extensive renovations before the Dewdneys could feel at home. Jane's mother, Mrs. Glennie, who had been living with them since their Regina days, was still part of the household. And they were now joined by Jane's niece, Louisa Allison, who was studying in Victoria.

Peter O'Reilly described the routines of the new viceregal couple to John Trutch with a hint of sarcasm: "She is to be seen every morning in the

Lieutenant governor of
British Columbia, 1893 (courtesy
Glenbow Archives NA-2307-4)

town, about 9 o'clock, shopping, marketing is more correct. He drives
about a good deal in a sort of tea cart and is generally accompanied by
Louisa Allison – the coachman wears a light drab fashionable livery and
cockade. Changed times for Ned, you will say."[4]

Two decades earlier, when Joseph Trutch had served as British Columbia's first lieutenant governor, the position had carried with it a modicum of
political influence, or at least Trutch had ensured that it had.[5] Reforms had
changed all of this, and the role was now almost purely ceremonial. There
were certain duties to perform – opening the legislature, signing bills, and
so forth; but most of the time was given over to social functions – opening
dog shows, entertaining visiting British naval officers, and other activities
at which Dewdney excelled.[6] It was the sort of prestigious sinecure with
few responsibilities and many privileges he had long coveted.

Goldwin Smith was not far wrong in his characterization of provincial
lieutenant governorships as "a decent retirement for those who have spent
their energies in public life but on whom the public refuse to bestow pensions."[7] The pay was not bad either. Dewdney received an annual salary
from the federal government of $9,000, making him one of the highest-
paid officials in the land. On top of this amount, the province provided his

"castle" and the expenses for maintaining it.[8] Small wonder that he had coveted the position for many years. The fact that Ottawa paid the salary underlined the fact that the lieutenant governor was not just a representative of the Crown, but also a federal officer. And the paymasters had certain expectations. In Dewdney's case, it seems that he was to be a source of information on local politics. He remained in regular contact with his old friend, John Thompson, passing on advice and commentary about diverse political matters. In these remarks, the interests of the Conservative Party were always paramount.

In November 1892, John Abbott resigned for medical reasons, and Thompson was asked to form a government. It was a move anticipated and welcomed by Dewdney who also saw it as an occasion to exert influence. He immediately advised the new prime minister to drop Adolphe Philippe Caron and John Carling from the cabinet, and the latter was indeed let go.[9] He also appears to have played a role in the forced superannuation around this time of old adversary Lawrence Vankoughnet, the deputy superintendent of Indian affairs, and in his replacement by old friend Hayter Reed.[10]

Politics in the Pacific province was a less than edifying enterprise in the 1890s, but it was definitely worth watching. With resources and lands seemingly inexhaustible, governments dispensed lavish grants of mineral rights, timber concessions, and so forth to themselves and their supporters. Most politicians were also speculators and viewed the bounty of the frontier as the road to riches and the political system as a legitimate mechanism of doing so.[11] It was a tradition with which the lieutenant governor could readily identify.

There were no political parties in the legislature, and governments consisted of shifting coalitions of individuals bound together by personal friendship or self-interest. Politics often fractured along the islander/mainlander divide, a rivalry that was intensifying in the early 1890s as the upstart city of Vancouver overtook Victoria in population. One of Premier Theodore Davie's most notable achievements was replacing the old birdcages with a new legislative building, "the marble palace," thereby permanently anchoring the provincial capital in Victoria.[12]

Dewdney saw Davie as a clever manipulator who was adept at a "little bit of sharp practice" to get his way, although he was personally pleased that the government would remain on the island. He told Thompson that the provincial ministers had "a most free and easy way of doing their business." If anything came up for which there was no order, they simply got a provincial warrant and went ahead whether the House was sitting or not. A large proportion of government expenditure was done that way.[13] There was no suggestion that Dewdney disapproved of such a modus operandi.

The séjour at Cary Castle provided ample time for leisure and travel, and Dewdney took full advantage of these perquisites of the job. In summer 1893, he took his wife on a sea cruise to Alaska. His written record of the trip shows his abiding love of nature, especially the magnificent landscapes of the Pacific coast which had captivated him as a young man almost forty years earlier.

"These inlets are beautiful," he observed, "like smooth dark green rivers, wooded to the water's edge, rocks perpendicular, no visible soil, a marvel how the trees and good-sized ones too obtain footholds." The mountains were "wrapped in comfortable grey clouds"; the sea "lead-coloured, smooth and glossy." He was fascinated by the small icebergs they encountered north of Wrangel that took on "fanciful shapes – chickens, blue rabbits with long white ears, Cleopatra's galley." Whales and porpoises then appeared and "gulls circling, squealing or sitting solemnly in rows on float-ing logs ... One little rocky inlet in the narrows was covered with them, as the vessel neared they rose in a body, and looked just like a shower of huge snowflakes floating down." On the return journey the boat entered Gardiner's Inlet, which provided the best scenery of all: "Grand, savage, untamable old nature! Man with all his inventions and scientific means of overcoming obstacles would have a poor chance of asserting himself in these parts." A fine tribute from one whose early career had been spent carving trails through the wilderness.

They visited numerous Native villages along the way, and there the lieu-tenant governor's observations were scathingly negative, mitigated only by the occasional acknowledgment of the Indians' genius for wood carving. At one village, he remarked that they were greeted by Indians in "gaudy attire." He was repulsed by their dirty faces and the "ancient and fish-like odours" that pervaded their houses. At Fort Simpson, they called at Rev-erend Thomas Crosby's mission, and Dewdney noted that the church was a large airy building "to make room for the smell as well as the Indians – they leave more than a soupçon of salmon in the air as they pass." On visit-ing a Tlingit village, he wrote that "dirt was rampant, mangy dogs and puppies, salmon offal and horrors of all sorts but with all of this the Indians themselves and their children were well clad and shod." Alert Bay was the most troubling: "But since the early days when I first arrived at Hope I have never seen such degraded worthless savages as the Alert Bay Indians and this in the face of a Government doing its best."[14]

A century later, such remarks with all their undisguised contempt may seem off-putting, but they were representative of the views of the Anglo-Canadian establishment at the time. And if the edge was sharp, that may have had to do with Dewdney's many years of difficult dealings with the

Native population in the North-West. The scars from those old battles had not completely healed. Of course, these remarks were private musings and not designed for public consumption. Shorn of the need for delicacy and decorum, a certain amount of which was expected in official documents and parliamentary discourse, they may be as true a reflection of his personal views as we could hope to encounter.

In an important sense, these comments mirrored vividly the increasing sensitivity to unpleasant odours characteristic of nineteenth-century bourgeois life. It was a sensitivity born of a moral crusade by sanitary reformers, of scientific theories that linked fetid effusions with disease, and of a desire by the respectable classes to distance themselves from those whose living and working conditions precluded such anxieties.[15]

Upon their return to Cary Castle, they discovered that Louisa Allison was seriously ill with typhoid fever. They spared no expense to get her the best medical treatment and she recovered.[16] The Dewdney hospitality was also extended to the other Allison children when they came to Victoria to pursue career training. One became a stenographer, another a nurse, and a third a school teacher. These young women were also able to enjoy the opportunities to meet young men that the numerous social functions at Government House afforded.

The dinners and dances were frequent enough, but they tended to be on a modest scale for the most part and confined to a circle of intimates. This pattern brought some grumblings of discontent from those who apparently expected to be invited but failed to be included on the guest list. Nonetheless, the Dewdneys remained a popular viceregal couple and, in Peter O'Reilly's estimation, "filled the bill" well. "Pretty hard work it must be," he remarked. "They are asked everywhere – dinners, dances, musical societies, etc. etc. etc., they I think never refuse."[17]

The O'Reillys were part of the Cary Castle circle, and their daughter Kathleen was a favourite of the Dewdneys. The two families were always dropping in on one another for lunch, dinner, or just a chat. Tennis parties were a regular diversion among Victoria's social elite, and the O'Reillys' court at "Point Ellice," their house on the Gorge, was a popular venue for these gatherings. Dewdney, who still liked to play, built his own tennis court at his residence.[18]

The elite was largely British and Irish-born, and they tended to look with some condescension on Canadians, although Dewdney, as noted, was never the worst offender in this respect. But the dominance of the immigrant group was beginning to slip away – a symptom of the growing Canadianization of the province. After the July 1894 election, Canadians for the first time outnumbered immigrants in the assembly.[19] But if their political power was waning, the elite retained its social prestige. Nothing, not even the prevailing economic recession, was allowed to interfere with the steady round of dinner parties, tennis parties, musical evenings, and shooting trips to the mountains with which the established families amused themselves.[20]

Ever mindful of the interests of the Conservative Party, Dewdney kept a close eye on Wilfrid Laurier when he toured British Columbia in September 1894. He informed John Thompson with some satisfaction that those who had heard the Liberal leader speak in Victoria reacted with disappointment and that "the miserable crowd he had with him did not make an impression here." Laurier, he noted disparagingly, made a long oration on the Manitoba school question to Saanich farmers who knew little about it and couldn't have cared less. In Vancouver and New Westminster, however, enthusiastic crowds greeted Laurier, and Dewdney admitted that the Conservatives would be hard pressed to defeat their rivals in those cities.[21]

The highlight of the year came in November when the governor general arrived in Victoria on an official visit. The Dewdneys were at the wharf to greet Lord and Lady Aberdeen. Ships in the harbour were arrayed in bunting and pipers played "Cock o' the North" for His Excellency's pleasure. Thousands lined the streets as the entourage of carriages made its way to Cary Castle. The route taken allowed the distinguished visitors to enjoy the "picturesque loveliness" of Beacon Hill Park. All that week, the castle was the scene of nightly elegant dinners with Victoria's prominent families on the guest list.[22] For social climbers and those given to snobbery (and Jane Dewdney was certainly of this inclination), hobnobbing with royalty was surely a crowning achievement.

Lord Aberdeen was not a month back in Ottawa when he telegrammed Dewdney with the "lamentable intelligence" of John Thompson's sudden death. The prime minister had collapsed and died at Windsor Castle on 12 December shortly after being sworn in as a member of the Privy Council. Dewdney was deeply grieved at the loss of his friend, and he and Jane journeyed by train to Halifax for the funeral early in January.[23]

Throughout 1895 the economic recession continued. Theodore Davie resigned the premiership that year to become chief justice of British Columbia. His successor, John H. Turner, was the former finance minister who had allowed the provincial debt to quadruple. He tried to encourage economic growth by advertising for farmers to cultivate fertile interior valleys such as the Okanagan. And he proceeded to hand out railway charters with reckless abandon. The charters, usually granted to those close to the government, often came with generous land grants attached, and many lines were never built or put into operation.[24] No real surprise here; this pattern of speculative "development" was already well established on the Prairies.

For Dewdney, it was a year much like any other: dinner parties, hunting trips to the mountains, and the like. In May, he spent a month in the Similkameen Valley at the Allison property in country he had loved since he had blazed a trail through it. Jane remained in Victoria, playing hostess at Cary Castle and looking after her mother who was recovering from a broken hip.[25]

In mid-August, the Aberdeens returned to Victoria on a private visit and stayed until early September. On this occasion, they brought their children along, and the Dewdneys moved into a hotel, giving the visitors full use of Cary Castle. There were the usual entertainments, the most memorable being a large garden party held in the castle grounds on 31 August. The weather was warm enough to be pleasant, but smoke in the atmosphere spoiled the view of the straits.[26]

In 1896, the provincial economy began to improve, with mining booms in Nelson and Rossland. Dewdney, his speculative instincts as keen as ever, invested money in the region and paid a personal visit to Rossland in May.[27] It was one of several ventures he had under way, one of which soon took him abroad.

In July, he took a leave of absence from his none-too-demanding duties and made a trip to England. The *St. James Gazette*, which interviewed him, informed its readers that he was "a bronzed, middle-aged gentleman whose manner has that pleasing mixture of English repose and Yankee alertness characteristic of the Canadian colonist of the West." Asked about the possibility of British Columbia being annexed to the United States, he offered a reassuring reply redolent with pride in the imperial connection: "We are very good friends with our Southern neighbours, but we joined Canadian Confederation of our own free will and for very sound reasons, and we are quite content to remain in it. To be partners of that great Dominion and loyal subjects of the Queen suits us very well on the Pacific, whatever others may feel. I believe there is no real annexation sentiment in any part of Canada."[28]

Politics, however, had little to do with his visit to London. He was trying to raise capital for the exploitation of copper claims near Princeton in which his brother-in-law, John Allison, had an interest. But Allison died on 28 October 1897, and it appears that the capital was not in place by then.[29]

Dewdney's other business venture around this time brought some negative publicity and again raised ethical questions about public officials engaging in entrepreneurial activities on the side. By the middle of the decade, the copper and gold mines at Rossland were a proven success, but the area remained isolated and ore had to be shipped to the United States to be smelted. In February 1896, a smelter in nearby Trail, built by American tycoon Fritz Heinze, began operations, giving the mines a great boost. Heinze was also the owner of the Columbia and Western Railway, a branch of which connected Rossland and Trail.[30] Dewdney accepted a directorship in the company, and around the same time the British Columbia government accepted bonds of $50,000 from Heinze, a sort of mortgage chargeable on the railway. The Victoria *Times* protested, accusing the lieutenant governor of exercising inappropriate influence. The *Colonist*, however, defended Dewdney, arguing that lieutenant governors did not influence government policy and that men holding the position were free to invest and speculate as they saw fit.[31]

By the time these stories appeared in the press in April 1897, Dewdney had only a few months to serve as viceroy and with his immense personal popularity could easily surmount what was a minor embarrassment rather than a scandal in any form.[32] But the episode reinforced his reputation as a speculator and served to remind the public that politics and business were not always a happy mix, a message which the regime of John H. Turner seemed to be unable to grasp.

Before his term expired, the lieutenant governor did exercise his constitutional powers in a potentially controversial way. In 1897, a private member's bill to restrict the employment of Chinese and Japanese workers passed through the legislature. The cabinet members, who upheld the interests of capital, opposed the Alien Labour Act, but anti-oriental prejudice was so strong at the time, they could not prevent it receiving the third reading. Dewdney consulted with Ottawa on the matter and was led to believe that the act was likely to be overturned by the federal government as a violation of agreements with Japan. He therefore withheld consent. His personal sympathies, in any case, had always been with capital, and he had once defended the employment of orientals during a speech in the House of Commons. Ultimately, the federal justice minister agreed that the bill was beyond the legislature's authority and that Dewdney's withholding of consent was vindicated.[33]

As these issues were being debated, an event took place that united all and sundry in a virtual orgy of imperialistic self-congratulation: 20 June marked the sixtieth anniversary of Queen Victoria's accession to the throne. Obviously in a city named after her and proud of its Britishness, the celebrations took on special meaning. Thousands flocked into the provincial capital for the great day, to be greeted by countless flags and banners and by festooned buildings. A huge parade made its way through the town, featuring proud contingents of Orangemen and Odd Fellows as well as marching bands of all descriptions. The parade led to Beacon Hill, where 10,000 people gathered for a Protestant church service. Dewdney was on the spot early, sporting his official uniform, proud to preside at the hymn singing and prayer reciting that filled the afternoon.[34]

Earlier that year, in January 1897, Mrs. Glennie had broken a leg in a bad fall at Government House and was confined to her bed with apparently no hope of walking again. Ever resilient, she refused to accept such a fate. By March, her thigh bones had knitted, and she was moving about on crutches. She continued to improve in the following months, in spite of one minor mishap as recorded by Peter O'Reilly: "The old lady is wonderfully well, and they are getting rid of the dogs – only one remains – and the parrot! But the latter now has to live in confinement (his cage) as he nearly broke the old lady's finger – by biting it!"[35]

Getting rid of the dogs was a prelude to a new phase in their lives that was now almost at hand. On 28 October, the new parliament buildings were informally opened when Dewdney occupied the three rooms assigned to the lieutenant governor. He only stayed for a couple of hours, greeting a few cabinet ministers and the American consul who had dropped in for a chat. Work continued around them to put the finishing touches to the "marble palace."[36] Within a month, Dewdney was out of office and out of Cary Castle.

The *Daily Colonist*, a partisan Tory newspaper that had never flinched from praising Dewdney, noted that he had acquitted himself in office in a manner above reproach and that he had been "in every way fitted for the post which he adorned." As for Jane Dewdney, she had "dispensed a genial hospitality that has greatly widened her circle of friends and well-wishers."[37] Such accolades were to be expected considering the source, but then acting as "Her Majesty's representative" was hardly a demanding job, and it is difficult to see how it might have been done incompetently.

After retirement, the Dewdneys went to live at Edgehill, the fine house they built on Rockland Avenue. Jane continued to look after her mother and also attended to the younger Allison children who lived with them while attending school.[38] Ned, freed from the constraints of public office, was now at liberty to pursue wholeheartedly his business interests. And what a good time to do so. As he left Cary Castle, British Columbia was in the throes of a new outbreak of speculative fever: the Klondike gold rush was on. The excitement that had lured him to the Pacific coast forty years earlier had propitiously returned. Would he at last achieve his elusive "competency"?

Dewdney had been aware of the Yukon's potential for some time. As early as April 1894, he had written to John Thompson warning of increasing activity of American miners in the district and of the possibility of a gold rush at any moment. He advised sending a confidential agent there to keep an eye on developments.[39] This was done and a year later a detachment of twenty Mounted Police was stationed in the Yukon. It was just in time. In August 1896, prospectors struck it rich on the Klondike, and news of the bonanza reached the world in June 1897, precipitating the rush.[40] Some fortune seekers made it to the Yukon that fall, but the real stampede was expected in 1898.

Many who hoped to profit from the new eldorado realized that they would be better off supplying and transporting the miners than in grubbing around in the diggings themselves. And so an intense rivalry developed among the merchants of Victoria, Vancouver, Seattle, and San Francisco for the lucrative Klondike trade. The Canadians were at a disadvantage because the major routes to the Yukon passed through the Alaska panhandle – territory claimed by the United States and subject to its customs duties. To better understand this problem, and the myriad others confronting the federal government because of the gold rush, Interior Minister Clifford Sifton visited the Yukon in October 1897 and inspected a number of routes into the district. He was appalled by conditions at the Chilkoot and White Passes and annoyed at the policies of American customs officials towards Canadian goods and travellers. He was impressed, however, by the potential of the Stikine River as an all-Canadian route to the gold fields devoid of American interference. While in Victoria in November, he discussed this idea with the provincial government and with Charles Tupper, leader of the Conservative opposition, who agreed with him.

Although the Stikine reached the ocean at Wrangel in the Alaskan panhandle, boats could enter the river without landing on U.S. territory and were entitled to do so without customs interference according to the Treaty of Washington of 1871. The river was navigable to Telegraph Creek, in Canadian territory. There, miners would disembark, go overland to Teslin Lake, from where they could travel by riverboat to the gold fields. Sifton and Tupper believed that a railway from Telegraph Creek north to Teslin Lake would make the all-Canadian route practical and desirable, and the government planned to have it built in 1898.[41]

On 11 December 1897, the Klondyke Mining, Trading and Transport Company was officially registered in British Columbia. The company planned to send experienced men to the Yukon in the new year to stake claims. It had purchased one ocean steamer and was planning to build boats for the Stikine and Yukon Rivers. The company was committing itself to transporting people and supplies on the all-Canadian route. Dewdney was on the board of directors and Charles Tupper was chairman of the board.[42] In January 1898, Dewdney went to Wrangel with a group of men whom he set to work building a warehouse and wharf for the company.

Ice choked the Stikine, but they would have everything in place when it cleared in the spring.[43]

Meanwhile, on 25 January 1898, the federal government signed a contract with William Mackenzie and Donald Mann to build the railway from Telegraph Creek to Teslin Lake. There was no cash subsidy, but the contractors were offered 25,000 acres of land for each of the 150 miles of railway constructed, for a total of 3.75 million acres. The job was to be finished by 1 September.[44] The contract needed approval by both Houses of Parliament, and there it ran into trouble. Charles Tupper, who had championed the Stikine route, and indeed had a vested interest in its success, opposed the Yukon Railway bill when it was introduced in the Commons in February. Powerful elements in the Conservative Party had forced his volte-face, and he now argued that the contract was too generous, had not been open to tender, and so forth. Wilfrid Laurier's comfortable majority enabled the bill to be approved early in March.[45] But in the Senate, where the Conservatives dominated, it was turned down at the end of the month. And when negotiations with Washington opened the possibility of international cooperation on a railway over the White Pass, the Stikine route was abandoned.[46]

As these events unfolded, several hundred gold seekers were trying out the Canadian route for themselves, hauling supplies on sleds over the frozen Stikine River and northwards overland towards Teslin Lake. Dewdney and a party representing the Klondyke Mining, Trading and Transport Company waited until ice cleared from the river and by mid-April were at Glenora, not far from Telegraph Creek. The company had a steamship plying the waters between Victoria and Wrangel and planned to take its customers on to Teslin using pack horses until the railway was built.[47]

In May, a squadron of 200 Canadian militia, the Yukon Field Force, arrived at Telegraph Creek on its way to the gold fields via the Stikine route. The militia members were to reinforce the nation's sovereignty in a district dominated by American miners.[48] The Hudson's Bay Company was contracted to supply the soldiers on their overland trek, and the company had commandeered most of the pack animals in the area for this purpose. Dewdney and his party discovered that horses were in short supply and the cost of goods and services had risen astronomically.[49] To make matters worse, when the ice and snow melted, the overland trail turned to mud and could be negotiated only with great difficulty.[50] These developments, combined with the news that there would be no railway, convinced the Klondyke Company to abandon the Stikine route.[51] His prospects of turning a profit fading, Dewdney resigned from the board.[52]

Bitterly disillusioned, Dewdney blamed the federal government for failing in its duty to support an all-Canadian route. That summer, he continued to champion the Stikine as the easiest and best way to the Yukon, if only Ottawa would construct a road.[53] But he was wasting his time. Another of his ventures had ended in failure.

If the experience did not dampen his entrepreneurial spirit, it may have encouraged him to try his hand at politics once more. In September 1900, he was asked to let his name stand for nomination as the Conservative candidate in the federal riding of New Westminster, which had been held since 1896 by a Liberal, Aulay Morrison. At first he hesitated, fearing that as an outsider, he would find the campaign a hard, uphill struggle.[54] But party organizers prevailed on him, and at the nominating meeting on 4 October, when other hopefuls withdrew, he was acclaimed as the candidate.[55] On 9 October, Parliament was dissolved and a general election called.

Dewdney issued a manifesto to explain his position to the voters on "the leading issues of the day." In fact, this statement was little more than a grab bag of promises designed to appeal to local self-interest. Among the matters he pledged himself to support were the following: assistance for a railway bridge across the Fraser at New Westminster; a grant of $6,400 per mile for construction of a Coast-Kootenay railway; tariff protection for agricultural and forest products to counter American dumping; and the establishment of a mint at New Westminster. But his most blatant attempt to capitalize on prevailing prejudices was his proposal to restrict fishing licences to provincial voters and Indians. Because the Chinese and Japanese were not entitled to vote, he explained, they would be denied licences, and their threatened takeover of the industry would be thwarted.[56] He was referring to the well-known fact that the coastal fisheries were increasingly dominated by the Japanese, a trend most pronounced on the Fraser River, alarming New Westminster fishermen.[57]

The election campaign had the aura of a triumphal march for Wilfrid Laurier and the Liberals. The country was prosperous, immigrants were filling up the West, government revenues flowed steadily, and the war in South Africa was coming to a conclusion favourable to the British imperial side. The Conservatives, under the aging Charles Tupper, could not erode the government's popularity. When the results came in from the 7 November polls, Laurier was not only returned, but several prominent Tory stalwarts had gone down to defeat. Tupper and George Foster lost in the Maritimes and Hugh John Macdonald, son of John A., failed in his bid to oust Clifford Sifton in Manitoba. It was the same in New Westminster; a margin of 145 votes separated Dewdney from Morrison, whom he was unable to unseat.[58]

It was the end of Dewdney's political career, but an opportunity soon arose for "the father of road making" in British Columbia to try his hand once more at his original occupation. The idea of building a railway from the coast to the Kootenays had been around since the silver boom in Nelson in the late 1880s. The need for such a line intensified in the 1890s with the Rossland mining excitement and the threat that American railroad companies would siphon off the trade to the south. By the turn of the century, with the CPR still dragging its feet on the matter, it looked as if aggressive American railroad tycoon James J. Hill was ready to build the Coast-Kootenay line. Powerful business interests in British Columbia wanted it built regardless of who undertook the job. James Dunsmuir, the Vancouver Island coal magnate who was premier of the province at the time, faced a dilemma. The CPR was a major customer for his coal, so he could ill afford to antagonize the national railway by supporting a rival company. At the same time, he could not ignore the clamour for the iron road.

The premier's solution was to commission a survey of the Hope Mountains (the Cascade Range east of Hope) to see if it were possible to build a railway through them.[59] In July 1901, Dewdney, who knew that country intimately, was asked to take charge of the survey. He hired two experienced engineers and a couple of dozen assistants and by the beginning of August had established his base at Hope. The fieldwork was done by mid-October, and he was able to submit his report to the government just before Christmas.

Dewdney marked out three possible routes over the mountains, two of them by way of the Coquihalla, another over Allison Pass. A railway by any of these routes would cost about $3 million to construct, he estimated. He pointed out that all lines involved heavy grades with numerous tunnels and protection works along the way and that snow would pose a problem at the higher altitudes in the winter. He advised against the project: "The result of the surveys shows that the Hope Mountains cannot be crossed without encountering serious engineering difficulties, which would necessitate a very large expenditure of money, and I know of nothing so pressing, either in the way of development along any line that might be determined on, to warrant its construction, outside of a few prospects that have been brought in by miners. There is nothing at present to give encouragement for this expenditure, except the existence of some very fine timber on the west slope."[60]

The report allowed Dunsmuir to procrastinate on the question. He had little taste for politics, however, and was soon out of office. Dewdney, while admitting the impracticality of a line over the Hope Mountains, believed that a Coast-Kootenay railway should be built but in a less direct way. In 1903, he openly advocated a route through the Similkameen and Nicola

Valleys, connecting with the CPR main line at Spence's Bridge. It was longer than any of the routes he had surveyed in 1901, but the easy grades it offered more than compensated for the extra distance. He was frustrated that an area with the economic potential of the Similkameen was virtually cut off from the rest of the province.

The provincial government was now led by Richard McBride, a man whose lengthy premiership would be marked by railway building at a breathless pace. In 1905, Dewdney got his wish when construction started on the line from Spence's Bridge to Nicola. Of course, he had a personal interest in this development: his sawmill in Allison townsite was soon cashing in on the economic stimulus provided by the railway. "One cannot help noticing the spirit of optimism throughout the whole of southern Okanagan, the Similkameen and Nicola districts," he exulted, "now that the people are on the eve of having their prayers answered for railway communication."[61]

His prediction that a line through the Hope Mountains would prove impractical and unjustifiably expensive was ultimately proven correct. Between 1913 and 1916, the Kettle Valley Railway, an affiliate of the CPR, drove a line over the Coquihalla Pass at the cost of $136,000 per mile, five times the prevailing average for railway construction. An engineering marvel of bridges and tunnels, it was constantly plagued by avalanches, landslides, and derailments until its abandonment in 1959.[62]

In 1905, Jane became seriously ill with cancer and was not expected to survive the year. Peter O'Reilly was one of the few family intimates who was given the news, and he passed it on confidentially to his brother-in-law, John Trutch: "You will be sorry to hear that Mrs. Dewdney is not at all well, they don't wish it known, so don't mention it please. We have always had the warmest regard for her – much more so than for him."

On 27 January 1906, Mrs. Glennie, who was then ninety-one years, died suddenly. Dewdney sent a telegram to Susan Allison informing her of her mother's death and mentioning that her sister could not last many days. Mrs. Glennie was buried on 29 January, and Jane died the following day.[63] Dewdney had lost his companion of forty years, the woman who had followed him faithfully to the various outposts his career had taken him and who had served as gracious hostess to the innumerable dinner parties and other events in their social calendar. They didn't have any children of their own, but Jane's sister, Susan, had given them an ample supply of nieces and nephews to whom they were devoted.

Jane's death was a tragic personal milestone and a loud reminder of what was now an unmistakable trend: the old generation of pioneers was passing on. Walter Dewdney died in 1892; Judge Begbie in 1894; Amor de Cosmos in 1897; Caroline O'Reilly in 1899; Joseph Trutch in 1904; and Peter O'Reilly in 1905.[64]

Alone now, Dewdney kept himself occupied with various business interests. He continued to visit the Similkameen Valley, always a favourite place of his, where he had investments to look after and the Allison family ranch to drop in on. He maintained an active interest in provincial politics, becoming a great champion of Premier Richard McBride, the man who had replaced the personal factionalism of the legislature with party labels. During the 1907 provincial election, he campaigned vigorously for the ruling Conservatives and even ventured the rather extravagant view "that John A. Macdonald, estimable gentleman that he was, would not make a better premier than Richard McBride." Nor would he countenance the charges of corruption (well founded, as it turned out) laid against the regime by the opposition.[65]

That same year, he sold his large house on Rockland Avenue and auctioned off much of the furniture and memorabilia. Two chairs he had received from Princess Louise and a collection of autographed photographs of the governors general since Lord Lorne were thus disposed of. He now went to live more modestly at Cogan's Farm on the Sooke Road. Early in 1909, he took a three-month holiday in England, spending most of the time with family and friends in his native Devonshire. While there, he married for the second time. His new bride was Blanche, the daughter of Colonel Charles T. Kemeys-Tynte of Halawell, Bridgewater, Somerset, the member of parliament who had introduced him to Colonial Secretary Bulwer Lytton almost fifty years earlier. By the end of April, the newlyweds were back in Victoria where they settled into a house on Cook Street.[66]

Contacted by the *Daily Colonist*, he provided a lengthy interview devoted almost exclusively to his impressions of British social and political conditions. At the time, there was growing unease at Germany's naval build-up, which threatened Britain's domination of the high seas. Dewdney was unequivocal: "The fact of the matter is that the people of England have been asleep, believing that some supreme guidance or prescriptive right will continue to maintain their navy up to the two-power standard. They suddenly awoke to find that it was slipping out of their grasp. The result has been a sort of panic."

In spite of the "Dreadnought crisis," for which he blamed the ineptitude of the Asquith government, Dewdney confidently predicted that "whatever emergency arises the British navy will be able to handle it just as it has done in the past." Canada would be willing and able to help, just as it had done in the past, he declared, "with men and money."

And on the question of money, he found Britain to be in a most unsatisfactory state: "The people give the impression of having lost faith in the country. Millions of pounds sterling are lying idle in the banks because the people are afraid to invest; not through any fear of international difficulties but on account of the socialistic element on the government benches. Money is always available for investment in Canada and the other overseas dominions and even in foreign lands. It is a curious anomaly that the English just at present seem to have more faith in other countries than their own."

Socialism was the problem, but he noted with relief that it was on the wane, a happy circumstance he attributed to the press, which had "treated it seriously and by common sense arguments shown the absolute impracticality of the doctrine." Indeed. And yet, perhaps with unintended irony, he remarked on the stark contrast between London's wealthy and poor. His solution to the potential social unrest was to encourage wholesale emigration "to the millions of acres we have available for settlement" in Canada. "It is just such people that we want to build up Canada," he observed. "Strong and able men, thousands of whom are now starving in the manufacturing centres of England."[67]

This heady mix of jingoistic imperialism and defence of class privilege was to be expected. Dewdney was not alone in his belief that Canada was merely a branch plant of Britain – a place to get a good return on your money, a safety valve to siphon off surplus population, and a ready source of cannon fodder in the event of another war.

He was still vigorous and active and played his last cricket game in 1910 at the age of seventy-five.[68] But many of his business ventures had proved disappointing, and money was an increasing source of concern. The defeat of Laurier's Liberals in the 1911 federal general election cheered him, and he lost no time in asking the new prime minister, Robert Borden, for an appointment to the Senate. There were no western vacancies at the time, and his request was turned down. The next few years he spent living quietly at 2840 Cadboro Bay Road.

On 11 August 1915, Dewdney suffered a minor stroke but was expected to recover. A second more serious attack two days later led his doctors to believe that there was little hope. He fought back, however, and although his left arm was paralyzed, he began to regain his strength. Blanche was convinced that the attack was brought on by financial worries. In September, on the advice of Hugh J. Macdonald, she wrote to Prime Minister Borden asking that her husband be granted a pension for his many years of service to the country and the Conservative Party. The reply was not encouraging. Borden was reluctant to act because requests for pensions were numerous and he feared creating a precedent if an exception were made.

By January 1916, Dewdney had sufficiently regained his health to take an active role in the appeal for political preferment. He wrote to Borden, Hugh J. Macdonald, Senator James Lougheed, Trade and Commerce Minister George E. Foster, and Agriculture Minister Martin Burrell, asking for help. He pointed out, among other things, that he had paid into the superannuation fund while Indian commissioner but had been a few months short of the required ten years of service to earn a pension. He proposed that he be refunded the $559.59 he had contributed. He also suggested an appointment to the Senate because one of British Columbia's representatives in that body, G. Riley, had recently died. And he even offered his services to help with soldier settlement on Vancouver Island, a scheme under Senator Lougheed's direction.[69]

With powerful friends such as Lougheed, Macdonald, and Joseph Pope working in the corridors of power on his behalf, some compensation would probably have been arranged. But time ran out for Edgar Dewdney. On 8 August 1916, he died suddenly of heart failure at his home on Cadboro Bay Road. His death came as a shock to friends, for he seemed to have recovered from the worst effects of the stroke and had been in the city centre the day before.

The *Daily Colonist*, full of optimistic reports from the European War and accompanying lengthy lists of local casualties, put the story of his passing on the front page, noting that the province had lost "another member of that fast-fading band of splendid pioneers who materially helped to mould her destinies." It was a time for eulogies, and the *Colonist*, which had long supported him, was not short in its praise: "The late Mr. Dewdney was exceedingly popular both in public and private life and was held in high respect by everybody. He was a man of incorruptible integrity, public-spirited and farsighted and one of the real builders of British Columbia whose name will ever be associated with the history of its development."[70]

The funeral was scheduled for Saturday, 12 August, and the public was encouraged to attend. The simple Church of England ceremony at Christ Church Cathedral attracted a large gathering. A group of surveyors and engineers acted as pallbearers, and the funeral procession featured a detachment of Mounted Police, a force he had always admired. Among the dignitaries present were old associates Charles H. Tupper and D.H. McDowall. Dewdney was interred at Ross Bay Cemetery.[71]

In his will, he left Blanche an estate worth $35,000 in British Columbia and $45,000 elsewhere, which included some lots he had acquired under suspect circumstances in Regina many years previously.[72] The estate was not an enormous fortune but was certainly substantial enough to live on comfortably.

Blanche stayed on in Victoria for a few years and gradually began to dispose of some of the properties and possessions her husband had accumulated. She donated his books to the legislative library in Victoria and sent Indian artifacts to the Royal Albert Memorial Museum in Exeter.[73] In the early 1920s, she returned to England and took up residence in Bath. She maintained correspondence with several friends in Canada and tried to find a historian who would write Edgar's biography, but there were no takers.[74] Later, she moved to live with one of her sisters in Leycroft, Exmouth, Devonshire, where she died on 27 March 1936.[75]

CHAPTER 8

A Frontier Capitalist

Edgar Dewdney's abiding ambition was to achieve a "competency." That meant having sufficient resources to live a life of comfortable independence. In nineteenth-century Canada, this goal was usually realized through property accumulation, viewed at the time as the key to security.

Like many young Englishmen of the age, Dewdney believed that overseas colonies offered a more rapid road to riches than the homeland. Well-educated and well-connected, he had the approved religion and accent to expect preferential treatment in a colonial outpost. Gold rushes are the ultimate manifestation of human greed and folly, and Dewdney's choice of British Columbia as his destination in the midst of such an outbreak says much about him. He had the instincts of a gambler and hoped to make a quick fortune from speculative ventures. Not for him steady accumulation through hard work and shrewd investment over a sustained period. Some of his enterprises paid off, but many didn't. *Le gros lot* continued to elude him, and there was never enough money in the pot to sustain him in a life of gentlemanly leisure. Disappointed at this failure, he turned to public life as a source of steady income and a vantage point from which to continue his quest for a competency.

While he was attracted to the new world by its economic opportunities, he was sufficiently a scion of imperial traditions to seek out or re-create the social relations of the older society. Privilege came easily to him, and he could never shed his craving for the outward marks of Victorian respectability. In a land without an aristocracy of birth, social status was tenuous at best. The prestige of high government office, even if we discount the avenues of personal gain it opened up, was as good as it got. In this respect at least, Dewdney's career was a resounding success.

His well-bred English civility bent to the realities of the frontier. Unlike some immigrants of his class, he adapted well to the tough conditions and crude amenities of the new society. Even when unrelated to his work, the lure of the outdoors often enticed him from the gentility of the salon and the garden party; he was equally at home in a remote campground as he was in the squalid luxury of a viceregal mansion. The frontier changed him, as it does everyone, and although he could never embrace egalitarianism as a political ideal, he was comfortable mixing with ordinary people. Indeed, many of the jobs he held, surveying contracts and the like, required him to do so. He had the "common touch," so to speak, and it served him well in his political career. There is no sense here of *noblesse oblige*, but a genuine affinity for those who, like himself, had braved the hardships and challenges of creating a new society.

Physically vigorous, especially during his youthful years on the British Columbia frontier, he was well suited to the outdoor life his surveying contracts demanded. The more sedentary life in Ottawa in the 1870s sapped some of his vigour, and by the time he was appointed Indian commissioner for the North-West Territories, he was already portly and plagued by back problems. His various appointments required that he travel extensively, and few people knew the geography of the West as he did. As the frontier receded, the revolution in transportation allowed him to move about with greater ease and rapidity. And even if he viewed the scenery increasingly from the comfort of a railway carriage, he remained a great lover of nature, especially of the stark splendours of the British Columbia landscape. Nature was not only an object of awe and adulation, it was part of his persona. In spite of the decline that age, comfort, and convenience inevitably wrought, he never failed to cultivate his own image as rugged pioneer, and on occasion, he even paraded around Ottawa in a fringed buckskin jacket. It was part of his stock in trade, a unique credential that set him apart from ordinary public figures. Who, after all, could claim to have crossed paths with James Douglas, Twelve-Foot Davis, Louis Riel, Sitting Bull, and countless others among the notable and notorious on the western frontier?

The frontier was one of the great myths of nineteenth-century imperial discourse. The hardships of an untamed land were an alleged source of regenerative power. Blazing trails, camping out, and shooting wild animals for food were acclaimed as ideal activities for the cultivation of the masculine virtues of courage, tenacity, forbearance, and practicality. The explorer/frontiersman was one of the great romantic figures of the age, the very embodiment of red-blooded heroism. Rugged, dashing, and fearless, he was the very stuff of which empires were made, a man whose escapades became moral lessons and models to be emulated. Most importantly, he was the antithesis of the decadent town dweller whose virility was sapped by luxury and vulgar amusements.[1] In the heyday of Victorian imperialism, it is hardly surprising that Dewdney would have exploited his frontier experiences to advantage.

The association of his name with Aboriginal affairs enhanced Dewdney's frontiersman image. Like most members of the Canadian establishment, he viewed Native peoples as a nuisance, an obstacle to development. As Indian commissioner in the North-West, he was responsible for corralling them onto reserves. It was a policy conducted with much bluff and bravado, backed by a small contingent of Indian agents and Mounted Police. Seriously outnumbered, they only succeeded in imposing their will on Natives with arrogant posturing, grandiose-sounding titles, and uniforms to match. A useful motif to this end was the mystique of Queen Victoria, who was held up to colonized peoples throughout the empire as their Great White Mother.[2] Matriarchal imagery was supposed to induce compliance and provide a reassuring sense of security to peoples whose familiar worlds were being rent asunder.

Dewdney's harsh measures appeared to work but provoked a sullen resentment that could not be repressed in spring 1885. He has often been blamed for the Rebellion, but in truth much of the responsibility lay in policies devised in Ottawa by men unfamiliar with western conditions. He had warned his superiors of the dangers and urged them to resolve Native grievances, but to little avail. His main achievement was in limiting Indian involvement in the hostilities, and his legacy was an administration that subjected Indians to strict surveillance and coercive tutelage.

Harsh personal experience hardened his attitude towards Natives with the passing years. And, like many of his contemporaries, he was influenced by racist ideology which, while always part of the colonialist baggage, became more refined and articulated in the pseudo-scientific discourse of late nineteenth-century social Darwinism. These ideas were at the root of the exclusionist policies of reserves and restrictive legislation central to Indian administration. Boundaries around the different were essential to placate respectable fears and to offer reassurances of certainty and stability in a society doubtful of its identity, a society transplanted imperfectly and partially from roots elsewhere.

In the world of politics, Dewdney never made a major impact. As MP for Yale in the 1870s, he pursued the narrow agenda of getting the transcontinental railway built with the terminal route via the Fraser Valley. This emphasis was in keeping with the localist tradition that has always plagued Canadian public life – a politics of whining that pitches trumped-up regional grievances against national interests. British Columbia MPs were not chosen in those days for their party allegiance, even if they had one, but rather for their ability to defend provincial and local interests in Ottawa.

As interior minister, Dewdney merely carried out existing policies and practices. There was no statesman-like vision, no spark of originality, no independent thought. If anything, his one great political passion was loyalty to John A. Macdonald, an unswerving sycophancy that endured to the old chieftain's deathbed.

True to the ideals of the Conservative Party, he was suspicious of democratization and assaults on privilege. Whether in British Columbia or in the North-West, he resisted the drive for responsible government. He believed that the low-born were unfitted for the reins of power and that high office was best reserved for those habituated to it by birth and formation. The gradual evolution of political institutions as a safeguard to mob rule was his political credo.

Being both a beneficiary and a practitioner of the patronage system made him a ready target of opposition indignation. Dispensing the spoils of public office to loyal supporters following electoral victories was one of the hallmarks of the Conservative Party. John A. Macdonald had refined this process, helping to keep his party dominant for decades. The expansion of government following Confederation greatly increased the possibilities of patronage and its use to advance party fortunes. The geographical challenges of the country and the acquisition of the West required massive state intervention to create modern transportation infrastructures and essential government services. The rapid creation of post offices, custom houses, Indian agencies, police barracks, and the like meant that the possibilities for patronage were enormous.[3]

Dewdney's appointments as Indian commissioner, lieutenant governor of the North-West Territories, and minister of the interior (in themselves rewards for party loyalty) put at his disposal a virtually unprecedented array of secure government jobs. And he never hesitated to ensure that these jobs were allocated only to the party faithful. Nor did he balk at warning voters of the consequences of opposing the government. In this context, the intensity of the attacks on his person by M.C. Cameron, Frank Oliver, and the Grit press in general can be readily understood. But these attacks also illustrate the uncompromising nature of party rivalry at the time, a hostility that was born in the heated debates over responsible government in the Canadas and tended to reinforce the patronage system. The opposition was genuinely despised, and it was almost a moral imperative to keep them from the spoils. There was nothing casual about party affiliation; it required an almost religious conviction and commitment.[4]

His penchant for mixing business and public office further marred his reputation in national politics and was a frequent source of embarrassment to his supporters. The western frontier abounded in real estate, railway, and mining investment opportunities that he simply could not resist, even when he had at his disposal decisions and information that enhanced the likelihood of a big payoff. While many other public figures were arguably also taking advantage of their positions, and strict rules governing conflict of interest did not exist at the time, there was a growing indignation at what were clearly corrupt practices. The selection of the site of the new territorial capital adjacent to his personal landholdings in 1882 was the most egregious example of self-serving opportunism. But Dewdney seemed oblivious to the difficulty. He could see no reason to fetter individualistic entrepreneurship in any way by ethical considerations.

It is no small irony that the main thoroughfare in Regina is called Dewdney Avenue. Could it be a deliberate tribute to the shady moral code of frontier capitalism with which the West was won?

Notes

Chapter 1: The Trailblazer

1 Barman, *The West beyond the West*, 56-7.

2 Ormsby, *British Columbia: A History*, 138-40.

3 Barman, *The West beyond the West*, 65-6.

4 BCR, M/D51, "Edgar Dewdney: Miscellaneous Information Supplied by Susan Louisa Allison, 26 February 1928." There is some dispute about Dewdney's birthplace. Madge Wolfenden, in a less than certain manner, says that it "was thought to have been Budleigh Salterton, a village adjoining East Budleigh, famous as the birthplace of the great Sir Walter Raleigh." Ibid., "Edgar Dewdney," seven-page typescript by Wolfenden.

5 "The Story of My Life – Hon. Edgar Dewdney," *Daily Colonist* (Magazine), 7 September 1913, 10-1. This article was actually the concluding episode of a six-part series on Dewdney that the *Colonist* ran in its weekend magazine between 20 July and 7 September 1913. The articles were written by Noel Robinson who interviewed the subject.

6 "The Story of My Life – Hon. Edgar Dewdney," *Daily Colonist* (Magazine), 20 July 1913, 10.

7 BCR, E/E/D51, Edgar Dewdney, "Reminiscences" (twenty-nine-page typescript, n.d.), 1-2.

8 Ormsby, *British Columbia*, 150-6, 171-2.

9 For a biography of Begbie, see Williams, *Man for a New Country*.

10 BCR, E/B/D51.9, Sir Edward Bulwer Lytton to Governor James Douglas, 28 February 1859.

11 Ibid., E/E/D51, Edgar Dewdney, "Reminiscences," 1-2.

12 Ormsby, *British Columbia*, 166-8.

13 Barman, *The West beyond the West*, 68-9.

14 Ibid., 73-87.

15 A man named Cochrane had originally been in charge of the survey. He was a friend of Moody but had been unable to get along with the men. The colonel had been obliged to dismiss him. Cochrane committed suicide shortly afterwards.

16 BCR, E/E/D51, Edgar Dewdney, "Reminiscences," 6-7.

17 "The Story of My Life – Hon. Edgar Dewdney," *Daily Colonist* (Magazine), 20 July 1913, 10.

18 Ormsby, *British Columbia*, 176.

19 BCR, GR 1372, Colonial Correspondence, F 916-14, Colonel R.C. Moody to Governor Douglas, 17 June 1859; F 461-1, Dewdney to Moody, 21 June 1859.

20 BCR, C/AB/30.6 (I), BC Royal Engineers, Letterbook, 1859, John J. Cochrane to Captain R.M. Parsons, 8 July 1859; Dewdney to Parsons, 8 July 1859.

21 BCR, E/E/D51, Edgar Dewdney, "Reminiscences," 9-14; "The Story of My Life – Hon. Edgar Dewdney," *Daily Colonist* (Magazine), 20 July 1913, 10. Sea Island is now occupied by Vancouver International Airport.

22 BCR, E/E/D51, Edgar Dewdney, "Reminiscences," 14-8; "The Story of My Life – Hon. Edgar Dewdney," *Daily Colonist* (Magazine), 20 July 1913, 10, and 10 August 1913, 10.

23 Barman, *The West beyond the West*, 76-8; Ormsby, *British Columbia*, 180-2.

24 BCR, Colonial Correspondence, F 461-2, Dewdney to Peter O'Reilly, 5 February 1860.

25 Ibid., F 461-2b, Dewdney to Colonel R.C. Moody, 18 April 1860; F 461-2c, Dewdney to Captain H.B. Luan, 19 April 1860; F 461-3, Dewdney to W.A.G. Young, 20 April 1860; F 461-3b, Dewdney to Moody, 5 May 1860; F 461-3c, Dewdney to Moody, 15 May 1860; F 461-3e, Dewdney to Luan, 5 June 1860; F 461-3h, Dewdney to Moody, 26 June 1860; F 461-3i, Dewdney to Luan, 7 July 1860.

26 BCR, Colonial Correspondence, F 461-3j, Dewdney to Colonel R.C. Moody, 21 August 1860; F 461-3k, Dewdney to Moody, 8 October 1860; F 461-3l, Dewdney to Moody, 13 November 1860;

F 461-3n, Dewdney to H.B. Luan, 21 November 1860; Dewdney and W. Moberly to Moody, 21 November 1860.

27 Ibid., F 461-3m, Dewdney to Colonel R.C. Moody, 21 November 1860.
28 BCR, J/B/B 86, "Building of the Dewdney Trail, 1865" (typescript, no author), 3-4.
29 GAI, M-454, Dewdney Papers, vol. II, 41-5, "Specification for a Waggon Road from Fort Hope to the N'Colomne Valley on the Similkameen Mule Road."
30 BCR, M/D51, "Edgar Dewdney," by Madge Wolfenden.
31 Ormsby, *British Columbia*, 184-8.
32 GAI, Dewdney Papers, vol. II, 52-3, contract for wagon road.
33 "The Story of My Life – Hon. Edgar Dewdney," *Daily Colonist* (Magazine), 3 August 1913, 10. "Celebrates His Jubilee in BC," *Daily Colonist*, 11 May 1907, 7. See also, Waite, *The Cariboo Gold Rush Story*, 97.
34 The young woman destined to become Dewdney's wife was born Jane Shaw Moir on 5 April 1843 at "Dhekinde," Ambegamoa, a plantation owned jointly by her father, Stratton Moir, and his cousin, Alexander Rogers. For further details of the family background and their voyage to the New World, see Ormsby, *Pioneer Gentlewoman*, ix-xii, 1-7.
35 Ormsby, *Pioneer Gentlewoman*, xv, xvi, 10-3.
36 Ibid., xvii.
37 Ibid., 16. See also, "Married," *British Colonist*, 31 March 1864, 3. "BC's First Lady of the 1890s Took Rough with the Smooth," *Daily Colonist*, 16 March 1958, 21.
38 "The Story of My Life – Hon. Edgar Dewdney," *Daily Colonist* (Magazine), 3 August 1913, 10. See also BCR, J/B D5 IG, R.E. Gosnell, "Bygone Days of British Columbia," 2-6. Dewdney described Tom Spence as "a bit of a character, very active, enterprising, honest and respected by all the old-timers of his day."
39 BCR, Colonial Correspondence, F 461-4, Dewdney to Thomas Spence, 27 March 1865.
40 Ormsby, *British Columbia*, 198-209.
41 BCR, J/B/B 86, "Building of the Dewdney Trail, 1865."
42 "The Story of My Life - Hon. Edgar Dewdney," *Daily Colonist* (Magazine), 24 August 1913, 10. BCR, Colonial Correspondence, F 461-5a, Dewdney to the colonial secretary, 3 April 1865.
43 Ormsby, *British Columbia*, 192-3. "The Story of My Life – Hon. Edgar Dewdney," *Daily Colonist* (Magazine), 20 July 1913, 10. Dewdney said of the Engineers: "Although at first the sappers were often laughed at by old Canadian woodsmen because they were not able to use an axe as they could use it out here, it was soon recognized that they were a splendid and practical body of men, including, as they did, all kinds of artisans and even men with much astronomical knowledge."
44 BCR, J/B D5 IG, R.E. Gosnell, "Bygone Days of British Columbia," 7. This seventeen-page typescript is taken from articles that appeared in *The Daily Province* (Vancouver), 14 November 1908, and the *Daily Times* (Victoria), 21 November 1908. Unless otherwise indicated, my account of the building of the Dewdney Trail is based on this source. Similar, but less detailed information is given in "The Story of My Life – Hon. Edgar Dewdney," *Daily Colonist* (Magazine), 24 August 1913, 10.
45 BCR, Colonial Correspondence, F 461-8, Dewdney to the colonial secretary, 27 May 1865.
46 "Adventure Rode the Trail that Helped Expand BC," *Vancouver Sun*, 4 July 1953, 20.
47 Fernie later discovered coal in the Crow's Nest Pass and extended the trail from Wild Horse to the town that now bears his name.
48 Highway No. 3 today follows more or less the route originally marked out by the Dewdney Trail.
49 Ormsby, *British Columbia*, 212.
50 J. Mayne Baltimore, "The Famous Dewdney Trail," *National Sportsman* (August 1901): 117-22. The trail has been the subject of a piece of doggerel by Charles E. Race. Here is a sample:

Tippity-toe and away we go,
Bunch grass flats or up in the snow,
Blizzard or heat, but a first-class show;
(Pull taut on that pack rope!)
Tippity-toe of the cayuse jog

Lowering peak and the beaver bog,
Balsam, sage and burnt pine log –
From old Fort Steele to Hope.

For the rest of it, see BCR, NW 906/041/V.20/c.2. Kathleen S. Dewdney, "Walter Robert
Dewdney," *20th Report of the Okanagan Historical Society, 1925:* 36-40.

51 BCR, Colonial Correspondence, F 461-12, Dewdney to the chief commissioner of lands and
    works, 24 March 1866.
52 "Celebrates His Jubilee in BC," *Daily Colonist*, 11 May 1907, 7.
53 Ormsby, *British Columbia*, 212.
54 BCR, Colonial Correspondence, F 461-17, Dewdney to the chief commissioner of lands and
    works, 8 November 1866.
55 Ormsby, *Pioneer Gentlewoman*, xxii.
56 "Celebrates his Jubilee in BC," *Daily Colonist*, 11 May 1907, 7.
57 Ormsby, *Pioneer Gentlewoman*, xxii-xxiii.
58 BCR, Colonial Correspondence, F 461-20, Dewdney to the chief commissioner of lands and
    works, 16 November 1867; F 461-22, Dewdney to the chief commissioner of lands and works,
    1 May 1868.
59 "Cariboo and the Interior," *British Colonist*, 20 August 1868, 3.
60 GAI, Dewdney Papers, vol. II, 25-9, newsclipping: R.E. Gosnell, "Bygone Days of British
    Columbia – Pioneer Mining in Peace River Country," *Daily Times* (Victoria), 29 August 1908.
    "The Story of My Life – Hon. Edgar Dewdney," *Daily Colonist* (Magazine), 31 August 1913, 10.
61 Loo, *Making Law, Order, and Authority*, 9.

Chapter 2: The Politician

1   Ormsby, *British Columbia*, 218-22.
2   Barman, *The West beyond the West*, 91-2.
3   For the early career of de Cosmos, see George Woodcock, *Amor de Cosmos: Journalist and
    Reformer*, 1-96. De Cosmos's real name was William Smith.
4   "The Story of My Life – Hon. Edgar Dewdney," *Daily Colonist* (Magazine), 31 August 1913, 10.
5   "Member for Kootenay," *British Colonist*, 3 December 1868, 3.
6   Ormsby, *British Columbia*, 227-8.
7   "Card from the Member for Kootenay – Why He Failed to Attend the Council," *British
    Colonist*, 16 March 1869, 2.
8   Woodcock, *British Columbia*, 106-8.
9   Hendrickson, "The Constitutional Development of Colonial Vancouver Island and British
    Columbia," 269-70. Ormsby, *British Columbia*, 229-42.
10 "Arrival of the Enterprise – News from the Mainland," *British Columbia*, 18 February 1870, 3.
11 Women, Indians, and Chinese were disfranchised at the time, which greatly reduced the num-
    ber of eligible voters.
12 *Journals of the Colonial Legislatures of the Colonies of Vancouver Island and British Columbia, 1851-
    1871. v. 5: Journals of the Legislative Council of British Columbia, 1866-1871.* Appendix A, Debate
    on the Subject of Confederation with Canada, 444-575. For Dewdney's speeches, see 482-3 and
    542-3. See also Derek Pethick, "The Confederation Debate of 1870," 165-94.
13 "Progress of Liberal Principles," *British Colonist*, 10 November 1870, 2.
14 BCR, Colonial Correspondence, F 461-32, Dewdney to B.W. Pearse, assistant surveyor general,
    21 June 1810; F 461-36, Dewdney to the chief commissioner of lands and works, 19 October 1870.
15 The reference here is to the legendary Dan Williams, a black man who squatted on land near
    Fort St. John. Dewdney's negative characterization was fairly typical. For further information,
    see the following excerpts in Bowes, *Peace River Chronicles:* W.F. Butler, "Fort St. John and Dan
    Williams," and A.C. Garrioch, "The Trial of Dan Williams."
16 GAI, Dewdney Papers, vol. II, 25-9, newsclipping: R.E. Gosnell, "Bygone Days of British
    Columbia – Pioneer Mining in Peace River Country," *Daily Times* (Victoria), 29 August 1908.
    "The Story of My Life – Hon. Edgar Dewdney," *Daily Colonist* (Magazine), 31 August 1913, 10.
17 BCR, Colonial Correspondence, F 461-38, Dewdney to B.W. Pearse, 20 May 1871. He

suggested that the trail be made to accommodate pack animals because the Indians were "a most independent and dishonest lot, charging exorbitant prices for packing – 10c p.h. from here to Babine and their food and 20c p.h. from Babine to Tatla."

18   Little, "The Foundations of Government," 81-3.
19   BCR, Colonial Correspondence, F 957-15, B.W. Pearse to Dewdney, 23 August 1871.
20   Ibid., F 461-40, Dewdney to B.W. Pearse, 28 August 1871.
21   Ormsby, *British Columbia*, 253.
22   Berton, *The National Dream*, I, 6-9.
23   For Houghton's background, see Ormsby, *Pioneer Gentlewoman*, 174.
24   "Yale-Kootenay," *Daily British Colonist*, 13 October 1872, 3. Dewdney received forty-three votes while his opponent, a man named Smith, received nineteen. There were only 127 qualified voters in the Yale constituency, often mistakenly referred to as Yale-Kootenay because it incorporated the former colonial electoral districts of Yale and Kootenay.
25   Creighton, *John A. Macdonald: The Old Chieftain*, 141.
26   GAI, Dewdney Papers, vol. II, 92, George Walkem to Dewdney, 20 November 1872; 93-7, undated draft of letter from Dewdney to Walkem.
27   Woodcock, *Amor de Cosmos*, 136-47.
28   GAI, Dewdney Papers, vol. II, 98, George Walkem to Dewdney, 25 November 1872; 101-6, Walkem to Dewdney, 4 December 1872; 100, Walkem to Dewdney, 9 December 1872.
29   "The Yale-Kootenay District," *Daily British Colonist*, 24 November 1872, 2.
30   Quoted in Gwyn, *The Private Capital*, 39.
31   BCR, A/E/Or/D51, O'Reilly Correspondence, Jane Dewdney to Mrs. O'Reilly, 18 March 1873.
32   "The Story of My Life – Hon. Edgar Dewdney," *Daily Colonist* (Magazine), 31 August 1913, 10.
33   Morton, *The Critical Years*, 268-77.
34   Waite, *Arduous Destiny*, 15-6, 25-7, 78.
35   Woodcock, *Amor de Cosmos*, 142-7.
36   "The Dewdney Scandal," *Daily British Colonist*, 20 February 1874, 3.
37   "Highly Reprehensible," *Daily British Colonist*, 25 February 1872, 2; "Victoria All Along the Line," ibid., 3.
38   "Our Little Rebellion," *Daily British Colonist*, 17 April 1874, 3.
39   Waite, *Arduous Destiny*, 28-9. See also the map of the various routes on p. 26.
40   Ormsby, *British Columbia*, 264-5.
41   BCR, NWp 971 B D515, "Speech on the Subject of the Canadian Pacific Railway, Delivered Recently by E. Dewdney, Esq., MP, to His Constituents at Cache Creek" (pamphlet published by the *Mainland Guardian*, New Westminster, 1875). The same speech was also published by the *Mainland Guardian* in excerpts on the following dates: 18, 25, 29 September; 2, 6, 9, 13, 16, 20, 23 October; and 10 November 1875.
42   Ormsby, *British Columbia*, 267.
43   "Mr. Dewdney on the Canadian Pacific Railway," *Daily British Colonist*, 17 September 1874, 3. "Complication," *Daily British Colonist*, 9 February 1875, 2.
44   Waite, *Arduous Destiny*, 31.
45   "Mr. Dewdney on the Canadian Pacific Railway," *Daily British Colonist*, 17 September 1874, 3; "Impugning Motives," *Daily British Colonist*, 18 September 1874, 2.
46   Berton, *The National Dream*, 174-81.
47   BCR, NWp 971 B D515, "Speech on the Subject of the Canadian Pacific Railway, Delivered Recently by E. Dewdney, Esq., MP, to His Constituents at Cache Creek."
48   Berton, *The National Dream*, 148-51.
49   BCR, NWp 971 B D515, "Speech on the Subject of the Canadian Pacific Railway, Delivered Recently by E. Dewdney, Esq., MP, to His Constituents at Cache Creek." Quite apart from their political differences, Dewdney's attack on Walkem may have been influenced by a lingering personal animosity. It was Walkem, after all, who had denied him the possibility in 1872 of becoming surveyor general of BC while retaining his seat in Parliament.
50   The letter, signed by Dewdney, James Cunningham, and Senator Clement Cornwall, was quoted by Lord Dufferin in his correspondence with Lord Carnavon, 31 March 1876. De Kiewiet and Underhill, *Dufferin -Carnavon Correspondence*, 204-6.
51   BCR, A/E /Or 3 /D 54.1, J.D. Edgar to Dewdney, 23 March 1876.

52   Canada, House of Commons, *Debates,* 5 April 1876, 1051-65.
53   Waite, *Arduous Destiny,* 84.
54   BCR, NW 971 B D515 C.2, "Report of a Public Meeting Held at New Westminster, BC, May
     10th, 1876." See also, "The Dewdney Welcome," *Daily British Colonist,* 14 May 1876, 3.
55   Berton, *The National Dream,* 200-8; Ormsby, *British Columbia,* 273-7.
56   Canada, House of Commons, *Debates,* 14 March 1877, 686-96.
57   Ibid., 17 April 1877, 1562-6.
58   Ibid., 18 April 1877, 1572-8.
59   Ibid., 24 April 1877, 1790-4.
60   See, for example, "Canadian Pacific Railway Routes," *Daily British Colonist,* 1 July 1877, 2. This
     was in fact a letter from W.F. Tolmie, MP for Victoria District, attacking Dewdney's Commons
     speech of 24 April. See also "Dr. Tolmie's Letter," *Mainland Guardian,* 11 July 1877, 2, for an
     editorial defending Dewdney's position.
61   Berton, *The National Dream,* 216; Ormsby, *British Columbia,* 277.
62   Canada, House of Commons, *Debates,* 25 February 1878, 495-8 and 510-25.
63   Berton, *The National Dream,* 216-7.
64   Canada, House of Commons, *Debates,* 8 May 1878, 2532-7.
65   Berton, *The National Dream,* 218; Ormsby, *British Columbia,* 277.
66   "No Uncertain Ring about Him," *Daily British Colonist,* 1 October 1878, 2.
67   Ormsby, *British Columbia,* 278-9.
68   Berton, *The National Dream,* 268.
69   BCR, NWp 971 B D515 p. "Pacific Railway Route, British Columbia," address to Senators and
     Members of the House of Commons by Edgar Dewdney, n.d.
70   Berton, *The National Dream,* 270; Ormsby, *British Columbia,* 279.
71   As noted, Dewdney's antipathy to de Cosmos originated in their differences over responsible
     government during the Confederation debate in Victoria. During the 1870s, the latter contin-
     ued to champion democratic reforms to the province's political structures while the former
     opposed them. In 1879, Dewdney joined with Senators C.F. Cornwall and W.J. Macdonald to
     protest to the prime minister about the rising democratic tide: "Unfortunately for British
     Columbia, what is known as universal suffrage is in force in the Province. The lower classes,
     those having no stake in the country, consequently control the elections, and the representation
     of the Province in the Legislative Assembly is, to say the least of it, most unfortunate. The pre-
     sent Legislative Assembly is perhaps taken together as inferior a body of the sort as could well
     be imagined; and if the Province is to be unmistakably given up to their tender mercies without
     the interposition of experienced guidance and to some extent repression from Ottawa, no
     thoughtful mind can view the picture without gravest apprehension" (quoted in Belshaw,
     "Provincial Politics," 135).

Chapter 3: Indian Commissioner

1   "The Story of My Life – Hon. Edgar Dewdney," *Daily Colonist* (Magazine), 7 September
    1913, 10.
2   NAC, RG 10, vol. 3671, file 10, 836-2, Constantine Scollen to Major A.G. Irvine, 19 April 1878.
    Father Scollen's lengthy letter was sent on to the minister of the interior in Ottawa. He
    described in detail the starving condition of the Blackfoot, noting, "We shall either have to pro-
    vide for the Indians or fight them; there is no other alternative." Ibid., vol. 3762, file 10, 853 1,
    M.G. Dickieson to R. Sinclair, 16 November 1878; L. Vankoughnet to John A. Macdonald, 12
    December 1878; Vankoughnet to Dickieson, 3 January 1879; Dickieson to Vankoughnet, 26
    February 1879.
3   Friesen, *The Canadian Prairies,* 149-52.
4   For details, see Brian Titley, "Unsteady Debut: J.-A.-N. Provencher and the Beginnings of
    Indian Administration in Manitoba."
5   Carter, *Lost Harvests,* 67.
6   NAC, RG 10, vol. 3686, file 13, 364, John A. Macdonald to the Privy Council, 16 May 1879.
7   GAI, Dewdney Papers, vol. III, 180-9, J.S. Dennis to Dewdney, 31 May 1879.
8   The details of the journey are found in Dempsey, "The Starvation Year," Part 1, 2-6.
9   NAC, RG 10, vol. 3693, file 14, 283, Dewdney to L. Vankoughnet, 21 June 1879.

10   Canada, *Sessional Paper No. 3, 1880*, Report of the Department of the Interior for the year ended 30 June 1879: 76-7.
11   Ibid., 77-83.
12   GAI, Dewdney Papers, vol. III, 1184-6, J.S. Dennis to Dewdney, 23 June 1879. NAC, RG 10, vol. 3692, file 13,955, Report to the Privy Council, no. 845, 12 June 1879.
13   NAC, RG 10, vol. 3698, file 16,142, Minutes of a conference on the destitution of the Indians in the North-West Territories, Battleford, 26 August 1879.
14   Dempsey, "The Starvation Year," Parts 1 and 2. Canada, *Sessional Paper No. 3, 1880*, Report of the Department of the Interior for the year ended 30 June 1879: 76-103. "The Story of My Life – Hon. Edgar Dewdney," *Daily Colonist* (Magazine), 7 September 1913, 10-1.
15   Leighton, "A Victorian Civil Servant at Work," 105. In Getty and Lussier, eds., *As Long as the Sun Shines and Water Flows*.
16   GAI, Dewdney Papers, vol. III, 198-203, L. Vankoughnet to Dewdney, 21 February 1880.
17   NAC, RG 10, vol. 3686, file 13,364, Dewdney to John A. Macdonald, 2 May 1880.
18   BCR, F. 5.2 D51A, v. 1, Diary of Edgar Dewdney, January-October 1880.
19   Canada, *Sessional Paper No. 8, 1880-81*, Report of the Department of Indian Affairs for the year ended 31 December 1880, 92.
20   Carter, *Lost Harvests*, 84-96.
21   Canada, *Sessional Paper No. 8, 1880-81*, Report of the Department of Indian Affairs for the year ended 31 December 1880, 94.
22   Tobias, "Canada's Subjugation of the Plains Cree," 527-9.
23   Pennanen, "Sitting Bull: Indian Without a Country," 134-6.
24   BCR, Diary of Edgar Dewdney, January-October 1880.
25   Canada, *Sessional Paper No. 5, 1882*, Report of the Department of Indian Affairs for the year ended 31 December 1881, 54. GAI, Dewdney Papers, vol. III, 1092-7, L. Vankoughnet to Dewdney, 14 December 1881.
26   Pennanen, "Sitting Bull: Indian Without a Country," 137-9. MacEwan, *Sitting Bull*, 184-95.
27   MacEwan, *Sitting Bull*, 208.
28   GAI, Dewdney Papers, vol. III. 1172-5, D.L. Macpherson to Dewdney, 15 July 1881.
29   Canada, *Sessional Paper No. 5, 1882*, Report of the Department of Indian Affairs for the year ended 31 December 1881, 41.
30   Ibid., 38-40.
31   Tobias, "Canada's Subjugation of the Plains Cree," 530.
32   GAI, Dewdney Papers, vol. III, 392-5, J.A. Macdonald to Dewdney, 19 August 1881; Dewdney to Macdonald, 2 October 1881.
33   GAI, Dewdney Papers, vol. III, 396-9, J.A. Macdonald to Dewdney, 28 October 1881; 205-11, Report of the Committee of the Privy Council, 31 October 1881. NAC, RG 10, vol. 3686, file 13,364, Report of the Committee of the Privy Council, 3 December 1881.
34   NAC, RG 10, vol. 3605, file 2950, C. Kettles to T.P. Wadsworth, 9 July 1882. Kettles was the farm instructor on the Peigan reserve. He was fired in October 1882 for his inability to keep accurate accounts, a frequent problem among department employees.
35   Canada, *Sessional Paper No. 4, 1883*, Report of the Department of Indian Affairs for the year ended 31 December 1882, 196.
36   NAC, RG 10, vol. 3574, file 167, N. Macleod to Dewdney, 12 December 1881; J. Howe to L.N.F. Crozier, 4 January 1882; Crozier to commissioner of NWMP, 5 January 1882; C.E. Denny to Dewdney, 23 January 1882. The Dickens involved in this incident was the son of author Charles Dickens.
37   Denny (1850-1928) was a well-born Englishman who had quite a career in Western Canada, serving as provincial archivist for Alberta in the 1920s. He was the author of two books, *The Riders of the Plains* and *The Law Marches West*. See the biographical note in Denny, *March of the Mounties*, a book excerpted from his two original works.
38   NAC, RG 10, vol. 3574, file 167, Dewdney to C.E. Denny, 12 January 1882; Dewdney to Denny, 17 February 1882; Dewdney to N. Macleod, 18 February 1882; vol. 3603, file 2043, Dewdney to the superintendent general, 8 August 1882; N. Macleod to N.C. Wallace, MP, 18 February 1884. Macleod had been appointed the first Indian agent for Treaty 7 in spring 1880. He was the brother of Colonel James F. Macleod, the Mounted Police commander.

39 Ibid., vol. 3609, file 3334, T.P. Wadsworth to E.T. Galt, 22 July 1882; Wadsworth to Dewdney, 24 July 1882; Galt to the superintendent general, 14 November 1882.

40 Ibid., T.P. Wadsworth to E.T. Galt, 29 July 1882; C.E. Denny to Wadsworth, 27 July 1882; Wadsworth to Dewdney, 2 August 1882; vol. 3609, file 3380, Wadsworth to Dewdney, 25 July 1882; Wadsworth to Galt, 13 and 15 August 1882.

41 Ibid., vol. 3610, file 3525, T.P. Wadsworth to Dewdney, 13 August 1882.

42 Canada, *Sessional Paper No. 4, 1883*, Report of the Department of Indian Affairs for the year ended 31 December 1882, 196-8; Dempsey, *Big Bear*, 104-11.

43 NAC, RG 10, vol. 3625, file 5470, F. Norman to Dewdney, 18 January 1883; Dewdney to the superintendent general, 22 February 1883; the deputy superintendent to Dewdney, 1 March 1883.

44 GAI, Dewdney Papers, vol. III, 1193-200, A.G. Irvine to Dewdney, 24 June 1882.

45 Ibid., 737-40, F. White to Dewdney, 29 August 1882.

46 For Reed's background, see Titley, "Hayter Reed and Indian Administration in the West."

47 Ibid., 113-4.

48 Canada, *Sessional Paper No. 3, 1884*, Report of the Department of Indian Affairs for the year ended 31 December 1883, 98.

49 Ibid., 99. Dempsey, *Big Bear*, 112-4.

50 Carter, *Lost Harvests*, 104-5.

51 NAC, RG 10, vol. 3603, file 2043, T.P. Wadsworth to Dewdney, 13 May 1882; Wadsworth, Report on Pincher Creek supply farm, 6 June 1882.

52 Ibid., vol. 3600, file 1752, L. Vankoughnet to Dewdney, 29 May 1882.

53 Carter, *Lost Harvests*, 98-9.

54 NAC, RG 10, vol. 3674, file 10, 958, return regarding home farms closed, 30 January 1884. Carter, *Lost Harvests*, 106-7.

55 NAC, RG 10, vol. 3686, file 13,364, memorandum of G.M. Matheson, 27 January 1925; vol. 3635, file 6567, Dewdney to the superintendent general, 23 March 1883. This letter is interesting in that Dewdney gives his personal evaluation of the work of most agents and several other employees under his direction. One of the recommendations acted upon by the government was the superannuation of James F. Graham, the man in charge of the Manitoba Superintendency. Graham had been "a very good officer" until his health had broken down. In putting him on the retirement list, Dewdney advised that the department keep in mind that he had thirteen children. This was done and the man was given an extra ten years of service for pension purposes. One of Graham's numerous offspring was William M. Graham, later a legendary figure in the Indian Department.

56 Ibid., vol. 3664, file 9834, L. Vankoughnet to J.A. Macdonald, 15 November 1883.

57 Ibid., file 9843, telegrams from headquarters to agents Denny, Pocklington, Anderson, Rae, and McDonald, 23 November 1883.

58 Ibid., file 9834, L. Vankoughnet to Dewdney, 30 November 1883.

59 Ibid., Dewdney to the superintendent general, 27 December 1883.

60 Ibid., vol. 3637, file 6882, Dewdney to the superintendent general, 29 December 1883.

61 Ibid., vol. 3664, file 9843, W. Anderson to Dewdney, 27 December 1883; C.E. Denny to Dewdney, 1 January 1884; Denny to the Indian commissioner, 14 January 1884; J.M. Rae to Dewdney, 19 January 1884.

62 Ibid., vol. 3637, file 6882, L. Vankoughnet to Dewdney, 16 January 1884; vol. 3664, file 9834, Vankoughnet to Dewdney, 26 January 1884; vol. 3664, file 9843, Vankoughnet to Dewdney, 2 February 1884.

63 Ibid., vol. 3671, file 10, 836-41, Dewdney to the superintendent general, 11 January 1884; L. Vankoughnet to John A. Macdonald, 31 January 1884; deputy superintendent to Dewdney, 20 May 1884.

64 GAI, Dewdney Papers, vol. III, 507-8, J.A. Macdonald to Dewdney, 18 July 1884; 509-10, Macdonald to Dewdney, 11 August 1884.

65 NAC, RG 10, vol. 3577, file 468, Dewdney to the superintendent general, 9 March 1882; Report of the Committee of the Privy Council, 11 April 1882.

66 Ibid., vol. 3647, file 8128, Dewdney to the superintendent general, 29 December 1883; L. Vankoughnet to J.A. Macdonald, 19 January 1884; Vankoughnet to Dewdney, 14 February 1884;

Dewdney to the superintendent general, 28 April 1884; J. McGirr to the deputy minister, 21 May 1884.

67 Titley, "Indian Industrial Schools in Western Canada," 133-6.

68 NAC, RG 10, vol. 3668, file 10,644, H. Reed to the Indian commissioner, 28 December 1883.

69 Canada, *Sessional Paper No. 3, 1885*, Report of the Department of Indian Affairs for the year ended 31 December 1884, 161.

70 NAC, RG 10, vol. 3668, file 10, 644, H. Reed to the Indian commissioner, 28 December 1883.

71 Carter, *Lost Harvests*, 121.

72 NAC, RG 10, vol. 3668, file 10,644, F. White to L. Vankoughnet, 28 March 1884; H. Reed to the superintendent general, 12 April 1884.

73 Ibid., vol. 3682, file 12, 667, Dewdney to the superintendent general, 28 April 1884.

74 Ibid., vol. 3086, file 13,168, A. MacDonald to the Indian commissioner, 13, 14, 15 May, 25 June 1884; H. Reed to the superintendent general, 20 May 1884.

75 Carter, *Lost Harvests*, 123-5.

76 GAI, Dewdney Papers, vol. III, 491-8, Dewdney to John A. Macdonald, 12 June 1884.

77 NAC, RG 10, vol. 3692, file 13,990, Dewdney to the superintendent general, 4 July 1884. The other letters and telegrams in this file offer a detailed description of the incident. See also the documents in vol. 3576, file 309A and B.

78 Ibid., vol. 3692, file 13,990, deputy superintendent to Dewdney, 24 and 29 July 1884.

79 GAI, Dewdney Papers, vol. III, 299-300, speech by Dewdney at opening of the North-West council, 3 July 1884.

80 NAC, RG 10, vol. 3694, file 14,624, Dewdney to the superintendent general, 19 July 1884.

81 GAI, Dewdney Papers, vol. III, 505-6, J.A. Macdonald to Dewdney, 16 July 1884.

82 Beal and Macleod, *Prairie Fire*, 114-6.

83 NAC, RG 10, vol. 3697, file 15,423, J.A. Macrae to Dewdney, 25 August 1884.

84 GAI, Dewdney Papers, vol. III, 1402-5, C. Rouleau to Dewdney, 5 September 1884.

85 Ibid., 1398-1401, H. Reed to Dewdney, 4 September 1884.

86 Ibid., 511-2, J.A. Macdonald to Dewdney, 2 September 1884; 513-4, Macdonald to Dewdney, 15 September 1884.

87 Ibid., 797-8, J.A. Macdonald to F. White, 15 September 1884.

88 NAC, RG 10, vol. 3701, file 17,169, P. Ballendine to the Indian commissioner, 21 November 1884.

89 GAI, Dewdney Papers, vol. III, 1104-10, L. Vankoughnet to Dewdney, 5 December 1884; 1111-6, Dewdney to Vankoughnet, 12 December 1884.

Chapter 4: Rebellion

1 NAC, RG 10, vol. 3705, file 17,936, P. Ballendine to the Indian commissioner, 2 January 1885; L. Crozier to the Indian commissioner, 14 January 1885. GAI, Dewdney Papers, vol. III, 1222-3, Crozier to Dewdney, 15 January 1885.

2 GAI, Dewdney Papers, vol. III, 520-1, Dewdney to J.A. Macdonald, 9 January 1885; 524, Macdonald to Dewdney, 27 January 1885; 1117-8, L. Vankoughnet to Macdonald, 28 January 1885; 533-4, Dewdney to Macdonald, 4 February 1885; 537-44, Dewdney to Macdonald, February 1885.

3 NAC, RG 10, vol. 3697, file 15,423, H. Reed to the superintendent general, 25 January 1885; deputy superintendent to Dewdney, 4 February 1885; Tobias, "Canada's Subjugation of the Plain's Cree," 542; Canada, *Sessional Paper No. 4, 1886*, Report of the Department of Indian Affairs for the year ended 31 December 1885, 144.

4 GAI, Dewdney Papers, vol. III, D.H. Macdowell to Dewdney, 14 January 1885; 529-30, Dewdney to J.A. Macdonald, 2 February 1885.

5 Beal and Macleod, *Prairie Fire*, 131.

6 NAC, RG 10, vol. 3576, file 309A, L. Vankoughnet to Dewdney, 5 February 1885; Dewdney to the superintendent general, 12 February 1885; Vankoughnet to Dewdney, 3 March 1885; vol. 3705, file 17,936, Vankoughnet to J.A. Macdonald, with marginal notes by Macdonald, 23 February 1885. GAI Dewdney Papers, vol. III, 546-7, Macdonald to Dewdney, 23 February 1885.

7 NAC, RG 10, vol. 3677, file 11,582-2, Sergeant J.A. Martin (Fort Pitt) to commanding officer, NWMP Battleford, 13 February 1885; Inspector F. Dickens (Fort Pitt) to commanding officer, NWMP Battleford, 15 February 1885. L. Crozier was in charge of the police detachment at Battleford, and he sent Dewdney regular reports on developments in the area.

8   GAI, Dewdney Papers, vol. III, 549-52, Dewdney to J.A. Macdonald, 12 March 1885.
9   NAC, RG 10, vol. 3715, file 21,264, T. Quinn to Indian commissioner, 13 March 1885; P. Ballendine to Dewdney, 19 March 1885.
10   Beal and Macleod, *Prairie Fire*, 135-43.
11   GAI, Dewdney Papers, vol. III, 1428, L.N.F. Crozier to the Indian commissioner, 18 March 1885; 1432, F. White to Dewdney, 19 March 1885; 1433, Dewdney to White, 20 March 1885.
12   Beal and Macleod, *Prairie Fire*, 154-9, 168-72.
13   Ibid., 177.
14   Ibid., 237-55.
15   NAC, RG 10, vol. 3709, file 19,550-1, W. McGirr to the superintendent general, 3 and 24 April 1885; headquarters to Dewdney, 8 April 1885.
16   Ibid., Pasquah and Muscowpetung to J.A. Macdonald, 21 April 1885; W. McGirr to the superintendent general, 2 May 1885; Macdonald to Dewdney, 11 May 1885.
17   Ibid., A. MacDonald to the Indian commissioner, 6 and 11 May 1885.
18   Ibid., A. MacDonald to the Indian commissioner, 6 May 1885; W. McGirr to the superintendent general, 15 May 1885.
19   Ibid., John A. Macdonald to A. Lacombe, 24 March 1885; Lacombe to Macdonald, 31 March 1885; vol. 3711, file 19,923, W. Sherwood to the Indian commissioner, 31 March 1885.
20   Denny, *March of the Mounties.*
21   NAC, RG 10, vol. 3709, file 19,550-1, Crowfoot to J.A. Macdonald, 11 April 1885; Dewdney to Macdonald, 12 April 1885.
22   GAI, Dewdney Papers, vol. III, 553-4, J.A. Macdonald to Dewdney, 29 March 1885; Beal and Macleod, *Prairie Fire*, 281.
23   Ibid., 277-80.
24   NAC, RG 10, vol. 3709, file 19,550-1, C.E. Denny to Dewdney, 17, 19, 24 April 1885.
25   Ibid., Dewdney to the superintendent general (enclosing copies of Strange's telegrams), 27 April 1885.
26   Ibid., C.E. Denny to Dewdney, 1, 6, 25 May, and 2 June 1885; Dewdney to Denny, 23 May 1885; W. Pocklington to Dewdney, 3, 10, 25, 31 May 1885.
27   Ibid., W. Anderson to Dewdney, 9 April 1885.
28   Titley, "Transition to Settlement," 178-9.
29   Beal and Macleod, *Prairie Fire*, 211; NAC, RG 10, vol. 3709, file 19,550-1, report of Reverend E.B. Glass, 23 April 1885; W. Anderson to Dewdney, 15 April 1885.
30   Ibid., James Seenum to W. Anderson, 16 and 21 April 1885; Anderson to the Indian commissioner, 7 May 1885; Dewdney to the superintendent general, 22 May 1885.
31   Ibid., W. Anderson to Dewdney, 20 May, 2 June 1885; Dewdney to the superintendent general, 15 June 1885. Dewdney was also responsible for Manitoba as Indian commissioner but not as lieutenant governor. During the course of the hostilities, he received reassuring reports from department officers in that province regarding Indian loyalty. See ibid., vol. 3713, file 20,888.
32   After the rebellion, Carlton was renamed the Prince Albert agency.
33   NAC, RG 10, vol. 3710, 19,550-3. This file contains a list of all the bands in the North-West with anecdotal remarks regarding their loyalty during the rebellion.
34   Beal and Macleod, *Prairie Fire*, 263-76.
35   GAI, Dewdney Papers, vol. III, 560-5, Dewdney to J.A. Macdonald, 2 June 1885.
36   Canada, *Sessional Paper No. 4, 1886,* Report of the Department of Indian Affairs for the year ended 31 December 1885, 139-41.
37   NAC, RG 10, vol. 3714, file 21,088-2, W. Anderson to the Indian commissioner, 3 June 1885; the deputy superintendent to Dewdney, 9 July 1885; vol. 3709, file 19,550-1, J.M. Rae to the Indian commissioner, 11 June 1885.
38   Ibid., vol. 3714, file 21,088-2, the deputy superintendent to Dewdney, 11 June 1885; Dewdney to the superintendent general, 19 June 1885.
39   Ibid., John A. Mitchell to the Indian commissioner, 23 July 1885.
40   Ibid., J.B. Lash to the Indian commissioner, 4 August 1885.
41   GAI, Dewdney Papers, vol. III, 1414, H. Reed to Dewdney, 29 July 1885. NAC, RG 10, vol. 3710, file 19,550-3, Dewdney to the superintendent general, 1 August 1885; the deputy superintendent to Dewdney, 28 October 1885.

42   Titley, "Hayter Reed and Indian Administration in the West."
43   Canada, *Sessional Paper No. 4, 1886*, Report of the Department of Indian Affairs for the year
     ended 31 December 1885, 218-23.
44   NAC, RG 10, vol. 3710, file 19,550-3, the deputy superintendent to Dewdney, 28 October 1885.
45   Ibid., vol. 3710, file 19,550-3, Dewdney to the superintendent general, 10 June 1885; Dewdney to
     the superintendent general, 21 August 1885.
46   Ibid., vol. 3710, file 19,550-4, Dewdney to the superintendent general, 8 October 1885.
47   Ibid., undated memo containing list of loyal Indians and the rewards they were to receive.
48   Beal and Macleod, *Prairie Fire*, 292-304.
49   Larmour, "Edgar Dewdney and the Aftermath of the Rebellion," 106. NAC, Macdonald
     Papers, Letterbook, 23, vol. 526, 241-2, J.A. Macdonald to Dewdney, 17 August 1885.
50   Ibid., vol. 107, 43252-59, Dewdney to J.A. Macdonald, 2 November 1885.
51   GAI, Dewdney Papers, vol. III, 1498, memo of Dewdney, 15 November 1885.
52   NAC, Macdonald Papers, vol. 107, 43318-20, Dewdney to J.A. Macdonald, 16 November 1885.
53   Beal and Macleod, *Prairie Fire*, 309-32.
54   GAI, Dewdney Papers, vol. III, 587-8, J.A. Macdonald to Dewdney, 20 November 1885.
55   Ibid., 589-90, Dewdney to J.A. Macdonald, 20 December 1885.
56   NAC, RG 10, vol. 3576, file 309A, Dewdney to P.G. Laurie (editor of the *Saskatchewan Herald*),
     30 January 1886.
57   GAI, Dewdney Papers, vol. III, 1165-6, Dewdney to C.E. Denny, 24 November 1885.
58   Denny, *The Law Marches West*, 228.
59   GAI, Dewdney Papers, vol. III, 1523-36, reports from James Anderson to Dewdney between 25
     November and 20 December 1885.
60   Ibid., 601-2, J.A. Macdonald to Dewdney, 19 February 1886; 606-7, Dewdney to Macdonald,
     2 March 1886; 610, Macdonald to Dewdney, 13 March 1886; 611-2, Dewdney to Macdonald,
     30 March 1886.
61   Ibid., 619-20, Dewdney to J.A. Macdonald, 22 July 1886. For further details on these security
     measures, see Larmour, "Edgar Dewdney and the Aftermath of the Rebellion."
62   Canada, *Sessional Paper No. 6, 1887*, Report of the Department of Indian Affairs for the year
     ended 31 December 1886, 109. NAC, RG 10, vol. 3671, file 10,836-1, Dewdney to the superinten-
     dent general, 4 June 1885, 7 July 1885. Titley, "Alexander McGibbon."
63   Canada, *Sessional Paper No. 15, 1888*, Report of the Department of Indian Affairs for the year
     ended 31 December 1887, 196.
64   NAC, RG 10, vol. 3647, file 8128, Dewdney to the superintendent general, 16 July 1887.
65   Ibid., J.A. Macrae to the Indian commissioner, 18 December 1886.
66   Titley, "Indian Industrial Schools in Western Canada," 138-9.
67   NAC, RG 10, vol. 3576, file 309A, H. Reed to the superintendent general, 28 January 1888.
68   Canada, *Sessional Paper No. 15, 1888*, Report of the Department of Indian Affairs for the year
     ended 31 December 1887, 188.

Chapter 5: Lieutenant Governor

1   GAI, Dewdney Papers, vol. III, 396-9, J.A. Macdonald to Dewdney, 28 October 1881.
2   Thomas, *The Struggle for Responsible Government in the North-West Territories*, 76.
3   Ibid., 89.
4   Ibid., 90-7.
5   Archer, *Saskatchewan: A History*, 99; Lalonde, "Colonization Companies in the 1880s," 26-7.
6   Thomas, *Struggle for Responsible Government*, 88, 104.
7   Brennan, *Regina: An Illustrated History*, 12.
8   For a more detailed account of this controversy, see Berton, *The Last Spike*, 113-25.
9   NAC, Macdonald Papers, vol. 211, 89712-32, Dewdney to J.A. Macdonald, 9 August 1882.
10   GAI, Dewdney Papers, vol. III, 216, "The Future of Regina," *Winnipeg Times*, 19 September
     1882 (newsclipping).
11   Ibid., 253, F. White to Dewdney, 29 March 1883, with enclosed correspondence regarding the
     site of the police barracks. Brennan, *Regina*, 12.
12   GAI, Dewdney Papers, vol. III, 403-4, J.A. Macdonald to Dewdney, 6 September 1882; 405-8,
     Macdonald to Dewdney, 8 September 1882; 250, W.B. Scarth to Macdonald, 2 January 1883.

13 Canada, House of Commons, *Debates*, 7 May 1883, 15-6.
14 NAC, Macdonald Papers, vol. 210, 89419-26, Dewdney to J.A. Macdonald, 5 May 1881. GAI, Dewdney Papers, vol. III, 388-91, Macdonald to Dewdney, 10 May 1881.
15 BRC, Dewdney Papers, A/E/Or 3/D54/W21, correspondence between Dewdney and W.C. Ward, 8 August 1884 to 27 November 1889; A/E/C 86/C 86/D511.1, correspondence between Dewdney and H.P. Crease, March 1884; A/E/Or 3/Or 3.15, correspondence between Dewdney and Peter O'Reilly, 30 October 1884 to 9 November 1885.
16 Morgan, "The Bell Farm." GAI, Dewdney Papers, vol. III, 1741-3, M.R. Bell to Dewdney, 25 February 1886; Dewdney to J. Boyle, 1 March 1886. NAC, Macdonald Papers, vol. 211, 89785-7, Dewdney to J.A. Macdonald, 15 May 1883.
17 Brennan, *Regina,* 21. NAC, Macdonald Papers, vol. 211, 89791-7, Dewdney to J.A. Macdonald, 3 June 1883. Dewdney spoke optimistically about the prospects of the branch line north of Regina.
18 NAC, Macdonald Papers, vol. 211, 89788-9, Dewdney to Macdonald, 21 May 1883; 89808-14, Dewdney to Macdonald, 11 July 1883.
19 Ibid.
20 Ibid., 89791-7, Dewdney to Macdonald, 3 June 1883.
21 Ibid.
22 Ibid., 89808-14, Dewdney to Macdonald, 11 July 1883; 89865-7, Dewdney to Macdonald, 14 August 1883.
23 Ibid., 89868-75, Dewdney to Macdonald, 30 August 1883.
24 *Journals of the Council of the North-West Territories, Session of 1883,* 7-15.
25 Thomas, *Struggle for Responsible Government,* 119.
26 NAC, Macdonald Papers, vol. 211, 89923-30, Dewdney to Macdonald, 27 September 1883; 89909-12, Dewdney to Macdonald, 24 September 1883.
27 Gray, *Booze,* 25-33.
28 *Journals of the Council of the North-West Territories, Session of 1883,* 17-20, 31, 57, 63. Thomas, *Struggle for Responsible Government,* 119-20.
29 Ibid., 64-8.
30 NAC, Macdonald Papers, vol. 211, 89923-30, Dewdney to Macdonald, 27 September 1883.
31 GAI, Dewdney Papers, vol. III, 477-80, Dewdney to J.A. Macdonald, 13 December 1883.
32 NAC, Macdonald Papers, vol. 211, 90005-8, Dewdney to Macdonald, 18 January 1884; 90013-29, Dewdney to Macdonald, 9 February 1884; 90033-4, Dewdney to Macdonald, 16 February 1884.
33 Ibid., 90045-55, Dewdney to Macdonald, 6 March 1884; 90056-64, Dewdney to Macdonald, 9 April 1884.
34 Thomas, *Struggle for Responsible Government,* 121-3.
35 GAI, Dewdney Papers, vol. III, 486-8, Dewdney to Macdonald, 3 May 1884.
36 While Macdonald agreed that breweries in the North-West were a good idea, he told Dewdney that it would be futile to proceed, given the temperance wave sweeping the country. Ibid., 501-2, Macdonald to Dewdney, 3 July 1884.
37 *Journals of the Council of the North-West Territories, Session of 1884,* 6-9.
38 Ibid., 16-17, 47-50, 60-3. Thomas, *Struggle for Responsible Government,* 124-7.
39 Lupul, *The Roman Catholic Church and the North-West School Question,* 9-20.
40 NAC, Macdonald Papers, vol. 212, 90100-7, Dewdney to Macdonald, 22 July 1884.
41 Lupul, *Catholic Church and the North-West School Question,* 21-5.
42 NAC, Macdonald Papers, vol. 212, 90115-9, Dewdney to Macdonald, 5 August 1884.
43 Thomas, *Struggle for Responsible Government,* 130-1.
44 NAC, Macdonald Papers, vol. 212, 90287-93, Dewdney to Macdonald, 7 August 1885.
45 GAI, Dewdney Papers, vol. III, 570-1, J.A. Macdonald to Dewdney, 17 August 1885.
46 Thomas, *Struggle for Responsible Government,* 131-3.
47 *Journals of the Council of the North-West Territories, Session of 1885,* 6-10, 43-6.
48 Canada, House of Commons, *Debates, 1885,* 3169-70.
49 Russell, "Cameron, Malcolm Colin."
50 Canada, House of Commons, *Debates, 1886,* 718-31.
51 NAC, RG 10, vol. 3743, file 29488-2, Dewdney to the superintendent general, 1 May 1886.
52 Canada, House of Commons, *Debates, 1886,* 1760-2. GAI, Dewdney Papers, vol. III, 570-1, J.A. Macdonald to Dewdney, 17 August 1885.

53 NAC, Macdonald Papers, vol. 213, 90782-4, Dewdney to Macdonald, 24 June 1886.

54 Canada, House of Commons, *Debates, 1887,* 1146-53.

55 *Journals of the Council of the North-West Territories, Session of 1886,* 6-10, 83-96. Thomas, *Struggle for Responsible Government,* 135-45. Koester, "The Agitation for Parliamentary Representation of the North-West Territories, 1879-1887."

56 GAI, Dewdney Papers, vol. III, 627-8, J.A. Macdonald to Dewdney, 19 October 1886.

57 NAC, Macdonald Papers, vol. 213, 90865-8, Dewdney to Macdonald, 25 October 1886.

58 See, for example, GAI, Dewdney Papers, vol. III, 629-30, J.A. Macdonald to Dewdney, 28 October 1886. NAC, Macdonald Papers, vol. 213, 90884-7, Dewdney to Macdonald, 9 November 1886; 90894-7, Dewdney to Macdonald, 13 November 1886; 90902-6, H. Reed to Dewdney, 23 November 1886.

59 NAC, Macdonald Papers, vol. 213, 90869-76, Dewdney to Macdonald, 26 October 1886; 90927-9, Dewdney to Macdonald, 19 December 1886. Ibid., vol. 214, 91017-8, Dewdney to Macdonald, 13 April 1887.

60 Ibid., vol. 213, 90874-5, Dewdney to Macdonald, 26 October 1886; 90917-20, Dewdney to Macdonald, 6 December 1886.

61 Ibid., 90880-3, Dewdney to Macdonald, 4 November 1886.

62 Waite, *Canada, 1874-1896: Arduous Destiny,* 192.

63 Thomas, *Struggle for Responsible Government,* 147.

64 *Journals of the Council of the North-West Territories, Session of 1887,* 6-10, 72-7.

65 NAC, Macdonald Papers, vol. 214, 91139-49, Dewdney to Macdonald, 20 November 1887.

66 Canada, *Sessional Paper No. 14, 1888,* Annual report of the Department of the Interior for the year 1887. E. Dewdney, "Report Concerning the Administration of the North-West Territories for the Year 1887."

67 Lupul, *Catholic Church and the North-West School Question,* 29-34.

68 NAC, Macdonald Papers, vol. 214, 91139-49, Dewdney to Macdonald, 20 November 1887.

69 For example, the composition of the Board of Education then became five Protestants and three Catholics. It was agreed that teachers would be examined for certification by a panel appointed by the two sections, with each section retaining exclusive responsibility for subjects of a religious/historical nature.

70 NAC, Macdonald Papers, vol. 214, 91228-34, Dewdney to Macdonald, 13 July 1888. He was referring to the recent victory of Thomas Greenway and the Liberal Party in the Manitoba provincial election. The Manitoba school crisis, precipitated by Greenway, almost tore the country apart.

71 Thomas, *Struggle for Responsible Government,* 152-5.

72 NAC, Macdonald Papers, vol. 213, 90812-8, Dewdney to Macdonald, 28 August 1886. GAI, Dewdney Papers, vol. III, 625-6, Macdonald to Dewdney, 1 September 1886.

73 NAC, Macdonald Papers, vol. 213, 90395-403, Dewdney to Macdonald, c. 1886.

74 Ibid., vol. 260, 118283-4, Joseph Royal to Macdonald, 14 September, 1886; 118293-4, Royal to Macdonald, 5 January 1887.

75 GAI, Dewdney Papers, vol. III, 649-50, J.A. Macdonald to Dewdney, 5 April 1887.

76 NAC, Macdonald Papers, vol. 214, 91009-15, Dewdney to Macdonald, 11 April 1887. It seems that Dewdney's antipathy towards French Canadians was shared by his wife. After a visit to Quebec in 1886, Jane complained to her friend Caroline O'Reilly that she felt in a foreign land. It seemed odd to her that "every tongue was chattering French." BRC, A/E/Or 3/D51, O'Reilly Correspondence, Jane Dewdney to Mrs. O'Reilly, 10 June 1886.

77 NAC, Macdonald Papers, vol. 260, 118323-5, Joseph Royal to Macdonald, 10 August 1887; 118338-40, Royal to Macdonald, 18 September 1887.

78 GAI, Dewdney Papers, vol. III, 656, J.A. Macdonald to Dewdney, 14 September 1887.

79 NAC, Macdonald Papers, vol. 214, 91160-3, Dewdney to Macdonald, 10 January 1888.

80 Waite, "Thomas White."

81 GAI, Dewdney Papers, vol. III, 661-2, J.A. Macdonald to Dewdney, 2 May 1888; 663-4, Dewdney to Macdonald, 14 May 1888; 665-6, Macdonald to Dewdney, 28 May 1888.

82 Ibid., vol. III, 2025-6, newsclippings: "Dewdney for the Interior," *Calgary Herald,* 9 May 1888; "The Minister of the Interior," *Saskatchewan Herald,* 26 May 1888; "Dewdney as Minister of the Interior," *Regina Journal,* 31 May 1888.

83   NAC, Macdonald Papers, vol. 214, 91222-5, Dewdney to Macdonald, 28 June 1888. Koester, *Mr. Davin, MP*, 104.
84   GAI, Dewdney Papers, vol. III, 672-3, J.A. Macdonald to Dewdney, 7 July 1888.
85   "Mr. Dewdney the Man," *Globe*, 2 June 1888, 1; "Sir John and Mr. Dewdney," 18 June 1888, 1.
86   GAI, Dewdney Papers, vol. III, 668-9, J.A. Macdonald to Dewdney, 12 June 1888. PAM, J.C. Schultz Papers, 23-4, Macdonald to Schultz, 25 June 1888.
87   NAC, Macdonald Papers, vol. 214, 91198-201, Dewdney to Macdonald, 2 June 1888; 91235-6, Dewdney to Macdonald, 30 July 1888. GAI, Dewdney Papers, vol. IV, 2037-8, G. Powell to Dewdney, 6 August 1888.
88   NAC, Macdonald Papers, vol. 214, 91240-3, Dewdney to Macdonald, 5 August 1888; 91256-65, Dewdney to Macdonald, 6 September 1888. NAC, Thompson Papers, vol. 75, 82777, Dewdney to Thompson, 6 September 1888.
89   "Telegraphic," *Edmonton Bulletin*, 15 September 1888, 1.
90   Ibid., 4 August 1888, 2.
91   NAC, Macdonald Papers, vol. 214, 91160-3, Dewdney to Macdonald, 10 January 1888.
92   Ibid., vol. 213, 90812-8, Dewdney to Macdonald, 28 August 1886.
93   BRC, A/E/Or 3/D51, O'Reilly Correspondence, Jane Dewdney to Caroline O'Reilly, 15 August 1884, 17 January 1885, 1 March 1886, 10 June 1886.
94   "Dewdney Played Big Part in Building Province," *Daily Times* (Victoria), 9 August 1952, 5.
95   NAC, Macdonald Papers, vol. 213, 90785-92, Dewdney to Macdonald, 27 June 1886; 90797-800, Dewdney to Macdonald, 6 July 1886.

Chapter 6: Minister of the Interior

1   Hutchinson, *Mr. Prime Minister*, 88-92.
2   Creighton, *The Old Chieftain*, 523-4.
3   The younger Tupper, Charles Hibbert, minister of marine and fisheries, was another matter. Dewdney disliked his self-important manner, a sentiment shared by Macdonald. "Tupper I fear does not make friends and is rather too fresh," he told the prime minister. "I think a letter from you would do Mr. Charlie some good." NAC, Macdonald Papers, vol. 213, 91353-6, Dewdney to J.A. Macdonald, 5 July 1889.
4   Spry and McCardle, *Records of the Department of the Interior*, 56-7, 129.
5   Hall, "The Pole-Star of Duty: A.M. Burgess and the Department of the Interior," 36-7.
6   GAI, Dewdney Papers, vol. III, 836-7, A.R.C. Selwyn to Dewdney, 5 November 1888.
7   BCR, A/E/Or 3/D51, O'Reilly Correspondence, Jane Dewdney to Mrs. O'Reilly, 22 December 1888.
8   See, for instance, NAC, Macdonald Papers, vol. 214, 91442-7, Dewdney to J.A. Macdonald, 20 November 1889. See also the considerable correspondence between Dewdney and Mackenzie Bowell, NAC, MG 26 E, Mackenzie Bowell Papers, vol. 7.
9   PAM, Schultz Papers, 8174-5, J.A. Macdonald to Joseph Schultz, 18 December 1888.
10   Canada, House of Commons, *Debates, 1889*, 1243-51.
11   Ibid., 1537-9.
12   "Most Obnoxious: Mr. Dewdney's Description of the Liquor Law," *Calgary Daily Herald*, 15 September 1888, 1.
13   Canada, House of Commons, *Debates, 1889*, 1537-9.
14   Ibid., *Debates, 1891*, 606-30.
15   Koester, *Mr. Davin, MP*, 113-4.
16   GAI, Dewdney Papers, vol. IV, 2177-83, J.W. Powers to Dewdney, 29 November 1889.
17   Canada, House of Commons, *Debates, 1890*, 3331-67.
18   Davin did get his way when Herchmer was investigated in 1893. Some of the complaints laid against the policeman were found to be justified, but none that would affect his leadership of the force. Koester, *Mr. Davin, MP*, 114-5.
19   Canada, House of Commons, *Debates, 1891*, 4736-47. The Blood may have been a special case, but the situation was not good for most prairie Natives. Dewdney had the following 1890 statistics in his files for the signatories of Treaties 4, 6, and 7:
     Population: 18,849
     Births: 582

Deaths: 785
Birth rate per thousand: 40.11
Death rate per thousand: 59.28
GAI, Dewdney Papers, vol. IV, 2198.

20   Canada, House of Commons, *Debates, 1889*, 1174.
21   Ibid., *Debates, 1891*, 4800-9.
22   Ibid., 4741-2.
23   Titley, "Indian Industrial Schools in Western Canada."
24   GAI, Dewdney Papers, vol. IV, 2186-92, Albert Lacombe to Dewdney, 25 November 1889; 2193-
     7, L. Vankoughnet to Dewdney, 4 December 1889. Lacombe wanted a new industrial school for
     the Blood and Peigan and volunteered to start it up. This interest is somewhat ironic because he
     was a failure as the first principal of Dunbow Industrial School, and that institution, established
     for Treaty 7, was still viewed with suspicion by Natives.
25   Canada, House of Commons, *Debates, 1889*, 1595-9. Ibid., *Debates, 1890*, 4043-60.
26   *Statutes of Canada 1890*, 53 Victoria, c. 29, *An Act further to amend "The Indian Act,"* c. 43 of the
     Revised Statutes.
27   Canada, House of Commons, *Debates, 1890*, 2718-39, 3604-22.
28   Creighton, *The Old Chieftain*, 534-9.
29   Canada, House of Commons, *Debates, 1890*, 932-6. There was some grumbling in the North-
     West at the position Dewdney took. The *Calgary Daily Herald*, usually very supportive,
     described his views as "unsatisfactory." "Mr. Dewdney's Position," *Calgary Daily Herald*, 14
     March 1890, 2.
30   Thomas, *Struggle for Responsible Government*, 185-7.
31   Ibid., 163-5.
32   Ibid., 171-5.
33   Ibid., 188-9.
34   Ibid., 198-9.
35   Canada, House of Commons, *Debates, 1891*, 3902-47.
36   NAC, Thompson Papers, vol. 143, 17642, Dewdney to J. Thompson, 15 December 1891.
37   Zaslow, *Reading the Rocks*, 134.
38   Canada, House of Commons, *Debates, 1890*, 2124-51.
39   Zaslow, *Reading the Rocks*, 133.
40   Canada, House of Commons, *Debates, 1890*, 2124-51.
41   Zaslow, *Reading the Rocks*, 144-5.
42   Lamb, *History of the Canadian Pacific Railway*, 214-5.
43   Hedges, *The Federal Railway Land Subsidy Policy of Canada*, 68-9.
44   Canada, House of Commons, *Debates, 1889*, 1717-20; *Debates, 1890*, 4667-94; *Debates, 1891*,
     3138-57, 4534-6, 4613-40, 5391-401, 5487-544.
45   NAC, Thompson Papers, vol. 90, item 10181, Dewdney to J. Thompson, 15 July 1889; item 10198,
     Dewdney to Thompson, 17 July 1889; item 10264, Dewdney to Thompson, 29 July 1889.
46   NAC, Macdonald Papers, vol. 214, 91383-9, Dewdney to J.A. Macdonald, 18 August 1889.
47   "Hon. Edgar Dewdney," *Vancouver Daily World*, 10 September 1889, 4.
48   "The Banquet," *Daily Colonist*, 17 September 1889, 4; "Victorian Men Whooped It Up in Swish
     Hotel Delmonico ... While Wives Stayed at Home." *Daily Colonist* (Magazine), 31 December
     1967, 2-3.
49   NAC, Macdonald Papers, vol. 214, 91402-12, Dewdney to J.A. Macdonald, 22 September 1889.
50   Ibid., 91516-22, Dewdney to J.A. Macdonald, 16 July 1890. "Mr. Dewdney in Winnipeg," *Cal-
     gary Daily Herald*, 15 July 1890, 1.
51   NAC, Macdonald Papers, vol. 214, 91523-30, Dewdney to J.A. Macdonald, 27 July 1890. "Cal-
     gary's Holiday," *Calgary Daily Herald*, 22 July 1890, 1.
52   "A Pleasurable Event," *Vancouver Daily World*, 2 August 1890, 4.
53   NAC, Macdonald Papers, vol. 214, 91523-30, Dewdney to J.A. Macdonald, 27 July 1890; 91533-7,
     Dewdney to Macdonald, 3 August 1890.
54   NAC, Thompson Papers, vol. 111, item 12934, Dewdney to J. Thompson, 28 August 1890.
55   NAC, Macdonald Papers, vol. 214, 91543-4, Dewdney to J.A. Macdonald, 10 September 1890;
     91546-8, Dewdney to Macdonald, 18 September 1890; 91550-3, Dewdney to Macdonald, 30

September 1890; 91554-5, A.M. Burgess to J. Pope, 14 October 1890; 91556, Dewdney to Macdonald, 14 October 1890. While in Devonshire, the Dewdneys had an address at Lothan Villas, St. Thomas, Exeter.

56 Creighton, *The Old Chieftain*, 552-4; Hutchinson, *Mr. Prime Minister*, 93-4.
57 GAI, Dewdney Papers, vol. IV, 2703, "To the Electors of Eastern Assiniboia (1891)." Thomas, *Struggle for Responsible Government*, 197.
58 Creighton, *The Old Chieftain*, 542-5.
59 NAC, Thompson Papers, vol. 129, item 15681, Jane Dewdney to J. Thompson, c. 19 and 31 May 1891; item 15682, E. Dewdney to Thompson, 31 May 1891; vol. 130, item 15734, Dewdney to Thompson, 6 June 1891.
60 Waite, *The Man from Halifax*, 295-331.
61 GAI, Dewdney Papers, vol. IV, 2609-11, T. Cunningham, MP, to Dewdney, 17 December 1891; 2612-9, Cunningham to Dewdney, 27 February 1892.
62 Canada, House of Commons, *Debates, 1891*, 1484-1513.
63 Ibid., 4736-47, 5067-72.
64 Hall, "The Pole-Star of Duty," 34-5.
65 Canada, House of Commons, *Debates, 1892*, 257-65, 825-55, 1154-9, 4206-9;
66 Brado, *Cattle Kingdom: Early Ranching in Alberta*, 45-55. Breen, *The Canadian Prairie West and the Ranching Frontier, 1874-1924*, 23-57. Jameson, "Partners and Opponents: The CPR and the Ranching Industry in the West," 71-8.
67 GAI, Dewdney Papers, vol. IV, 2147-50, J.W. Power to Dewdney, 16 December 1888. Breen, *Canadian Prairie West*, 59-60.
68 Canada, House of Commons, *Debates, 1891*, 6147-66.
69 Ibid., *Debates, 1892*, 223. GAI, Dewdney Papers, vol. IV, 2312-3, D. McEachran to Dewdney, 13 August 1891; 2314-7, McEachran to Dewdney, 28 March 1892; 2319, A.M. Burgess to Dewdney; 2470, J. McMullen to Dewdney, 12 April 1892. Breen, *Canadian Prairie West*, 74.
70 "The Government and the Grazing Leases," *Calgary Daily Herald*, 7 March 1892, 1. Ibid., 2, "Interview Between Ranch Representatives and Mr. Dewdney." Breen, *Canadian Prairie West*, 75-6.
71 "A Change for the Better," *Calgary Daily Herald*, 25 March 1892, 1. Canada, House of Commons, *Debates, 1892*, 1648-55, 4210-2.
72 Hall, "The Pole-Star of Duty," 31-2.
73 GAI, Dewdney Papers, vol. IV, 2440-1, C. Pooley to Dewdney, 17 March 1892; 2442-4, D. Oppenheimer to Dewdney, 23 March 1892; 2612-9, T. Cunningham to Dewdney, 27 February 1892; 2631-3, Cunningham to Dewdney, 2 July 1892.
74 NAC, Thompson Papers, vol. 164, item 20388, Dewdney to J. Abbott, 1 October 1892.
75 "Capital Notes," *Daily Colonist*, 16 October 1892, 1.
76 See, for example, GAI, Dewdney Papers, vol. IV, 2521-2, E. Coatsworth to Dewdney, 8 July 1892. Coatsworth was an Ontario MP who admitted that he had originally blamed Dewdney for the North-West Rebellion because of prejudiced reports in the newspapers. But having worked with him for several years, he realized he had been mistaken and came to have the highest respect for Dewdney's character and abilities, a view shared by other Ontario MPs.
77 "Capital Notes," *Daily Colonist*, 16 October 1892, 1.

Chapter 7: Semi-Retirement

1 "Duly Sworn In," *Daily Colonist*, 10 November 1892. BCR, O'Reilly Diaries, entry for 9 November 1892.
2 Reksten, *"More English than the English": A Very Social History of Victoria*, 73-4.
3 Reynolds, *Agnes: The Biography of Lady Macdonald*, 144.
4 Ormsby, *Pioneer Gentlewoman*, xli.
5 Belshaw, "Provincial Politics, 1871-1916," 135.
6 BCR, GR 443, BC Lieutenant Governor, Letterbook, Copies of Correspondence Outward, vol. 1, 32, Dewdney to the secretary of state for Canada, 18 April 1896. Ibid., O'Reilly Diaries, entry for 17 January 1893. "Guests of the Governor," *Daily Colonist*, 9 February 1897, 7.
7 Saywell, *The Office of Lieutenant-Governor*, 261.
8 Ibid., 20.

9 NAC, Thompson Papers, vol. 167, item 20872, Dewdney to J. Thompson, 21 November 1892; item 20943, Dewdney to Thompson, 26 November 1892. Waite, *The Man from Halifax*, 350.

10 Titley, "Hayter Reed and Indian Administration in the West," 134.

11 Ormsby, *British Columbia*, 307.

12 Belshaw, "Provincial Politics, 1871-1916," 142-3.

13 NAC, Thompson Papers, vol. 180, item 22525, Dewdney to J. Thompson, 22 April 1893.

14 GAI, Dewdney Papers, vol. IV, 2671-701, Journal of a trip to Alaska, 1893. NAC, Thompson Papers, vol. 184, item 22838, Dewdney to J. Thompson, 10 August 1893.

15 Corbin, *The Foul and the Fragrant*, 143-5.

16 Ormsby, *Pioneer Gentlewoman*, xli. NAC, Thompson Papers, vol. 184, item 22838, Dewdney to J. Thompson, 10 August 1893.

17 Ormsby, *Pioneer Gentlewoman*, xlvii.

18 BCR, O'Reilly Diaries. Reksten, "*More English than the English*," 129-30.

19 Belshaw, "Provincial Politics, 1871-1916," 136.

20 NAC, Thompson Papers, vol. 211, item 26544, Dewdney to J. Thompson, 7 June 1894; item 26568, Dewdney to Thompson, 9 June 1894; vol. 215, item 27180, Dewdney to Thompson, 26 July 1894.

21 Ibid., vol. 220, item 27557, Dewdney to Thompson, 12 September 1894; item 27563, Dewdney to Thompson, 16 September 1894.

22 "Old Homes and Families," *Daily Colonist* (Magazine), 16 July 1950. Ormsby, *Pioneer Gentlewoman*, xlvii. "The Governor-General," *Daily Colonist*, 4 November 1894, 1. "Our Parting Guests," *Daily Colonist*, 10 November 1894, 1.

23 GAI, Dewdney Papers, vol. V, 2793, Lord Aberdeen to Dewdney (telegram), 12 December 1894; 2797A, Dewdney to governor general (telegram), 13 December 1894. Waite, *Man from Halifax*, 429-30.

24 Belshaw, "Provincial Politics, 1871-1916," 142-3, 149. Ormsby, *British Columbia*, 314.

25 Ormsby, *Pioneer Gentlewoman*, xli, xlii.

26 "The Governor General," *Daily Colonist*, 16 August 1895, 6; "Garden Fete," *Daily Colonist*, 1 September 1895, 6.

27 BCR, O'Reilly Diaries, entries for 9 and 14 May 1896.

28 "Old Homes and Families," *Daily Colonist* (Magazine), 16 July 1950.

29 Ormsby, *Pioneer Gentlewoman*, xxxix-xl.

30 Mouat, *Roaring Days: Rossland's Mines and the History of British Columbia*, 19-28.

31 "The Attack on the Governor," *Daily Colonist*, 3 April 1897, 4; "The Lieutenant Governor's Critics," *Daily Colonist*, 4 April 1897, 4.

32 There is little evidence to suggest that Dewdney did well from his investments. Only four mines at Rossland were really profitable, and they were owned, at least initially, by Americans. Yet thousands of shares in hundreds of worthless properties were sold during the height of the boom. Like most "gold-rush" situations, a few early stakeholders did exceedingly well while latecomers usually lost. Mouat, *Roaring Days*, 35-7.

33 Roy, *A White Man's Province*, 124-5; "The Oriental Labour Bill," *Daily Colonist*, 8 May 1897, 4; "The Oriental Labour Bill," *Daily Colonist*, 2 June 1897, 4.

34 "The Jubilee Has Come," *Daily Colonist*, 22 June 1897, 4, 5.

35 Ormsby, *Pioneer Gentlewoman*, xlii, xlviii.

36 "Informally Opened," *Daily Colonist*, 29 October 1897, 5.

37 "The Lieutenant-Governors," *Daily Colonist*, 4 December 1897, 6.

38 Ormsby, *Pioneer Gentlewoman*, xlvii.

39 NAC, Thompson Papers, vol. 205, item 25726, Dewdney to J. Thompson, 4 April 1894.

40 Morrison, *The Politics of the Yukon Territory*, 8-10.

41 Hall, *Clifford Sifton*, 168-73.

42 "Klondyke Transport," *Daily Colonist*, 11 December 1897, 5.

43 "Ex-Governor Dewdney Returns," *Daily Colonist*, 11 January 1898, 2.

44 Fleming, *The Railway King of Canada*, 76.

45 Canada, House of Commons, *Debates, 1898*, 1481-574, 1521-91, 1734.

46 Fleming, *The Railway King of Canada*, 77-9. Hall, *Clifford Sifton*, 185-8.

47 "The Canadian Route," *Daily Colonist*, 15 April 1898, 6.

48   Greenhous, *Guarding the Goldfields*, 28-35.
49   "The Road to the Yukon," *Daily Colonist*, 5 July 1898, 3.
50   Berton, *The Klondike Fever*, 228-30.
51   NAC, Tupper Papers, 8869-70, C. Tupper to C.H. Lugrin, 4 May 1898.
52   BCR, O'Reilly Diaries, entry for 2 April 1898.
53   "The Road to the Yukon," *Daily Colonist*, 5 July 1898, 3.
54   GAI, Dewdney Papers, vol. V, 2808, H. Ladner to Dewdney, 21 September 1900; 2809-10, Dewdney to Ladner, 23 September 1900.
55   "Westminster Wants Dewdney," *Daily Colonist*, 5 October 1900, 6.
56   GAI, Dewdney Papers, vol. V, 2817-8, "To the Electors of the Electoral District of New Westminster."
57   Roy, *A White Man's Province*, 143-4.
58   "The Battle Is Over," *Daily Colonist*, 9 November 1900, 1. Schull, *Laurier: The First Canadian*, 397.
59   Sanford, *Steel Rails and Iron Men*, 6-9.
60   BCR, NWp 971.46 B862 re, "Coast-Kootenay Railway Survey, Mr. Dewdney's Report, 23 December 1901." "The Mystery of Hope Mountain," *Daily Colonist*, 23 July 1901, 3.
61   "Coast-Kootenay Railway," *Daily Colonist*, 24 November 1903, 4.
62   Sanford, *Steel Rails and Iron Men*, 61-73, 118-9.
63   Ormsby, *Pioneer Gentlewoman*, xlvii-xlviii. "Mrs. Dewdney Dead," *Daily Colonist*, 31 January 1906, 5.
64   Ormsby, *Pioneer Gentlewoman*, xlviii. Williams, *"The Man for a New Country,"* 256. "Despondency Causes Death," *Daily Colonist*, 27 January 1892, 1.
65   "Liberal-Conservatives Name Their Standard-Bearers," *Daily Colonist*, 8 January 1907, 1. "Liberals Realized Hopeless Position," *Daily Colonist*, 22 January 1907, 1. "Big Development in Similkameen Country," *Daily Colonist*, 23 July 1907, 7.
66   Jackman, *The Men at Cary Castle*, 62.
67   "Conditions in Great Britain," *Daily Colonist*, 30 April 1909, 3.
68   Jackman, *The Men at Cary Castle*, 62.
69   BCR, A/E/Or3/D54/D54.1, Hugh J. Macdonald to Blanche Dewdney, 8 September 1915; B. Dewdney to R. Borden, 16 September 1915; Macdonald to B. Dewdney, 20 September 1915; Borden to B. Dewdney, 29 September 1915; Macdonald to B. Dewdney, 4 October 1915; Macdonald to B. Dewdney, 18 October 1915; Macdonald to B. Dewdney, 21 October 1915; E. Dewdney to Macdonald, 21 January 1916; Macdonald to E. Dewdney, 24 January 1916; E. Dewdney to Macdonald, 31 January 1916; E. Dewdney to Borden, 31 January 1916; E. Dewdney to M. Burrell, 7 February 1916; E. Dewdney to G.E. Foster, 7 February 1916; E. Dewdney to J. Lougheed, 11 February 1916.
70   "Helped to Mould Destiny of BC," *Daily Colonist*, 9 August 1916, 1.
71   "Public Privileged to Attend Funeral," *Daily Colonist*, 12 August 1916, 7; "Many Pay Tribute to Hon. E. Dewdney," *Daily Colonist*, 13 August 1916, 7.
72   Jackman, *The Men at Cary Castle*, 62.
73   GAI, Dewdney Papers, vol. V, 2840, J. Hawkes to B. Dewdney, 5 October 1917; 2844-5, F.R. Rowley to B. Dewdney, 25 March 1920.
74   Ibid., 2848-50, H.J. Macdonald to B. Dewdney, 24 January 1923; 2851-2, G. Brown to B. Dewdney, 4 January 1924; Macdonald to Dewdney, 12 January 1926.
75   "Mrs. Dewdney Passes Away," *Daily Colonist*, 28 March 1936, 2.

Chapter 8: A Frontier Capitalist

1   MacDonald, *Sons of Empire*, 33-4. Field, *Toward a Programme of Imperial Life*, 37, 48-55.
2   Hyam, *Britain's Imperial Century*, 157-9.
3   Stewart, *The Origins of Canadian Politics*, 65-82.
4   Ibid., 89.

Bibliography

Archival Sources

National Archives of Canada (NAC)

Charles Tupper Papers.
MG 26 A. John A. Macdonald Papers.
MG 26 D. John Thompson Papers.
MG 26 E. Mackenzie Bowell Papers.
MG 27 1 C4. Edgar Dewdney Papers.
MG 29 E 106. Hayter Reed Papers.
RG 10. Records of the Department of Indian Affairs.
RG 15. Records of the Department of the Interior.

British Columbia Records (BCR)

A/E/Or/D51. O'Reilly Correspondence.
C/AB/30.6. BC Royal Engineers. Letterbook, 1859.
F. 5.2 D51A. Diary of Edgar Dewdney.
GR 443. BC Lieutenant Governor. Letterbook.
GR 1372. Colonial Correspondence.
J/B D5 1G. R.E. Gosnell. "Bygone Days of British Columbia."
J/B/B 86. "Building of the Dewdney Trail, 1865."
M/D51. Edgar Dewdney Papers.

Glenbow Archives Institute (GAI)

M-454. Edgar Dewdney Papers.

Provincial Archives of Manitoba (PAM)

Mg 12 E1 J.C. Schultz Papers.

Government Publications

Canada. House of Commons. *Debates*.
_____. *Sessional Papers: Annual Reports of the Department of Indian Affairs*.
_____. *Sessional Papers: Annual Reports of the Department of the Interior*.
Journals of the Colonial Legislatures of the Colonies of Vancouver Island and British Columbia, 1851-1871.
Journals of the Council of the North-West Territories.
Statutes of Canada, 1890.

Newspapers

British Columbia.
Calgary Herald.
Daily Colonist (Victoria. Also known as the *British Colonist* and the *daily British Colonist*).
Daily Province (Vancouver).
Daily Times (Victoria).
Edmonton Bulletin.
The Globe (Toronto).
Mainland Guardian.
Regina Journal.

Saskatchewan Herald.
Vancouver Daily World.
Vancouver Sun.
Winnipeg Times.

Articles and Books

Adam, G. Mercer, ed. *Prominent Men of Canada.* Toronto: Canadian Biographical Publishing, 1892.

Archer, John H. *Saskatchewan: A History.* Saskatoon: Western Producer Prairie Books, 1980.

Baltimore, J. Mayne. "The Famous Dewdney Trail." *National Sportsman* (August 1901): 117-22.

Baptie, Sue. "Edgar Dewdney." *Alberta Historical Review* 16, 4 (1968): 1-10.

Barman, Jean. *The West beyond the West: A History of British Columbia.* Toronto: University of Toronto Press, 1991.

Beal, Bob, and Rod Macleod. *Prairie Fire: The 1885 North-West Rebellion.* Edmonton: Hurtig, 1984.

Begg, Alexander. *History of British Columbia from Its Earliest Discovery to the Present Time.* Toronto: McGraw-Hill Ryerson, [1894] 1972.

Belshaw, John D. "Provincial Politics, 1871-1916." In *The Pacific Province: A History of British Columbia,* ed. Hugh M. Johnston. Vancouver: Douglas and McIntyre, 1996.

Berton, Pierre. *The Great Railway, 1871-1881: The National Dream.* Toronto: McClelland and Stewart, 1970.

_____. *The Great Railway, 1881-1885: The Last Spike.* Toronto: McClelland and Stewart, 1971.

_____. *The Klondike Fever.* New York: Alfred A. Knopf, 1972.

_____. *The Wild Frontier.* Toronto: McClelland and Stewart, 1978.

Bowes, Gordon E. *Peace River Chronicles.* Vancouver: Prescott Publishing, 1963.

Brado, Edward. *Cattle Kingdom: Early Ranching in Alberta.* Vancouver: Douglas and McIntyre, 1984.

Breen, David H. *The Canadian Prairie West and the Ranching Frontier, 1874-1924.* Toronto: University of Toronto Press, 1983.

Brennan, J. William. *Regina: An Illustrated History.* Toronto: James Lorimer, 1989.

Carter, Sarah. *Lost Harvests: Prairie Indian Reserve Farmers and Government Policy.* Montreal: McGill-Queen's University Press, 1990.

Corbin, Alain. *The Foul and the Fragrant: Odour and the French Social Imagination.* Cambridge, MA: Harvard University Press, 1986.

Creighton, Donald. *John A. Macdonald: The Old Chieftain.* Toronto: Macmillan, 1955.

Cruickshank, Ken. *Close Ties: Railways, Government, and the Board of Railway Commissioners, 1851-1933.* Montreal: McGill-Queen's University Press, 1991.

De Kiewiet, C.W., and F.H. Underhill, eds. *Dufferin-Carnavon Correspondence, 1874-1878.* Toronto: Champlain Society, 1955.

Dempsey, Hugh. *Big Bear: The End of Freedom.* Vancouver: Douglas and McIntyre, 1984.

_____. "The Starvation Year: Edgar Dewdney's Diary for 1879," Part 1. *Alberta History* 31, 1 (1983): 1-12.

_____. "The Starvation Year: Edgar Dewdney's Diary for 1879," Part 2. *Alberta History* 31, 2 (1983): 1-15.

Denny, Cecil E. *March of the Mounties.* Surrey, BC: Heritage House, 1994.

_____. *The Law Marches West.* Toronto: Dent, 1972.

Dewdney, Kathleen S. "Walter Robert Dewdney." *20th Report of the Okanagan Historical Society, 1929:* 36-40.

Dunae, Patrick A. *Gentlemen, Emigrants: From the English Public Schools to the Canadian Frontier.* Vancouver: Douglas and McIntyre, 1981.

Field, H. John. *Toward a Programme of Imperial Life: The British Empire at the Turn of the Century.* Westport, CT: Greenwood Press, 1982.

Fleming, R.B. *The Railway King of Canada: Sir William Mackenzie.* Vancouver: UBC Press, 1991.

Friesen, Gerald. *The Canadian Prairies: A History.* Toronto: University of Toronto Press, 1984.

Getty, Ian A.L., and Antoine S. Lussier, eds. *As Long as the Sun Shines and Water Flows: A Reader in Canadian Native Studies.* Vancouver: UBC Press, 1983.

Gray, James H. *Booze: When Whiskey Ruled the West.* Saskatoon: Fifth House, 1995.

Greenhous, Brereton. *Guarding the Goldfields: The Story of the Yukon Field Force.* Toronto and Oxford: Dundurn Press, 1987.

Gwyn, Sandra. *The Private Capital: Ambition and Love in the Age of Macdonald and Laurier.* Toronto: McClelland and Stewart, 1984.

Hall, D.J. *Clifford Sifton: Vol. I – The Young Napoleon, 1861-1900.* Vancouver: UBC Press, 1981.
_____. "The Pole-Star of Duty: A.M. Burgess and the Department of the Interior." *Prairie Forum* 16, 1 (1991): 21-40.
Hedges, James B. *The Federal Railway Land Subsidy Policy of Canada.* Cambridge, MA: Harvard University Press, 1934.
Hendrickson, James. "The Constitutional Development of Colonial Vancouver Island and British Columbia." In *British Columbia: Historical Readings,* eds. Peter Ward and Robert A. McDonald. Vancouver: Douglas and McIntyre, 1981.
Howay, F.W. *British Columbia: The Making of a Province.* Toronto: Ryerson Press, 1928.
Hutchison, Bruce. *Mr. Prime Minister, 1867-1964.* New York: Harcourt, Brace, 1964.
Hyam, Ronald. *Britain's Imperial Century, 1815-1914.* London: Batsford, 1976.
Inwood, Damien. *Fort Steele: The Golden Era.* Langley, BC: Sunfire Publications, 1986.
Jackman, S.W. *The Men at Cary Castle.* Victoria: Morriss Printing, 1972.
Jameson, Sheilagh S. "Partners and Opponents: The CPR and the Ranching Industry in the West." In *The CPR West: The Iron Road and the Making of a Nation,* ed. Hugh A. Dempsey. Vancouver: Douglas and McIntyre, 1984.
_____. "The Agitation for Parliamentary Representation of the North-West Territories, 1879-1887." *Saskatchewan History* 26 (1973): 26.
Koester, C.B. *Mr. Davin, MP: A Biography of Nicholas Flood Davin.* Saskatoon: Western Producer Prairie Books, 1980.
Lalonde, André. "Colonization Companies in the 1880s." In *Pages from the Past: Essays on Saskatchewan History,* ed. D.H. Bocking. Saskatoon: Western Producer Prairie Books, 1979.
Lamb, W. Kaye. *History of the Canadian Pacific Railway.* New York: Macmillan, 1977.
_____. "Edgar Dewdney and the Aftermath of the Rebellion." *Saskatchewan History* 23, 3 (1970): 106-17.
Larmour, Jean. "Edgar Dewdney: Indian Commissioner in the Transition Period of Indian Settlement, 1879-1884." *Saskatchewan History* 33 (1980): 13-24.
Little, J.I. "The Foundations of Government." In *The Pacific Province: A History of British Columbia,* ed. Hugh M. Johnston. Vancouver: Douglas and McIntyre, 1996.
Loo, Tina. *Making Law, Order, and Authority in British Columbia, 1821-1871.* Toronto: University of Toronto Press, 1994.
Lupul, Manoly. *The Roman Catholic Church and the North-West School Question: A Study in Church-State Relations in Western Canada, 1875-1905.* Toronto: University of Toronto Press, 1974.
MacDonald, Robert H. *Sons of Empire: The Frontier and the Boy Scout Movement, 1890-1918.* Toronto: University of Toronto Press, 1993.
MacEwan, Grant. *Sitting Bull: The Years in Canada.* Edmonton: Hurtig, 1973.
McGregor, D.A. *They Gave Royal Assent.* Vancouver: Mitchell Press, 1967.
Morgan, E.C. "The Bell Farm." In *Pages from the Past: Essays on Saskatchewan History,* ed. D.H. Bocking. Saskatoon: Western Producer Prairie Books, 1979.
Morice, A.G. *The History of the Northern Interior of British Columbia.* Fairfield, WA: Ye Galleon Press, 1971.
Morrison, David R. *The Politics of the Yukon Territory.* Toronto: University of Toronto Press, 1968.
Morton, W.L. *The Critical Years: The Union of British North America, 1857-1873.* Toronto: McClelland and Stewart, 1964.
Mouat, Jeremy. *Roaring Days: Rossland's Mines and the History of British Columbia.* Vancouver: UBC Press, 1995.
Ormsby, Margaret. *British Columbia: A History.* Toronto: Macmillan, 1958.
_____, ed. *A Pioneer Gentlewoman in British Columbia: The Recollections of Susan Allison.* Vancouver: UBC Press, 1976.
Pennanen, Gary. "Sitting Bull: Indian Without a Country." *Canadian Historical Review* 51, 2 (1970): 123-40.
Pethick, Derek. "The Confederation Debate of 1870." In *British Columbia and Confederation,* ed. W. George Sheldon. Victoria: Morriss Printing, 1967.
_____. *Men of British Columbia.* Surrey, BC: Hancock House, 1967.
Reksten, Terry. *"More English than the English": A Very Social History of Victoria.* Victoria: Orca Books, 1986.

Reynolds, Louise. *Agnes: The Biography of Lady Macdonald.* Ottawa: Carleton University Press, 1990.

Robin, Martin. *The Rush for Spoils: The Company Province, 1871-1933.* Toronto: McClelland and Stewart, 1972.

Roy, Patricia E. *A White Man's Province: British Columbia Politicians and Chinese and Japanese Immigrants, 1858-1914.* Vancouver: UBC Press, 1989.

Russell, Peter A. "Cameron, Malcolm Colin." *Dictionary of Canadian Biography, XII.* Toronto: University of Toronto Press, 1990.

Sanford, Barrie. *Steel Rails and Iron Men: A Pictorial History of the Kettle Valley Railway.* Vancouver: Whitecap Books, 1990.

Saywell, John T. *The Office of the Lieutenant-Governor.* Toronto: University of Toronto Press, 1957.

Schull, Joseph. *Laurier: The First Canadian.* Toronto: Macmillan, 1965.

Scott, David, and Edna Hanic. *East Kootenay Chronicle.* Langley, BC: Mr Paperback, 1979.

Spry, Irene M., and Bennett McCardle. *The Records of the Department of the Interior and Research Concerning Canada's Western Frontier of Settlement.* Regina: Canadian Plains Research Centre, 1993.

Stewart, Gordon T. *The Origins of Canadian Politics: A Comparative Approach.* Vancouver: UBC Press, 1986.

Thomas, Lewis H. *The Struggle for Responsible Government in the North-West Territories, 1870-97.* Toronto: University of Toronto Press, 1978.

Titley, Brian. "Alexander McGibbon." *Dictionary of Canadian Biography, XIII.* Toronto: University of Toronto Press, 1994.

_____. "Hayter Reed and Indian Administration in the West." In *Swords and Ploughshares: War and Agriculture in Western Canada,* ed. R.C. Macleod. Edmonton: University of Alberta Press, 1993.

_____. "Indian Industrial Schools in Western Canada." In *Schools in the West: Essays in Canadian Educational History,* eds. Nancy M. Sheehan, J. Donald Wilson, and David C. Jones. Calgary: Detselig, 1986.

_____. "Transition to Settlement: The Peace Hills Indian Agency, 1884-1890." In *Canadian Papers in Rural History,* vol. 8, ed. D.H. Akenson. Gananoque, ON: Langdale Press, 1992.

_____. "Unsteady Debut: J.-A.-N. Provencher and the Beginnings of Indian Administration in Manitoba." *Prairie Forum* 22, 1 (1997): 21-46.

Tobias, John. "Canada's Subjugation of the Plains Cree, 1879-1885." *Canadian Historical Review* 64, 4 (1983): 519-48.

Waite, Donald E. *The Cariboo Gold Rush Story.* Surrey, BC: Hancock House, 1988.

Waite, P.B. *Canada 1874-1896: Arduous Destiny.* Toronto: McClelland and Stewart, 1971.

_____. *The Man from Halifax: Sir John Thompson, Prime Minister.* Toronto: University of Toronto Press, 1985.

_____. "Thomas White." *Dictionary of Canadian Biography, XI.* Toronto: University of Toronto Press, 1982.

Williams, David R. *"The Man for a New Country": Sir Matthew Baillie Begbie.* Sidney, BC: Gray's Publishing, 1977.

Woodcock, George. *Amor de Cosmos: Journalist and Reformer.* Toronto: Oxford University Press, 1975.

_____. *British Columbia: A History of the Province.* Vancouver: Douglas and McIntyre, 1990.

_____. *Faces from History.* Edmonton: Hurtig, 1978.

Zaslow, Morris. *Reading the Rocks: The Story of the Geological Survey of Canada, 1842-1972.* Toronto: Macmillan, 1975.

Index

Set in Caslon by Brenda and Neil West, BN Typographics West
Printed and bound in Canada by Friesens
Copy editor: Maureen Nicholson
Proofreader: Rachelle Kanefsky